# Reason and the Nature of Texts

# Reason and the Nature of Texts

James L. Battersby

**PENN**

University of Pennsylvania Press

Philadelphia

Copyright © 1996 by the University of Pennsylvania Press
Printed in the United States of America

Library of Congress Cataloging-in-Publication data

Battersby, James L.
  Reason and the nature of texts / James L. Battersby.
     p.     cm.
  Includes bibliographical references and index.
  ISBN 0-8122-3359-X
  1. Criticism.   2. Criticism, Textual.   I. Title.
PN81.B385 1996
801'.95—dc20                                                                96-21300
                                                                                  CIP

for
Lisa and Julie

# Contents

# Acknowledgments

With some justification and with the benefit of rhetorical license, Samuel Johnson could respond to Lord Chesterfield's late notice of the forthcoming *Dictionary* by remarking, "I hope it is no very cynical asperity not to confess obligations where no benefit has been received, or to be unwilling that the Publick should consider me as owing that to a Patron, which Providence has enabled me to do for myself." Earlier, he asked, "Is not a Patron, my Lord, one who looks with unconcern on a man struggling for life in the water, and, when he has reached ground, encumbers him with help?" I am perhaps not alone in finding something in these sentiments from which I do not withdraw in repugnance or on which the phrase "sympathetic reverberation" is not wasted, but once the intoxication of self-importance yields to decent sobriety, I, like most academics, am obliged to recognize that in the midst of my fitful struggles close to shore many have brought useful aid and needed assistance. And I only hope it is no very criminal degree of impertinence or ingratitude to give public attention to those who either assisted my efforts or removed my encumbrances.

To the Trustees of the Ohio State University, to the wise and generous people at the Office of Research, and to the members of the Research Committees of the Graduate School and the College of Humanities, I am, in the language of litotes, not a little grateful for calculable financial assistance and the incalculable gift of released time from teaching and administrative duties.

As I make clear in the introduction, this book is based in greater and lesser degrees on previously published work, and I am genuinely grateful to all the editors and publishers identified below for their willingness to allow me to reprint material. Chapter 1 originally appeared in a slightly revised version in *Beyond Poststructuralism: The Speculations of Theory and the Experience of Literature*, ed. Wendell Harris (University Park: The Pennsylvania State University Press, 1996), 177–201 (copyright 1996 by The Pennsylvania State University Press; reproduced by permission of the publisher). In Chapters 1, 4, and 5, I have occasionally appropriated material from my earlier book on pragmatic pluralism, *Paradigms Regained: Pluralism and the Practice of Criticism* (Philadelphia: University of Pennsylvania Press, 1991), to make crucial points efficiently and clearly. Chapter 2 is an extensively revised and supplemented version of an essay that appeared in the *Bucknell Review* volume entitled *Criticism, History, and Intertextuality*, ed. Richard Fleming and Michael Payne (Lewisburg: Bucknell University Press, 1988), 61–76. Chapter 3 is a modestly revised version, a fraternal twin, of an essay originally published in *PMLA* 107 (1992): 51–64; it is here reprinted by permission of The Modern Language Association of America. Although Chapter 6 now bears very little resemblance to its forebear, substantial sections of it betray their genetic filiation with "Elder Olson: Critic, Pluralist, and Humanist," which appeared in *Chicago Review* 28 (1977): 172–86. Chapter 7 is a somewhat distant cousin of an article, "Coded Media and Genre: A Relation Reargued," that appeared in *Genre* 10 (1977): 339–62; the passages that the two pieces have in common are reprinted with the permission of the University of Oklahoma. A much shorter and very different version of Chapter 8, under the long and cumbersome title "Exercises in the Criticism of Narrative for the First Few Days in an Introductory Literature Course," had a debut outing in *Literary Theory in the English Classroom*, a special edition of *FOCUS: Teaching English Language Arts* 7 (1981): 25–31; the relevant portions of this essay are reprinted with the permission of the Southeastern Ohio Council of Teachers of English.

In the preparation of the bibliographical material I had the able, diligent, and assiduous assistance of Irmgard Schopen, and when the onerous tasks of proofreading and index-compiling needed to be done now and not next week or a day later, I was the extremely fortunate and immoderately delighted beneficiary of the sound wisdom and expert talents of my colleague and friend Lisa Kiser. There are undoubtedly good and capable people working at other presses around the country and around the world, but it would be a damnable lie, I think, to say that any one of them is wiser, more capable or competent, more generous, or more efficient than those I have dealt with at the University of Pennsylvania Press, especially Mindy Brown, who, combining tact and graceful diplomacy with rigorous attention to sense, style, and syntax, did everything in her power to make smooth the corrugations in my argument and the wrinkles in my prose, and Jerome Singerman, whose learning and toughmindedness are surpassed only by his decency, honesty, and fairmindedness; to his generosity, every reader of this book can attest.

Of course, I have also benefited immensely from the gentle and rough suggestions and counterarguments that the students, colleagues, and colloquia members on whom I imposed or inflicted my views, opinions, and arguments over the years have been far from unwilling to share with me, have sometimes insisted on not letting me leave the room without. But, amidst the many helpful advisors, I am especially and deeply indebted to Reed Way Dasenbrock and Wendell V. Harris, who by careful reading, good advice, and friendly but tough criticism did much to sharpen my thought, gladden my heart, and save me from embarrassment. Moreover, to three colleagues—James Phelan, David Riede, and Lisa Kiser—I owe more than I can easily repay; they read my work in virtually every stage of its evolution and gave unsparingly of their time and intellectual energy to make this work fit for public scrutiny. If I have not always heeded their wise counsel (and every reader will discover where I have not), I have everywhere profited by it, and I shall continue to make it my study to deserve their care.

Finally, there is the "without whom" of "without whoms," the last named colleague above and the first mentioned dedicatee of this book; to this scholar, critic, editor, teacher, friend, wife, who has taught me all there is to know (or all one needs to know) about truth and textuality and from whom I have learned how to read classical tales, I am indebted for all that I have mentioned and for so much more that must go unnoticed here but will be acknowledged elsewhere and, I hope, in a style of answerable worth—in acts of commensurate generosity.

# Introduction: Language in Use, or the Semantics of Presence

When I began the project that became this book, I thought, rather na-ively as it turned out, that by putting together a couple of recent articles and some earlier pieces written in the late seventies and in the eighties I could expeditiously and without much labor advance the campaign in behalf of intentionality, determinate meaning, and objective knowledge of the internal interests of literary texts that I had waged in my *Paradigms Regained: Pluralism and the Practice of Criticism*. In addition, I thought that these essays would nicely supplement and complicate the debate by tak-ing up matters either peripheral to or neglected by the book. I was sus-tained, at least initially, by the conviction that despite their parochial interests and obligations the essays were argument-ready for their new assignment. I am perhaps not the first person who has listened "with credulity to whispers of fancy and pursued with eagerness the phantoms of hope," as Johnson says at the opening of *Rasselas*. As dream yielded to morning and morning to effort, however, I realized that, while each piece had a contribution to make to the project, all but the two most recent essays would have to submit to substantial retraining (indeed, in some cases, genetic reprogramming would be in order) if they were to reflect accurately my current thinking and to respond effectively to the prevailing assumptions in critical theory.

Although in their extensively reworked form the essays occasionally address specific critical positions (for example, those of Stanley Fish, Mikhail Bakhtin, Elder Olson, and Jacques Derrida), they speak most im-mediately to current concerns by directing attention to conceptions of language, mind, and meaning that run counter to those expressed or assumed in most theoretical and practical discussions today. In short, this book argues against some specific approaches and doctrines but focuses principally on explaining, developing, and applying to literary concerns a body of principles and arguments that has emerged in recent years in the philosophical literature on language and mind and that, by giving prominence to intentionality in the production of meaning and to intersubjectivity in the production of understanding, renders problematical, at the very least, all—or most of—the truths that the vast majority of poststructualists hold to be unalienable.

By unalienable "truths" we have in mind those "truths," for example, that depend directly or indirectly on a conception of meaning, not as a product of mental states in individuals, but as an *effect* of one or another system of differential relations among signs, and those "truths" that depend on some (essentially Foucauldian) notion of "thinking without a subject"; or on those that seek to substitute "social relations" for intentionality in the construction of meanings; or on those that suppose that interpretations are inevitably and necessarily the creations of interpreters (one of the latest costumes with which self-refuting relativism has adorned itself); in short, on all those truths that are consequences of eliminating the "agent" point of view in the discussion of meaning production and of adopting the view that meanings are (temporary) markers within systems of difference and/or (usually "and") representational effects of contingent social/political forces. In one way or another, each of the chapters of this book works against the grain of the prevailing truths and in support of quite different "truths," those sponsored by alternative views of language, thought, and mind and given compact and summary expression in Michael Dummett's view that "any adequate philosophical account of language must describe it as a rational activity of creatures with intentions and purposes." It is "essential both to our use of language and to any faithful account of the phenomena of human language that it is a rational activity, and that we ascribe motives and intentions to speakers." [1]

A brief examination of the deep sense and complex entailments of this view—which expresses nothing more than conventional wisdom to most philosophers of thought and language and, undoubtedly, nothing but hopelessly naive simplemindedness to most critical theorists—will be temporarily deferred, so that I can quickly situate this book within the concerns that have occasioned it and forestall certain potential objections to the overall project by meeting them at the gate. Initially, however, every reader should understand that while most poststructuralist approaches render invalid or make impossible what I would be about, since what I would be about assumes as a condition of meaning what they cannot admit (a grounding purposiveness in a conscious agent), the approach I everywhere argue for and support—pragmatic pluralism—not only allows but also recognizes the value of much of what they would be about, if not the value of the principles that sets them about it.

The concerns that activate the interests of this book arise from the virtual consensus among literary theorists regarding the following claims:

Because everything we say and do is socially constructed, individuals do not write but are written (that is, the nature and limits of expression and understanding are determined by the prevailing cultural and political conditions).

Because language has no certifying and ultimate warrant in some fixed signified and because language owes whatever apparent determinacy it has to its "units of meaning" being marked within a system of differences in the language system, there is no way for meanings to achieve fixity of reference or meaning.

Because meanings are theory-laden or paradigm-dependent, are transparent within communities of interpreters and users and inscrutable from without them, there is no way to translate from one system to another, to get out of the prisonhouses of incommensurable discourses.

Because our interpretations are various and many, indeed, not only different but conflicting and contradictory, because texts are nothing in themselves and something only in their interpretations, and because no reading can claim any privileged status (for the reasons specified in the preceding claims), there is nothing left to do but to study the conflicts, to study our ways of knowing texts and the various conflicting things we say about them; and so on.

Each of these concerns is addressed in detail in the chapters that follow: the construction of meaning by social conditions in Chapter 4; the limitations of relational conceptions of linguistic differentiation in Chapter 5, which considers the continuing influence of deconstructionist linguistic assumptions on cultural materialist and other forms of poststructuralist theorizing; the incoherence of incommensurability hypotheses in Chapter 3; and the ascertainability of the justification conditions determining the specific content, emphases, and values of literary works in virtually every chapter, but especially Chapters 1, 2, 7, and 8.

In brutally brief summary, then, the first five chapters critique currently prevalent views of language, mind, meaning, and interpretation in the light of alternative views, those central to what might, in grotesquely crabbed shorthand, be called postanalytic, Anglo-American philosophy, especially as articulated by Donald Davidson, Hilary Putnam, John McDowell, Nelson Goodman, John Searle, Akeel Bilgrami, and others, to whom "thinking without a subject" is a flat contradiction in terms and for whom the construction of reality by anything other than a conscious, intelligent agent a form of magic, since content of any kind—whether concerning things either concrete or abstract, material or ideal—depends on intentional states or propositional attitudes. To think about anything, we have to be able to refer to it, and reference is a semantic entailment of a conscious intentional state of an agent (as in "I *believe* that there's a *chair* supporting me"). The last three chapters descend somewhat from the metatheoretical altitudes to explore some sights on the fertile plain of criticism. Specifically, these chapters take up for consideration three distinct matters of critical concern: (1) the felicitous correspondence in the views of the so-called "Chicago critics" and the philosophers of language and mind noted immediately above (Chapter 6); (2) the relevance of previously outlined conceptions of mind and language to the discussion and definition of genre (Chapter 7); and, finally, (3) the practical classroom benefits of an agent- and intention-based conception of artistic production (Chapter 8). The progress, in short, is from the consideration of broad theoretical issues to the elucidation of such specific critical concerns as intellectual affinity, genre definition, and practical interpretation.

What makes all the shibboleths of current theory so troublesome is not that they lead to practices that are utterly trivial or worthless, practices that have no value or justification, but that they prohibit or make impossible, in principle—that is, by principled commitment to certain views about language or power relations—much that we know in our bones and by our daily activities to be not only possible but inevitable. Indeed, many theorists themselves consistently violate in practice what they proclaim in principle. They are caught up in what Susan Hurley has characterized as "pragmatic inconsistency," in that some aspect of what they do from day to day is inconsistent with their views: They read with understanding marvelously diverse texts answerable to richly different and often conflicting justification conditions, make choices in their writing that satisfy their interests and purposes (the interests of their self-created systems of intentionality), evaluate writings produced by colleagues and students in terms of effectiveness and achievement, considered apart from the hegemonic power structure from which the writings necessarily emerged and the instability of language as such, and so on. The problem here, of course, is not merely one of logical inconsistency; rather, their practices affirm the truth of what is inconsistent with their views and demonstrate the falsity of what they profess.[2]

At times, it seems that many academics tend to assume that something—for example, some claim, statement, or view from some neo-marxist, new historicist, poststructuralist perspective—is so counterintuitive, so inconsonant with accepted opinion and practices that it must be right. It is so perversely contrary to what we seem to know or think that it must be correct: for example, there's no author, only texts;

there's nothing outside of texts; people do not speak but are spoken, and so forth. And often what is partially true or true in some limited or qualified sense is taken as true generally: for example, that because words are capable of entering into a virtually infinite number of relationships or bearing countless meanings, they necessarily do so in every context, or that because signs are iterable, they always already mean more or other than they locally say, and so on. Indeed, on the basis of my acquaintance with what constitutes literary study today and of what my colleagues say about their teaching, it seems clear that the only place in literature departments where literature as a unique product of artistic making is being discussed is in the creative writing program. It is in this program that choice at every level is seen as relative to the furthering or functioning of the interests of the composition under construction; that hard decisions about what works and doesn't work, what fits and doesn't fit are made; and that student-writers are brought to some understanding of the rigors of craftsmanship and the imperatives of systems of intentionality. They come to learn that getting it right is different from getting it wrong, that writing well is different from writing poorly, and that the former is easy and the latter hard.

One unfortunate consequence of the focus on politics, ideology, and power relations in literature classes is that it forces out of consideration what in our innocence and by our former standards we had recognized to be distinct and superior achievement. Certainly it cancels the need to read what we had once been willing to call "great" literature again and then again for the pleasure of reacquainting ourselves with its rich formal and moral satisfactions. Under the new ordinance what is truly significant about literature is exhibited as clearly in many other productions of the era (such as postcards, prisons, dance-halls, trade routes, and so forth), and exhibited in them perhaps more clearly and uncomplicatedly. Unless the theorist has some view about the special concentration or purity of political or ideological representation in literary works, as Bakhtin has with respect to novels, there is no reason today to focus on literature at all in literature classes.

From the standpoint of this book, however, there would be nothing philosophically impossible or unrespectable in spending some part of literary training in working cooperatively with students in the difficult but deeply pleasurable process of understanding how some works, as concrete and superlative achievements of practical reasoning, manage to satisfy in humanly rich and interesting ways the standards that their interests and purposes have internally generated. But, alas, the very suggestion that some works are better, richer, deeper, more artistically successful than others is today regularly treated by our theorists as bordering on some form of criminality (sexism, racism, Westernism, colonialism, logocentrism, or whatever). That such a suggestion is an indictable offense today is, to say the least, alarming. That rationality, intentionality, coherence, consistency, and logic are considered by many theorists to be cultural prejudices of . . . what?, humanism, bourgeois capitalism, and so on (as though, short of lobotomization, these could be evaded or eliminated) is, to say the least, unsettling. Of course, as we shall see, even the mere experience of something *as* something depends on a rich network of intentionality, and any denunciation of such intentionality—as of rationality, coherence, and so forth—entails pragmatic inconsistency, inasmuch as the act of denunciation is itself an instance of what is denied.

Nevertheless, from the above remarks and the book as a whole, no one should conclude that because I am encouraging theorists to moderate some outsized claims and to consider devoting some attention, especially at the lower levels of instruction, to what works realize at the level of their interests and intentionality, I am simultaneously interested in proscribing the discussion of literature in terms of social forces, of what is excluded or suppressed, of implicit contradictions or tensions, or of anything else in relation to which literature or any given work may stand, as consequence, cause, or instance. We are certainly historically situated creatures, upon whom the interests and priorities of our culture impinge in marvelously complex ways. In any period, certain beliefs and assumptions are widespread, and many questions go unasked, because they seem unaskable, given what is generally accepted as true, natural, or right. Clearly it is always fruitful—and sometimes politically necessary—to think about what is not being said, as well as what is implied in what is being said, and about what the prevailing assumptions do to limit our views and possibilities. And since literary works, like many other artifacts, both popular and elite, are rich sources of information about prevailing standards and practices and about prevailing assumptions, they certainly should not be exempted from, say, political or ideological scrutiny.

Still, it should be clear that, while in some sense nothing that we say or do or think is possible apart from our culture and, thus, everything is in some sense socially constructed (nothing comes from nothing), cultures and societies can construct nothing in particular. The prevailing terms, concepts, and assumptions of any culture can be used in the construction of an indefinitely large number of positions, views, hypotheses—some inconsistent, some even contradictory. Similarly, just as many disparate statements may be formulated from a single vocabulary, so from different vocabularies similar or substantially identical hypotheses can be articulated. Since no culture or society can preclude the expression of diverse, disparate, conflicting, and contradictory views, everything expressed or expressible in any era belongs to the constructible potentiality of the society or culture. Thus, culture or society, in permitting so much and precluding so little, provides very few constraints on expression or imagination (however severe its constraints on our activities may be).

Of course, there are trends and proclivities in every era (some notions and categories get into circulation and attract the attention of whole flocks of people for a while), but it is always useful to bear in mind that nothing surfeits like success; that is, nothing is more likely to instigate oppositional or antithetical views or what Kenneth Burke calls "perpectives by incongruity" than the success of a discourse or a power structure (if only in forms of parody). The force of the negative or the merely different is always with us. Even modest familiarity with the productions of any era reveals an enormous diversity of views, opinions, and structures, a diversity sometimes concealed by ostensible similarities in the doctrines expressed and by the persistence of common terms and concepts. By isolating shared doctrines and common terms from whole works, we often obscure the real differences among productions, differences deriving from differences in the systems of intentionality in virtue of which the doctrines have specific content and meaning.

It is useful to remember that to the extent that we can discuss that by which we are structured, that by which our thinking is thought, we must operate from standards of rationality outside those of the prevailing power relations, since no system can be *discussed* from within the system itself. Thus, we must give up the incommensurability thesis, which is not much of a loss, since it is incoherent. To talk about what is "true" according to the standards of a given culture (as Rorty is inclined to do), to talk about what is necessary, true, or right relative to this or that culture or according to this or that language game, we must be outside the culture or game (not trapped within it), inasmuch as there's no talking *about* it from within it. To say, as many were fond of doing not so very long ago, that I can see "where you are coming from" is to speak while coming from somewhere else. Additionally, incommensurability is a *comparative* judgment that is obviously based on a standard that is not intrinsic to the systems being examined for alignment; incommensurability as a judgment involves knowing what two (or more) systems are trying to explain and then determining by some noncombatant criterion the lack of commensurability. To say that two systems are incommensurable is to make a judgment from within neither system. Finally, as imaginative creatures (as well as socially situated ones), we must recognize that it is always possible to imagine new structures or to reinvest with new immediacy and relevance those of earlier periods. This view, consonant with common experience and daily practice, is supported by many, including Thomas Nagel, who notes that the "capacity to imagine new forms of hidden order, and to understand conceptions created by others, seems to be innate."[3]

It is undoubtedly fair to say that modern theory in all of its branches is deeply indebted to a theory of language that originates with Saussure, a theory complicated and enriched by Derrida (and other "deconstructionists") and then applied in various ways to mind, history, and social formations. The limitations of the theory are discussed at several points in this book (particularly in Chapters 1 and 5), but with some of its assumptions almost every reader today must agree, most particularly with those that call into question at least one form of the correspondence theory of truth, the view that some special metaphysical relation obtains among words, thoughts, and things and that our meanings and references have their fixity guaranteed by preexistent, language- and mind-independent things, the view, in short, that the "world" or "reality" has semantic preferences or its own preferred linguistic choices. With all poststructuralist theorists, we must also agree that there is no limit on the number of relations in which language units at every level (from phonemic or graphemic units all the way up to sentence or proposition units) may participate and that we cannot know what something (temporarily) is without knowing how it is marked off from other things. Further, it is clear that for something to be marked off from other things (other sounds, words, sentences, for example), it must stand in some relation to them, a relation of difference, if you will. But beyond these grounds of agreement we cannot go. Indeed, this entire book is based on views of the relations among words, thoughts, minds, and worlds that regularly affirm what our theorists regularly deny: determinate meaning, fixity of reference, ascertainable warrant for assertions, the objectivity of our judgments of meaning, valid interpretation, secure knowledge of truth, and so on.

Each of the chapters attempts to make good on one or more of the preceding claims, but in the remainder of this introduction I will attempt to present a brief overview of the principles and assumptions relating to language, thought, and meaning that underlie the book as a whole and that distinguish its philosophical underpinnings from those of most modern literary theorists. Initially, we would note that if it is true that language is a system of differential relations that makes it possible for words (or even sentences) to have the "effect" of reference or meaning, it is also true that "philosophy is not concerned with what *enables* us to speak [or write] as we do, but what it is for our utterances [or inscriptions] to have the meanings that they have," and nothing that happens in or is made possible by the *langue* can explain that.[4] Moreover, however crucial *langue* may be to the possibility of utterance or inscription, it can play no epistemological role in establishing the referential or meaningful *contents* of those utterances or inscriptions (in other words, *langue* as a system of relations cannot really establish even the temporary *effect* of meaning and reference), since *content* is impossible apart from some intentionality. As Quine has famously observed relative to reference, there are no facts about reference beyond those fixed by our use of language, and use is determined, of course, by mental state, intentionality, purpose. The very indeterminacy of language, of all linguistic units, outside some system of intentionality is what makes it impossible for *langue* to have any bearing on specific content.

All this, I suppose, can be granted by our theorists (though they must be careful here), since, as they admit, logocentrism is inescapable, and logocentrism is, if not just another name for, at least cognate with, intentionality. The trouble, we are told, is not that there's no centering going on, but that, because of the relational nature of language, no center will hold (and, hence, no meaning is stable). But, of course, in current theorizing there is no emphasis on the intentionality of logocentrism. The emphasis falls, rather, on a conception of language that minimizes or eliminates individual purposes and that stresses relations among terms and categories independently of their local functions in discrete conceptual systems. On the other hand, intentionality, understood as that in relation to which fixity is established and outside of which there is no determinacy, has no principle of fatality (of self-cancellation or whatever) within it. Indeed, as we shall see, intentional systems have a vested interest in satisfying their interests and have some trouble violating or abusing themselves, if only because they tend to see what their interests enable them to see, and to believe and want what, under the circumstances of interest, is true and desirable. What is cryptic here the ensuing discussion will, I trust, make clear.

Like things, words in themselves have no semantic preferences (or, perhaps more exactly, too many). It is only in relation to interests and beliefs that words have particular representational content. John Searle has persuasively argued that semantics is not intrinsic to syntax, and syntactical relations, as simply relations among signs, have no representational content, no directedness to something beyond, no aboutness about them. They have, in short, no intentionality (that is, no object- or concept-directedness).[5] In most modern discussions, argument focuses largely on syntactical operations, that is, on the relations of signs to other signs (to those to which they are related by some form of association, usually antithesis; this is the opposite of that and is thus implicit within it). In formal logics as in current theory, syntax (or, in theory, prior assumptions about the relational character of signifiers) "specifies the shapes of the symbols [units of the signifiers] and how they can be combined into strings, and gives a set of rules for moving from given well-formed strings to others." Admittedly, the "rules" in theoretical discussions hardly get beyond the notation of binary opposites or antithetical categories: "from the point of view of syntax, the symbols may as well be counters in a game, and the rules a set of allowable moves."[6]

What gives plausibility (and, to some, persuasiveness) to many critical statements produced by current theorists is that they are clearly *allowable moves* in a relational system of signs. One problem with these moves, however, is that they shift counters (signs) that are assumed to have *representational* (that is, intentional) content, not only in their original placement (which they have, as a result of participating in a system of intentionality, of representation) but also in their newly assigned relation (which they have not, because the new "meaning" is merely a relational possibility of a signifying system, not a content of a system of intentionality, which alone can endow the signs with representational content). It is by means of such moves that something comes to imply or mean something other than it says in current theory. In short, for our theorists, meaning—or the *effect* of meaning—resides in the sign (in its relational and iterative possibilities), not, as it does for pragmatic pluralists, in the intentional, representational acts of language users who have particular purposes in specific situations. Since the number of relations in which one thing can stand to another is limitless, the number of "plausible" meanings we can generate by such moves is similarly limitless. But "it is semantics [not syntax] that attributes representational significance to . . . symbols, that tells us that they are words which refer to certain objects or classes, that they are sentences which are true or false," right or wrong, fitting or not fitting.[7] And where there are semantic relations and functions, there is intentionality and, hence, specific content. Syntactic relations have no semantic content.

As Alvin Goldman has noted, "to say that something has content is to say that it has semantic properties," such properties, for example, as reference, meaning, truth-conditions, and satisfaction conditions.[8] As we have noted, where there are semantic properties, there is intentionality, because intentionality is the condition of "aboutness," and intentional states are nothing more than attitudes about contents or states of affairs. To think about the chair I am sitting on I have to be able to refer to it, and I have to believe that what I am sitting on is a chair; I have to have some attitude (in this case belief) about some object. Moreover, this intentional state—like all such states, like all mental contents—has conditions of satisfaction or normative standards built into it, in that my belief could be true or false (I could be hallucinating, or the lighting conditions could be such that what seemed to be a chair turned out to be juxtaposed boxes). Had the intentional state been one of desire rather than belief, then the condition of satisfaction would have been met or not depending on whether the good was supplied, on whether I got what I wanted.

Since we cannot think about or see anything except in some particular way, and since our "seeing it as" one thing or another determines what else fits with our seeing, the constraints on satisfaction are governed by the aspectual or perspectival nature of our intentional states. What is true or false, satisfying or unsatisfying, fitting or not fitting for us is contingent upon whether the conditions of satisfaction of our intentional states (our propositional attitudes) are met or not, and, thus, truth and fittingness are not metaphysical issues but semantic issues. Reference and meaning are not fixed relative to some system of signs (nothing internal to sounds, words, gestures, notes, etc., can determine a relation to something external), but relative to intentional states. As Donald Davidson observes, "only things with content"—such as mental states and linguistic acts, "such as beliefs and interpreted sentences"—"can be evidence for beliefs." Furthermore, "we cannot get outside our beliefs" to some uninterpreted given or mind-independent reality, "and only a belief can be a reason for another belief." [9]

From the preceding we should not be led to suppose that there is nothing but language or mental states, for clearly some of our beliefs are true and some of our desires are satisfied. Although we cannot get beyond our beliefs, the fact remains that while the conditions of satisfaction are in some sense up to us, the satisfaction of those conditions is not something that is left to our discretion, and this is true whether we are talking about our relations to the physical realm or the mathematical or moral realm (that is, any realm in which meaning is possible), since meaning depends on fittingness, on belongingness within some system of intentionality or rationality. In short, we determine what counts as a platypus, what traits a platypus has, but only a platypus satisfies our specifications, fits our definition. Focusing on the physical realm, Hilary Putnam's maxim is that because we "cannot describe the world without describing it . . . does not mean that reality is hidden or noumenal." "Some facts are there to be discovered, but this is something to be said when one has adopted a way of speaking, a language, a conceptual scheme." [10] And even though we have no linguistically unmediated connection with, say, abstractions, we can create something genuinely believable out of them, and we cannot string them together any way we please. Intentional states, of course, can be existence-independent (since hallucinations are contentful states, and we have marvelously complex attitudes about fictional characters), but for them to have any meaningful content they must be justified relative to the interests of those states. Finally on this point, the rightness of how we string things together is not up to our interpretive communities. Rightness is a matter of satisfying the criteria that are the conditions of the possibility of our meaning, a matter, that is, of making our terms and categories serve our interests, of making our moves advance or enhance our practices, our, as one wag has put it, our "forms of life."

What this book in various ways and in various chapters assumes and argues for is a focus on literary works as products of art, as forms of behavior or action. As consequences of action, of practical choices and decisions, of beliefs, desires, and so on, literary works have content and meaning only within systems of intentionality, rationality, and justification. Content is impossible apart from some system of justification, and the understanding of literature depends on coming to grasp its justification conditions, those conditions only in relation to which there is any specific meaning at all. John Pollock's view in *Knowledge and Justification* is that "To learn the meaning of a concept is certainly not to learn its 'definition.' It is to learn how to use it, which is to learn how to make justifiable assertions involving it. Thus it seems to me inescapable that the meaning of a concept is determined by its justification conditions." [11] Since there is no essence to reference and reference is fixed by use and use by intentionality, meaning is a function of mental states within a system of relationships, a system, in short, of justification conditions.

All this is simply another way of getting at the insight that originates with Frege, namely, that words have meaning only within a context of a sentence (the reference and function of words are determined by the intentional conditions they satisfy) and that sentences (and words) have meaning only within a particular language system, a context of use within a larger intentional system. The insight is also given in Wittgenstein's view that we understand utterances or statements only by grasping the "practices" in which they have their functions. It is relative to justification conditions that words (and sentences) have specific content, have determinate meaning. As Davidson says, "It is at the sentential level [not the level of the word, sign, signifier] that language connects with the interests and intentions language serves, and this is the level at which the evidence for interpretation emerges. . . . There is no harm in assigning meanings to sentences, but this must always be a meaning derived from the concrete occasions on which sentences are put to work." [12]

It is important to recognize that specific content comes to us trailing clouds of significances or associations in the form of underlying subsidiary beliefs and background assumptions. Specific content, then, is part of a network of intentionality, and, hence, is implicated in meaning holism. Propositional attitudes and any behavior or events based on them—actions and verbal productions—are intrinsically holistic. Linguistic actions, based as they are on propositional attitudes, have definite content, in Davidson's scheme. They have what Davidson terms "semantic opacity," which is simply fine-grainedness of meaning, definiteness and specificity of content, determinate meaning. This opacity can be shown in relation to any of the attitudes. As Davidson notes, "One way of telling that we are attributing a propositional attitude is by noting that the sentences we use to do the attributing may change from true to false if, in the words that pick out the object of the attitude, we substitute for some referring expression another expression that refers to the same thing."[13] For example, to borrow an example from John Searle, if we were to describe some behavior as $H_2O$-seeking behavior, instead of as what it was (water-seeking behavior), the content of the desire responsible for the behavior would be misrepresented. In intentional states conditions of satisfaction are represented under specific aspects, the aspects in terms of which things are seen, believed, wanted, represented. The person is seeking water, not $H_2O$, or wants to climb the oak tree in the front yard, not the largest object on Maple Court. And because we want satisfaction under the aspects of our representations, only some conditions will be right, or true, or fitting for our states.

Further, to believe that a mouse ran up the clock (to have this specific content, this specific representation), I must have many subsidiary, unexpressed, but nevertheless necessary beliefs about mice and clocks, and timepieces, and the appearance and characteristics of mice and clocks, about animate creatures and time, and so on. The centrality of belief to all the propositional attitudes is apparent when we consider that all these background beliefs in the network of intentionality are required if I *wonder* whether the mouse went up the clock, *fear* that it did, *hope* that it did, *intend* to chase it up the clock.

The point, of course, is that it is only against this vast backdrop of beliefs and assumptions that our utterances and inscriptions have determinate meaning. But, because this network is operating in the background of specific content and supplying our representations with semantic opacity, it is difficult—though certainly not impossible—to violate the integrity of our developing utterances, to cancel or undo what we are in the process of representing in certain ways according to specific justification conditions (along with their trailing clouds of content-limiting beliefs and assumptions). Indeed, the tendency of systems of representation, as it is the tendency of the propositional states of which they are comprised, is to satisfy themselves, especially since for the moment there is no way the world is (no way for the representation to go), no way to have a satisfaction or a fulfillment, apart from that way implicated in the unfolding system of intentionality. Meaning comes not in single spies, but in battalions, and semantic opacity and meaning holism tend to insure that the bough does not break and the cradle does not fall. (Still, mistakes can be made, and weakness of will always watches in wait.) At any rate, it should be clear that there is nothing in the use of language that determines and makes inevitable the *undoing* of whatever is represented or expressed because of the unstable, relational nature of language as such.

The way we see things or represent them determines what further things will go with them or what will satisfactorily answer to them or fulfill them. Similarly, or by extension, a person with such and such beliefs and desires will tend to act in such and such ways (the ways that are reasonable under the governance of those beliefs and desires, the only reasonable ways to behave if you want what you want, if you have propositional attitudes); and a person acting in such and such ways will do so because she has such and such beliefs and desires. In some sense this is the whole point of Wittgenstein's rabbit-duck example. I see something as a shoe (or a rabbit, or a duck), say, and I see it only as a shoe, and because I see it as I do, it fits some things and not others.

Much recent philosophic opinion is converging on the view that meaning is a matter of specific or determinate content and that content is determined by knowable systems of intentionality or distinguishable justification conditions. James Harris, for example, notes that "any meaningful use of language must take place against the context of a rule-governed situation within which there are recognizable proper and improper moves," and such rules and moves are dependent on operative systems of intentionality; there are no semantic obligations in the signs themselves.[14] Hilary Putnam argues convincingly that "without the cognitive values of coherence, simplicity, and instrumental efficacy," the values associated with intentional-state relations, "we would have no facts" or meanings whatsoever.[15] And Wittgenstein makes our understanding of language use dependent on grasping the the practices or "forms of life" in which it has a part. In a context focusing on justification conditions, Michael Luntley affirms that "the only grasp we have of the way some utterance is connected inferentially with others is via the idea of the structure of the utterance [and there is, for Luntley, no structure apart from our mental states]. Our grasp of inferential connections proceeds via our discerning structure."[16] For Michael Dummett, whose views Luntley is both examining and endorsing, "the fundamental fact . . . is that our understanding of language is the grasp of a system or structure." Elsewhere he says that "the sentence expresses a thought in virtue of its having semantic properties," and the specific content of "thought is grasped in grasping the semantic properties of the sentence."[17] Within a discussion of meaning relative to purposes, Mark Johnson indicates that "there can be no meaning without some structure or pattern that establishes relationships," or, as he elsewhere suggests, where there is content, there is rationality.[18] This list of citations undoubtedly does not add up to a proof of anything, but together with the preceding analysis it does add weight to conceptions of meaning and language and mind, especially to conceptions of the fixity of reference and meaning relative to systems of intentionality, that are viable alternatives to those prevailing in current theory.

Of course, although there is no meaning, no specific content, apart from some system of rationality, there is no way that in our role as interpreters we can determine the meaning of the activity of the author, or distinguish the significant from the incidental features of a literary work, merely by looking hard at the work's verbal features, just as there is no way we can determine merely by looking at behavior—considered apart from some mental structure, some rationalizing network of belief and desire—whether a person wants to sit by a tree or to be adjacent to cylindrical fibrous material. Reference is behaviorally inscrutable, since the same action can be accounted for by an extraordinarily wide range of hypotheses. Signs, like actions, have no meaning or reference intrinsically, as Wittgenstein and others have persistently reminded us. Echoing Wittgenstein, John Searle, for example, notes that "nothing internal to the picture of the man walking uphill—or is he sliding downhill—forces the interpretation that we find natural" (that is, that he is walking uphill).[19]

Nothing inside an object or action, nothing in a word or line or sentence, is sufficient to determine a meaning relation to something outside it; nothing just is the correspondence relation, since meaning does not transcend use, and use is a function of rationality, justification conditions. As Putnam observes, we cannot "specify in an effective way what *the* justification conditions for the sentences of a natural language are. . . . The assertibility conditions for an arbitrary sentence are not surveyable." To get some sense of the variability of the justification conditions of an arbitrary sentence simply repeat "I didn't say he stole it" six times, giving emphasis to a different word with each repetition. Now take any one of those repetitions and say it ironically, solemnly, gloomily, comically, portentously, and so on. "If assertibility conditions are not assertible, how do we learn them? We learn them [as Wittgenstein, Michael Dummett, and others have suggested] by acquiring a practice."[20]

But, of course, there is no algorithm for acquiring practices, for learning which system of rationality we are confronting. We must rely on our imaginative capacities to construct and understand new structures, on our rich experience with making and understanding a variety of systems of rationality, guided by some such assumptions as these: that there is no content at all in the absence of intentional states, that only rational creatures have intentional states with full-blown content, that people do not try to shoot themselves in the foot (that is, they act in conformity with their beliefs and desires, thereby making their behavior an action, not a mere happening), that words and actions do not normally lose their customary, conventional, or "default" values and emphases when they appear in literary works, that people believe what is true and want what is answerable to their need or desire, and that . . . (here supply all those "rules" on which you customarily rely in making sense of all the linguistic and nonlinguistic actions encountered in any given day; by supplying such "rules," you satisfy what Davidson calls the "principle of charity").

Beliefs are justified relative to other beliefs, and it is in coming to know the network of beliefs and assumptions underlying linguistic action and determining specific content that we come to an understanding of the determinate meaning of the texts we encounter. In all our encounters with language, we are involved in the process of coming to understand a new practice, a new language game, but we never have to begin from scratch. We begin with our accumulated competencies for understanding, that is, our developed and developing capacities for rationalizing behavior, improvising as we go, but sustained by the knowledge that where there is specific content, there is rationality, rationality precisely of the sort that we ourselves use in forming our beliefs, getting what we want, doing what we intend, and so on. John Heil, expanding on and clarifying one of Davidson's points, notes that in "delivering an utterance, I produce something that possesses a definite sense, one that I can reasonably expect my audience to recover." "The recovery of sense, interpretation, is a matter," says Davidson, "of bringing to bear a 'theory of truth.'" Further, "the production of an utterance is something in part because it expresses a definite, recoverable, intentional content. [And] productive capacities go hand in hand with interpretive capacities, we have reason to assume."[21] What Davidson calls a "theory of truth," Michael Dummett calls a "theory of meaning" and what we, focusing on the interpretation of literary works, might call a tentative, working hypothesis, a controlling conception of the operative justification conditions, which functions to render the unfolding words and sentences intelligible and meaningful, and only in relation to which are the words and sentences intelligible. In essence, we are talking about the conditions of the possibility of a "practice," those conditions that in a holistic network of intentionality give the work its specific content, its determinate meaning. Thought and language are inextricably joined, as are truth (that is, meaning and reference) and justification conditions.

All the chapters of this book attempt in one way or another to endow with force and emphasis the conception of linguistic action outlined in this introduction. The chief assumption underlying this book and distinguishing it from all the modern theories and practices emanating from what is ultimately a Saussure-based conception of language (that is, virtually all modern theories) is that "any adequate account of language in use must consider it as a rational activity by individuals who have specific intentions and purposes"; "use of language is . . . the primary manifestation of our rationality—it is the rational activity par excellence." [22] Each of the chapters has its own specific concerns, and each could stand alone, but the book as a whole is unified by a common set of concerns and by a view of meaning and language that is a clear alternative to the one prevailing in contemporary critical discourse.

# Chapter 1
## Authors and Books: The Return of the Dead from the Graveyard of Theory

Common theoretical wisdom has it that authors have given up the ghost and literary works have deferred pride of place to language or been dissolved into ideology or politics, especially the politics of race, class, and gender. Given the prevailing assumptions in critical studies today, to express an interest in the literary text as a unique product of artistic making and an eagerness to focus attention on works within the system of their interests would be to express what many would undoubtedly take to be an antedeluvian quaintness or perverse stubbornness. By and large, literary critics today produce not literary criticism or literary studies, but theory and metacriticism. They talk not about literary works or artistic products (that is, unique products of art, verbal structures reflecting the representational and expressive interests of rational agents), but about writing, semiotics, the play of codes and conventions. Or, speaking even more broadly, they talk about texts as instantiations, signs, exemplifications, or consequences of the more basic linguistic or social (political, ideological, gender, etc.) forces that serve as the conditions of possibility for the speaker, speaking, and spoken.

Interestingly enough, the language that is seen to the bottom of—or the bottomless abyss of—is one that gives special prominence to what we would old-fashionedly call syntax, as distinct from semantics or pragmatics, that is, to that branch of semiotics which studies the relations of signs to one another apart from their contentful relations to the "world." Semantic relations, after all, are those concerned with reference, meaning, and truth-conditions, with that to which the signs point or direct attention, with the representational content of agents' intentional states (their belief, desires, hopes, etc.). Modern theorists also tend to neglect pragmatics, the study of the relations between speakers and interpreters and, more broadly, of the ways we *use* signs. The current theoretical neglect of authors and individual purposes undoubtedly derives much of its impetus from its Saussurrean heritage, with its neglect of reference and its emphasis on language, not as a representational system, but as a formal system of sign relations.

In *On Deconstruction: Theory and Criticism,* Jonathan Culler enthusiastically welcomes the liberation of criticism from a concern with works of literature, believing that the view of theory as the handmaiden to literature has tended to debase critical thought or, more properly, theory, a rigorous independent discipline. To Culler, it is a totally discredited and thoroughly outmoded view which insists that "the test of critical writing is its success in enhancing our appreciation of literary works, and [that] the test of theoretical discussions is its success in providing instruments to help the critic provide better interpretations."[1] As the natural sons and heirs of Carlyle, Emerson, Nietzsche, et al.—that is, of those doing theory, not criticism—Culler celebrates such modern writers as Saussure, Marx, Freud, Gadamer, and Derrida, all of whom, along with Lacan, Bakhtin, Althusser, and many others, make problematic what critics had hitherto treated as given, by bringing to reflection what had before only been used. And in *Topographies,* J. Hillis Miller deplores any tendency to revive "thematic or mimetic readings of literature" or to "return to 'history' "; he opposes any effort to reinstate "traditional ideas about personal identity, agency, and responsibility."[2]

The views of Culler and Miller are entirely compatible, of course, with the widespread, if not quite pervasive concern, not with the book, but with the *text,* and with the text not as a discrete or isolable locus of meaning and value, but as a complex of intertexts, or, in Julia Kristeva's terms, a "mosaic of quotations."[3] The text, as another critic would have it, "emerges as interpretive discourse caught up in a network of other interpretive discourses."[4] Once everything goes textual (and signs are seen principally in terms of their relations to other signs), it is easy to show that no center or stable locus of meaning will hold. In short, once what *is* becomes only *semes,* once the sign of the thing becomes the "thing" of attention, it is difficult not to conclude that everything is intertextual, since interimplication is inevitable in a world where marks or inscriptions are, as Derrida insists, iterable in illimitable contexts and always and already other than themselves. We are informed, further, that books, unlike texts, aspire to tell the truth about things, whereas texts are and can be nothing more than comments on other texts. (Of course for many critics, books—that is, literary works—aspire not to *tell* truths but to *express* and *depict* them by showing us, for example, how it would be to live such and such humanly interesting times and situations with such and such beliefs, hopes, problems, and so on.) As Derrida insists, "the idea of the book is the idea of a totality, finite or infinite, of the signifier; this totality of the signifier cannot be a totality, unless a totality constituted by the signified preexists it, supervises its inscriptions and its signs, and is independent of it in its ideality." (That is, the totality of the signified is the ultimate center or ground of meaning that authorizes and makes valid what is said or done, but since neither signifier nor signified is stable—everything is relational, and stability is always deferred—there can be no fixed meaning; other meanings and uses are always and necessarily implicated in current meanings and uses.) "The idea of the book, which always refers to a natural totality, is profoundly alien to the sense of writing." [5]

The idea of the book has gone, of course, with the loss of the Transcendental Signified, the sure grounding of the fixed relation between word and thing, leaving us only with relations among signs. At best, with the loss of real correspondences between words, thoughts, and things, we are left with various systems of thought, each legitimate and none privileged. As Hilary Putnam observes, "For deconstructionists, metaphysics was the *basis* of our entire culture, the pedestal on which it all rested; if the pedestal has broken, the entire culture must have collapsed—indeed, our whole language must lie in ruins." [6] (It is perhaps worth noting for the sake of my subsequent argument that Putnam goes on immediately to say, "But of course we can and do make sense of the idea of a reality we did not make, even though we cannot make sense of the idea of a reality that is 'present' in the metaphysical sense of dictating its own unique description.") Just because "reality" (or "realities," since, with Putnam and many others, I assume that there are innumerable correct or right "realities" or descriptions of the world) cannot be seen or understood independently of our descriptions, we should not be led to suppose that there are only descriptions. From Putnam's anti-relativist, "internal realist" viewpoint—which runs counter to the relativism and nihilism of most literary theorists—"some facts are there to be discovered . . . but this is something to be said [only] when one has adopted a way of speaking, a language, a 'conceptual scheme.' " [7]

But if we have lost the possibility of providing a single, unique description of the way things just are, we have not lost our ability to make and live in real worlds of fact and value, nor our ability to produce artifacts, including poems, with determinate references and meaning, with internal interests and effects that are knowable, as we shall see. And it is worth remembering at the outset that for our purposes and for purposes of literary study we, if not Derrida and others, can separate the issue of realism, an ontological matter, from the issues of truth and meaning, semantic matters.

Indeed, it is important to recognize that there is no inherent inconsistency in one's believing both in conceptual relativity (the idea that reality is determined by *our* categories and concepts, that the only access we have to "reality" is by means of interest-relative, language-dependent conceptual schemes) and in external realism (the idea that reality exists independently of our representations of it, that we can distinguish between our representations and what is represented). After all, in our diurnal, workaday experience we recognize that though we decide what traits a pigeon must have to be a pigeon, we do not decide whether the odd bird in front of us is or is not a pigeon. Our terms apply to or fit the creature or they do not, and we can do nothing to coerce the creature to enroll under our categorical rubric, our conceptual scheme. To insist that there simply are no pigeons independently of our definitional system of necessary traits is to be stuck with a conceptual scheme that can have neither application nor confirmation. Or, as John Searle, observes, "the interest-relativity of our representations of reality does not show that the reality represented is itself interest relative." [8]

Despite their many differences, modern theorists by and large share the view that there is no single mind- or discourse-independent world of things that authorizes or validates our claims and against which our assertions must be squared. If this view amounts to no more than saying that it makes no sense to talk about references, objects, or facts except in relation to some conceptual scheme or that content-bearing mental states depend on some particular use of language, then there can be no disagreement with the theorists. But it does not follow from this view, as the theorists seem to think, that as the world of unique descriptions (as the Transcendental Signified) goes, so goes the text as a bearer of stable, determinate meanings to which our interpretive statements can be adjusted and against which our opinions must be tested for accuracy and appropriateness. Still, the prevailing view is that once meaning goes immanent (once things and thoughts and all the rest go inside conceptual schemes, inside the language by which they are constituted what they are) and "reality" presumptively stands aloof in noumenal hauteur or is willing, for its own high ironic purposes, to wear any outfit supplied by any logodaedalic courturier, while steadfastly refusing to endorse or approve of any one conceptual suit, then such things as determinate meaning, truth, justification and so on disappear from the scene, along with authors, stable texts, and standards of value, which are nothing but precipitates of always-already-in-place categories and systems of meaning that shift from interpretive community to interpretive community and from period to period.

Many, if not all, modern relativists/poststructuralists apparently believe that if there is no Transcendental Signified, no one independently existing maker good and true of our assertions, then no writing is better, more valuable, or more negotiable than any other. An impatient citizen, outside the loop of theory, might protest at this point that a scheme that enabled her to form true beliefs, to satisfy desires and meet needs would certainly be preferable to one that made possible none of these or that was self-refuting or otherwise incoherent, but she speaks out of turn here. Though no scheme, according to these theorists, has any privilege over any other scheme, some schemes, it is affirmed, have greater authority and, hence, legitimacy than others do. This authority derives not from the adequacy of the scheme to some needs or values or from its truth, but from its power. In a world of immanent meaning, emphasis is regularly placed on the constitutive energy of various more and less powerful paradigms, social formations, ideologies, or interpretive communities. Emphasis is placed, in short, on the determination of facts, things, values, and so on by the conceptual categories of one or another entrenched or influential community or power elite and, usually, on the "incommensurability" of the various schemes—the impossibility, that is, of speaking or understanding outside the historical-ideological framework through which not only "reality" but also the speaker is spoken (though this latter view, taken in its general sense, would seem to invalidate or refute itself in its articulation or expression).

The issues which occupy today's literary theorists and to which they subordinate artistic works are nothing other than local discipline-specific manifestations of more general and pervasive concerns of modern philosophy, both Continental and Anglo-American. The Continental side is preoccupied *either* with the endless deferral of meaning, the loss of stability in signifier and signified, and the emergence of the Other to undermine or subvert what is affirmed on the surface (what is logocentrically asserted) *or* with the determination of the speaking and the spoken, the writing and the written, by social, political, cultural, and ideological conditions. The Anglo-American side concentrates *either* on the *incommensurability of languages* (theories, conceptual schemes), the view that each language is unique and, thus, not translatable into any other language, *or* on the *indeterminacy of meaning*, the view that too many statements (theories, meanings) are compatible with the data. In the philosophical debates, as in those strictly focused on literary theory, the primary disesteemed antagonists are objectivity, intentionality, determinate meaning, stability of reference, the authority of the author to structure meanings and determine effects—all those terms and categories upon which the discussion and analysis of the discrete products of the creative, artistic imagination depend or rely.

In the space of a single chapter it would be impossible, of course, to put into question (as the popular phrase has it) all that the theorists have emphasized, impossible, and also unwise, since there are obviously many attractive neonates in the bathwater of modern theory. Still, to the extent that some of the prevailing principles and assumptions make impossible (or seem to make impossible) what we would most earnestly be about—namely, a discussion of some of what is involved and entailed in an approach to literature based on a conception of language in *use*—it is necessary to do a little ground-clearing and to reclaim some territory for tillage that has been deemed (at best) infertile. Elsewhere in this book I attempt to provide full-scale arguments in support of what I must here lay claim to by force of enthymeme and authoritative fiat, a kind of pointing in the right direction, directing the attention to the critics and philosophers with big shoulders and muscular arguments.

The philosophical literature on *incommensurability* (the impossibility of talking across paradigms or interpretive communities, or of translating from one discourse to another) and *indeterminacy of meaning or translation* (the inability of terms to describe uniquely the ways things are or to remain fixed in reference) is vast, but no one should assume that these issues have been settled once and for all in favor of the theorists. Quite the contrary, the accumulating evidence and argument lean the other way. Against the notion of incommensurability, which finds its strongest advocates in literary theorists influenced, both directly and indirectly, by Thomas Kuhn's *The Structure of Scientific Revolutions*, such as Stanley Fish (and many others), the strongest case has undoubtedly been made by Donald Davidson in "On the Very Idea of a Conceptual Scheme." In addition to showing how field linguists regularly overcome the difficulties of translating languages radically different from their own (languages grounded in and informed by values and assumptions that they do not share), Davidson forcefully argues that the notion of a scheme beyond our capacity to understand is incoherent, since to know that it is an alternative scheme is already to be well into the process of translation and understanding. In another compelling essay, Davidson argues that "we really do not understand the *idea* of such a foreign scheme," because

We know what states of mind are like, and how they are correctly identified; they are just those states whose contents can be discovered in well-known ways [i.e., by attending to the rational or logical links between actions and the mental states that are their necessary preconditions and causes]. If other people or creatures are in states not discoverable by these methods, it can be, not because our methods fail us, but because those states are not correctly called called states of mind—they are not beliefs, desires, wishes, or intentions. The meaninglessness of the idea of a conceptual scheme forever beyond our grasp is due not to our inability to understand such a scheme or to our other human limitations; it is due simply to what we mean by a system of concepts.[9]

Moreover, it is clear, I think, that we regularly discuss the conflicting claims of rival views. In doing so, we are representing both views from a position outside either view (managing in the process, it should be noted, to be fair to both but partial to neither), since no position can be discussed within the position itself. Within the position, we *use* the conditions of its expression; we do not *discuss* them. Even to say in Wittgensteinian fashion that something is "true" in such and such a "language game" is to speak a truth about the "language game," but not a "truth" within the game, or, as Hilary Putnam notes: "If we say that it is a *fact* that acceptance of a given statement or theory is 'justified relative to the standards of culture A' " (as Richard Rorty does, and as Fish says of "interpretive communities"), "then we are treating 'being the standard of a culture' and 'according with the standard of a culture' as something *objective*, something itself *not* relative to the standards of this-or-that culture." [10] A similar point, with Kuhn's paradigm-locked view as the focus, is made by James Harris in *Against Relativism*, when he argues that

> To say that two paradigms are incommensurable requires one to assume an intellectual position such that one can "stand outside" the totality of any single paradigm. . . . Since rules and criteria for paradigm evaluation (including presumably even logical consistency) are clearly supposed to be internal to a paradigm, according to Kuhn, then "incommensurable" is a predicate which can only take on a meaning relative to a single paradigm. Obviously, however, incommensurability is a relationship between or amongst paradigms; so it must follow as a result of criteria or rules which are *not internal* to any given paradigm. [11]

Further, it is useful to remember that "rationality and justification are presupposed by the activity of criticizing and inventing paradigms and are not themselves defined by any single paradigm, certainly not by any existing paradigm (or what would be the point of critique or invention?)." [12] Without rationality, randomness would rule, sense would be inexpressible (inconceivable even), and intelligibility would be impossible. Just as each expression is a specific realization of a particular "rationality," so rationality is itself a precondition (a logical precondition, that is) of any and all meaningful expressions. Although there is considerably more to say about our ability to understand and participate in structures of meaning and reference not of our (or our interpretive community's, our episteme's, our archive's, etc.) own making, we can conclude this discussion by noting that we can always talk *about* what we talk *with*, we can always go "meta-" on any discourse or work. Without the sharing of content, the sharing of some references and meaning, there can be no agreement or disagreement.

Like incommensurability, *indeterminacy* is a vexed question, one not likely to be stripped of all vexation in a brief discussion. But for our immediate purposes we can say enough about it to justify and legitimize our concern with determinate art products. As W. V. Quine and others have shown us, there is a strong sense in which, since "nature" has no semantic preferences and has no point of view on "things" that determines which descriptions are uniquely true, and since every object of any kind is like Wittgenstein's rabbit/duck figure—in that logically it can be described in many ways and participate functionally in innumerable conceptual schemes—reference is fundamentally and inescapably inde- terminate. If we were metaphysicians of daily life, we might worry about our ability to negotiate our way through each day in a world without bounded entities (i.e., fixed objects) or a Foundation. But the fact that the contents of our experience have no fixed reference does not mean, of course, that we can't bump into them or that they are not "real." They are real enough for all our interests and purposes, since they are in large part the products of those interests and purposes. Although it is perhaps impossible to say where "things" would be *for us* without our interests in and descriptions of them, it is possible to say that what is true and right and fitting is not simply a matter of language. There is for us no one way the world independently is, although there is an independent world (or, more properly, there are independent worlds), as Mark Sacks, echoing Putnam, suggests.[13]

What is true, right, or fitting is not simply up to us, since we can dis- tinguish "conditions of reference," which we supply, from "reference," which we do not supply. As Michael Devitt observes, making the word "rose" refer in certain conditions (the conditions that we specify) "is not *making those conditions obtain,* and, hence, is not making roses."[14] This basic point is given even more emphatic expression by John Searle when he notes: "[that] we use the word 'cat' the way we do is up to us; that there is an object that exists independently of that use, and satisfies that use, is a plain matter of (absolute, intrinsic, mind-independent) fact."[15] Nevertheless, with Quine and the theorists, we recognize that reference is nonsense except "relative to a coordinate system," a frame of reference, a conceptual scheme.[16] Objects, facts, references, values, explanations, then, are context-sensitive, interest-relative, and purpose- conditional. On these matters most parties are largely in agreement.

But if we can agree on this much—that meaning and reference are relative to conceptual scheme—then we should be able to agree on more (indeed, we have already agreed to considerably more in fact). We should agree, for example, that our endorsement of such conceptual relativity entails no ontological commitments, no commitments pertain- ing to Transcendental realms or noumenal orders of existence; that such schemes as have content are knowable (see the comments above on radical interpretation and on understanding systems not of our own making); that whatever has content has semantic properties (such as meaning, reference, and truth-conditions); and that there are only con- tents where there are systems of intentionality, since "aboutness" is the essential feature of intentionality, and since only creatures with content-bearing mental states have intentionality and use language. Simply, there is no directedness to the world (and, hence, no content to focus on or be interested in) apart from such contentful states as belief and desire. Content depends on the intentional states of individuals, who believe, desire, hope, intend that such and such is, will be, could be the case. And it is only because we believe, desire, hope, *about* this or that thing or state of affairs that we act (or write, or speak) as we do. Agents, authors, folks like you and me—not cultures, ideologies, epistemes, communities, and so on—are capable of marking things off from one another and having interests and systems of meaning.

The web of interlocking concepts is very tight here, but a few strands more will provide the conceptual strength we need to pursue our interests in literary works with a clear conscience in this contentious era of theory (that is, the prevailing theory that has made authors and works suspect, indeed, phantasmagorical notions). To be interested in something is to be able to think about it and refer to it (whatever it is); such directing of the attention to something is what we mean, in large measure, by intentionality (to have any world at all or anything at all to think about is to be caught up in intentionality). Since all forms of intentionality (beliefs, desires, intentions, doubts, fears, thirsts, hungers, experiences, understandings, and so on) have conditions of satisfaction (truth is the satisfaction of belief, drinking the satisfaction of thirst, and so on), intentionality is inescapably normative; its conditions are satisfied *or not* (or satisfied more or less). Now, to take one instance of intentionality, for a belief to be satisfied is for it to be justified, to be true. And what something is depends on the conditions justifying it, as we learned above when with Quine and others we recognized that reference is relative to scheme.

What is referred to in a sentence is determined and justified (or not) by its fittingness to a scheme. More simply, "there can be no meaning without some form of structure or pattern that establishes relationships." [17] It is only relative to justification or truth conditions, for example, that a "bill" belongs to a baseball cap rather than to a restaurant check. And for Michael Dummett, as Ernest Lepore and Barry Loewer remind us, "the justification [or truth] conditions of a sentence are its meaning, and since understanding a sentence is just knowing its meaning, it follows that anyone who understands a sentence knows its justification conditions, that is, the canonical conditions such that if they were satisfied the sentence would be true." [18]

From all this, it is not a big leap to the understanding that a literary work (like a critical essay or an editorial) is a system of justification or rationality, a system of self-satisfaction, one that is knowable from within its interests and conditions of satisfaction. To have any world at all, including the world of specific conceptual and emotional entailments that make up a literary work, we must have standards of justification or standards of rational acceptability. Just as there are many ways of wrecking a ship in a storm and very few ways of bringing it home safely, as Aristotle observed, so there are many ways for a piece of literature to go wrong and very few ways for it to go right, to fit its internal conditions of satisfaction or justification. Since we, along with Davidson and others, are concerned with a psychological, semantic, truth-conditional view of truth and meaning, we acknowledge the wisdom of the notion that without rationality there is no content, no truth, meaning, or reference. We tend to see things in literary and other works the way they are intended to be seen, because that is the way they are justified, that is the way the contents have justification, and once we start "seeing as," we tend to work within what "seeing as" makes possible. On this point, Wittgenstein, as elucidated by Eddy M. Zemach, is instructive:

[As I initially see the content] it fits some things and not others. That is why Wittgenstein compares meaning in language to the meaning of a musical phrase; of course you can do anything at all with that motif [considered in isolation], but given the way we see it, having heard [or read] the work up to this point, some developments would look absolutely wrong to us. The phrase in that work has a meaning: it "asks" to be dealt with in certain ways and not others.[19]

In sum, meanings are determinate within systems, and such systems are, if not given to the understanding as immediately as the leaves are given to the tree, accessible to understanding, in just the ways that Davidson has suggested.

The consequences of the foregoing remarks for critical practice are, I think, quite remarkable, if only because they enable us to reinvest with dignity and appropriateness many critical activities that have undergone the lash of excoriation and suffered the shame of excommunication in recent years, the years dominated by what Jonathan Culler and others calls Theory. From the heights of philosophical reflection, we can now descend to more mundane observations and concerns. In the interests of expedition, I shall be brief, presenting the case in truncated form (at least initially) as articles of commitment, with only some of the implications spelled out.

1. Language in *use* is always centered, is always selective and restrictive. We cannot talk about what we cannot mention or distinguish, and we cannot talk about or imply all the attributes that what we talk about may have. As Quine has persistently reminded us, we cannot know what something is without knowing how it is differentiated from other things. (For Quine, of course, this means that identity is coextensive with ontology.) More pointedly, as John Searle notes, "intentional states repre-

sent their conditions of satisfaction only under certain aspects, and those aspects must matter to the agent." [20] Intentionality is aspectual or perspectival, a matter of seeing something "as" something from some point of view, and "representation" is a matter of intentionality. In any given use of the word "chair," for example, I do not imply that it is my property or was made in North Carolina. Simon Blackburn has provided an interesting example of how "chair" satisfies conditions under one rather than another aspect (and, incidentally, of the interest-relativity of explanation): "The natural or best explanation of a physical thing having a physical property need not belong to physics. In most contexts, the best explanation of this chair being within three miles of Carfax may be that it belongs to me, and this is where I live." [21] Furthermore, once we have selected and, hence, restricted our terms, we can say no more, while those restrictions are in place, than what falls within the logical and semantic range of those terms as used. Among other things, we affirm here that no problem or situation can be completely formulated or represented, that any problem or representation is "relative to its formulation, and that any solution," to the extent that it is a solution to the problem or situation as formulated, "must also be relative to the formulation." [22]

2. The constraints on usage are not *always already* in place, as the popular theoretical phrase goes; the constraints are not an automatic consequence of, for example, the nature of language, prior texts, ideologies, social formations, or gender. We are never locked into the prisonhouse of any language (any particular system of justification). Understanding depends on the sharing of many concepts, and the coreferentiality of terms is common; for example, we can have many different views of *Hamlet*, the French Revolution, psoriasis, department chairmen, and so forth. Indeed, our understanding of common references across paradigm shifts, across systems of meaning, can find a down-home illustration in our immediate grasp of the meanings of such ambiguous sentences as "Alphonse likes exciting sheep." Here references remain stable while truth conditions shift. When we move from the homely to the lofty, the point is preserved, for in the comparison of theories, understanding or mutual intelligibility depends not on two theories sharing *meanings*, but on their sharing (at least some) *references*, some concepts. [23] Moreover, as we have seen, we can always talk *about* what we talk *with*, always transcend our formalizations. Without such imaginative capacities of transcendence, mindless repetition would be our only expressive possibility. Now, as in the past, we all coexist more or less comfortably within a variety of interpretive communities.

3. Our plenty makes us poor. That is, our various codes and conventions—whether derived from the analysis of language, culture, history, politics, or whatever—supply us with little more than a large stock of

terms capable of entering into a multiplicity of substitutional, combinatorial, meaning, or referential relations, a stock of terms rich in meaning possibility or potentiality. But these codes and conventions, however refined and elaborated, cannot determine the boundary conditions of their own operation, for, as we have seen, truth-, assertibility-, or justification-conditions are prior to reference (and meaning). They are rich in possibility, but poor in determination. Thus, just as the system of rules governing the relations in which chess pieces may enter does not and cannot determine the strategy of any particular game (as Michael Polanyi observes), so the conditions of language, considered as a relational system of possible substitutions and combinations, considered as a formal system, cannot determine the nature of any particular work.[24]

The game cannot be played outside the rules, but the rules cannot organize a strategy. Even though it would be a mistake to assume that people are not played by systems—in the sense that we are all creatures of the terms available to or forced upon us and, as such, all limited to working out what falls within the logical and semantic range of those terms—it would be a greater mistake to fail to realize that, no matter how severe the constraints on expression may be, an unlimited number of purposes are realizable within them, or that the boundary conditions for the operation of the relational systems cannot be supplied by the systems themselves. Hence, it is the very *indeterminacy of language* that obliges us to locate the constraints on possibility in the textually embedded intentional acts of agents.

4. Codes and conventions make writing possible. Writers make codes and conventions meaningful and representational, make them answer to the bidding of mental states, of various intentionalities. Neither a sentence nor a work derives its specific meaning or emphasis from the words considered in themselves (indeed, they have no determinate reference considered in themselves) or in their possible relations (apart from justification conditions, which make them relations of something to something); in other words, no work can come into being or carry a determinate meaning (or have a particular expressive content of moral choice and emotional emphasis) unless its medium (its language) is deliberately arranged in some fashion for some reason or purpose. Consequently, it is not possible in our engagement with the work to avoid the sorts of interpretive assumptions about agents and intentions that modern critical theory, in most of its branches and franchises, has denounced or proscribed. For example, in reading *Othello*, we are most profitably rewarded by asking repeatedly of greater and lesser linguistic units not "What do these words mean?" but, borrowing from Ralph Rader, "What significant creative intention must I assume to make these words intelligible?"[25] In posing the question this way, we are seeking to understand

the justification conditions or, in slightly older, more "literary" terms, the principles of construction embedded in the text as products of choice, only on the assumption of which can we account for all the particulars of the text.

Making what is to me a compatible point, Hilary Putnam states that "what is *true* depends on what our terms *refer to*, and—on any picture—determining the reference of terms demands sensitivity to the referential intentions of actual speakers and an ability to make nuanced decisions as to the best reconstruction of those intentions." [26] Similarly, Martha Nussbaum views "literary texts as works whose representational and expressive content issues from human intentions and conceptions." Nussbaum goes on to discuss how Richard Wollheim, in *Painting as an Art* and in *Art and Its Objects*, shows that "the standard of correctness for the spectator's (or reader's) activity must be found by reference to the artist's intention; but that only those intentions are relevant that are causally involved in the production of the work." [27] At this level of inquiry, we are interested in the representational and expressive content as determined by the author's controlling system of intentionality. The problem, as posed here, depends on the recognition that, as Michael Dummett observes, "the concept of intention can be applied only against a background of a distinction between those regularities of which a language [user], acting as a rational agent engaged in conscious, voluntary action, *makes use* from those that may be hidden from him and might be uncovered by a psychologist or neurologist" (or a Marxist or cultural historian). The writer can "make use only of those regularities of which he may be said to be in some degree aware, those, namely, of which he has at least implicit knowledge," those which "fit" and "belong to" the text's interests.[28]

Of course, in our reach for artistic intention, we may guess wrong, may misunderstand the creative intention, but the text, in its reluctance to accommodate itself to our constitutive hypothesis, has the capacity to force a revision of our assumptions. Our guess is propensive, not tyrannical. Finally, it is useful to remember that in perhaps most of our dealings with most of our literature, we are concerned with language, not as organized into propositional networks or systems of truth claims, but as systems of moral perplexity, moral choice, and moral action. What most frequently needs to be grasped is not what the words mean, but what act by what sort of person in what sort of situation the words make possible. "Character," for example, must be inferred from its actualizations, and unless we make such inferences about "character" (the sort of person we are dealing with), the work has no significant moral or emotional effect.

5. The final commitment has several codicils attached to it, but basically it affirms a sharp division among interpretation, poetics, and criticism and sees them as hierarchically arranged in a regular order of dependence: criticism is dependent upon poetics, and poetics upon interpretation (the last, in turn, depending upon linguistics and, broadly considered, philology). Each of these divisions (along with ethics) will be quickly considered in turn below in the conclusion to this essay, but here we can briefly chart the terrain. Once we have grasped the significant artistic intention that both implies and is implied by the details of this work and then that work and the next one (interpretation), we can begin to consider a variety of texts in terms of likenesses and differences (along several lines of differentiation).

Since we can make relevant statements about essential aspects of two or more texts—aspects essential under distinct intentional conceptions (we are not limited to particulars)—and since every work uses its medium in distinguishable ways, we can begin to outline the poetics of discrete artistic forms. Only when we have mastered these tasks (however casually or deliberately) are we in a position to see texts in their larger artistic, social, political relations, only then are we in a position to do criticism. For all our current talk about transcending works and authors and moving beyond interpretation, no one, it seems to me—not Derrida or Foucault or Greenblatt or whoever—can do any work with literature at all without first performing acts of interpretation (something must be understood as something before it can be talked *about*). Interpretation, however unimportant ultimately to the critic, is the necessary basis of larger speculation, to the extent that that speculation is concerned at all with *literature* and what it reveals about, say, history, mind, language, politics, or culture. We need not focus on interpretation, of course, but we cannot do literary criticism of any kind prior to or in the absence of interpretation.

In the following concluding section on the divisions among critical enterprises, the emphasis will be less on definition and theoretical defense of categories than on elaboration of the importance and value of the categories (given the analyses of meaning, reference, intentionality, and rationality presented above). Our task here, at the rudimentary or propaedeutic level, is merely to show that celebrations (or "funferals," as James Joyce would say) on the occasion of the death of the author or of the work (at least as a determinate structure of intentionality) are premature. Consequently, with our focus on agents (authors) and intentionality (as embedded in works), we will not be able to give full or even sufficient consideration to the difficulties involved in coming to a strong understanding of justification conditions (or, in an older terminology, principles of form) or to deal in detail with conflicting conceptions of those conditions (with, in other words, rival or multiple interpretations).

## Interpretation

Interpretation, in our view, involves coming to an understanding of the text's categories of intelligibility (its contents) in their functional relations within a system of rationality or justification. In the literature we have come most to value (in every culture), our understanding is enlarged with each renewed contact and perhaps never enlarged to fullness or completeness. In reading *Othello* for the fortieth time, we are struck by a new rightness or appropriateness that we had not noticed before. This understanding is at the center of interpretation and is crucial to what W. V. Quine and Joseph Ullian call the training of taste: such training "proceeds by emphasizing skillfully selected elements of an object," and this "increased familiarity with the structure of the aesthetic object," with what we have been calling its conditions of satisfaction, "can engender a liking, granted a suitable choice of object in the first place." [29] The skill part of such an understanding can be developed and refined and, to a large extent and in its main features, taught, principally by regularly asking questions about how these and those discernible elements *fit* or *satisfy* the intentional conditions of their possibility. Moreover, those to whom it is taught can develop and refine the skill on their own, largely because the questions it permits and encourages can be right *or* wrong, because the hypothesis (the controlling conception of "seeing as," in Wittgenstein's sense) from which we project meanings and possibilities is right and adequate to the (always already) justified structure, *or it is not*; our projections can be *disconfirmed* as well as confirmed. (I present a more detailed discussion of the satisfaction of a text's internal, intentional conditions in Chapter 8, where I distinguish between—and provide examples of—the internal and external "goods" of texts.)

And surely those of us who give days and nights to the study of literature can be forgiven for focusing at least some of our attention on what we ought not to be embarrassed to call the "internal goods"—the satisfied needs of the artistic structure—of texts, on the rather uncommon, wonderful, and remarkable fittingness and workingness of things in certain texts, once they are considered under this or that conception of justification. Perhaps we can even be forgiven for allowing ourselves to value more highly than other works those which not only manage to fit much of interest in but to make so much of what fits in contribute significantly to the working of the whole work. Surely we can be forgiven for continuing to admire and value *Paradise Lost*, the *Essay on Man*, *The Prelude*, and *King Lear* as "masterpieces," as monuments of unaging intellect. And we continue to admire them even though propositionally, as bodies of ideas or systems of thought, they are, if not philosophically bankrupt, at least intellectually poor or suspect, and even though most of what is politically, ideologically, or historically interesting in them can be found in many other earlier, contemporaneous, and later works (both serious and comic, both popular and elite) as well as in other cultural artifacts, like trade routes or jokes, and perhaps in purer, starker, bolder form.

In addition to admiring these works for the largeness of their conception, the extent of their understanding, the importance of the matters they raise and deal with, we recognize as we applaud in each of them a superior kind of formal or artistic achievement. We discern in each rightnesses and appropriatenesses that are widely distributed and deeply embedded and that, by *enhancing the workingness of the whole*, make the realized work a rare and, hence, especially valuable achievement. Indeed, this formal richness is inseparable from the intellectual and moral achievement of the works; the verbal, imagistic, and structural echoings, entailments, and interlacings are the conditions of possibility, in a sense, of the conceptual reach, moral significance, and emotional power of the works.

In *Othello*, for example, every scene, virtually every word, not only contributes to the forwarding of the action and to our understanding of the bases of jealousy, but also enhances and enriches our sense of the internal integrity, of the architectonic cohesiveness of the work as a whole. One after another, each image, phrase, or scene finds itself involved with predecessors or successors in a complexly appropriate system of interimplication. (Consider, for example, the wonderfully rich interlacings of "wit," "witchcraft," and "jealousy" throughout the text.) If the making of such deeply self-satisfied, formally and morally rich works as, for example, *Othello, Paradise Lost, The Essay on Man, The Prelude*, and so on) is a huge accomplishment (as it clearly is when measured against the standards established over the years by the accomplishments of other toilers in the same fields), then the participation, by means of understanding, in such achievements at the level of their interests and justifications is a huge pleasure. Many today, alas, do not experience this pleasure, but fortunately (in the odd sense in which ignorance is bliss), their theoretical principles and assumptions keep them from knowing what they are not experiencing.

To talk of these pleasures and these accomplishments to the knowledgeably well-pleased is undoubtedly to talk unnecessarily; that is, it is to talk to the sailor of the sea, to talk to those who already know what one is talking about and who do not need to be convinced of the pleasure of pleasure. But something is surely awry when one is repeatedly invited to deny the pleasure, or to confess that it is second-rate, insignificant, illusory, or impossible, because language is such and such or because what really counts or what everything finally boils down to is ideology, undoing, colonialism, or whatever. Or, if the pleasure is allowed, it is allowed only as a guilty pleasure, one inseparable from one's tolerance of or complicity with oppression, racism, sexism, or whatever. In this chapter, my aim, in part, has been to reclaim the pleasure (to establish at least its possibility) and to take the guilt out of it by showing that the text, as a product of a rich network of interested human and humanly interesting intentionality (and not as a mere consequence, sign, instance of something else, such as history, ideology, gender, class, etc.), is already an uncommonly rich system of justification and that the system it is is knowable as that system (though coming to know it is no easy or automatic task). It is a system made and recovered by the more or less strenuous exercise of practical reasoning upon conceptual materials within our grasp or available to our reach.

## Ethics, in Brief

Any differentiable part, any isolable element of the work can become the focus of independent interest and inquiry, and anything so isolated for attention can be examined and discussed in connection with any number of things linguistic, social, political, philological, ideological, anthropological, horticultural, musical, patriotic, mechanical, biographical, or psychological. Nevertheless, high among our interests in those works not motivated or justified by a system of *ideas* or *themes* but focusing on morally differentiated individuals in humanly interesting situations is an interest in what speaking broadly we can call "ethical quality."

Most of our novels, dramas, narrative poems, as well as the majority of our lyric poems, for example, invite us to note clearly and then to consider carefully, apart from self-interest, what it would be like to think and feel in such and such a frame of mind and live in such and such circumstances. We are allowed to see vividly and to participate imaginatively in moral perplexities, in situations of moral choice and moral action, confronting those perplexities not as a system of ideas or as a corpus of theses or moral propositions, but as a complex of social, personal, emotional circumstances impinging on or otherwise affecting and affected by particular character. What we witness and are moved by are ethical possibilities of living. We are interested in what it would be like to live in them and live them out (i.e., to know the consequences of their adoption and use). For many simple reasons within easy reach, all of which are undoubtedly connected in some way or another with our insatiable interest in ourselves, we are tirelessly interested in "new" exhibitions of moral perplexity and possibility. Such exhibitions enable us to add to the stock of our conceptual storehouse, to enlarge our understanding, and to fit ourselves for further and future understanding.

Life is short, and, like Bottom, we cannot be in all roles or know much about the roles available or possible. Literary works, however, provide us with "ethical samples" of ethical possibilities, and they are, in a very large and untrivial sense, the schools of our moral sensibilities, teaching us surreptitiously much about the nature and bases of right behavior. As we read these works, the line of our sustained interest is the line of moral entanglement, complication, and, usually, resolution. In other words, the line of *our* interest and satisfaction follows the line of the text's moral concerns, and these concerns supply the categories of rightness and the conditions of justification that make up the text's interest and make for artistic fulfillment. But as we move beyond the texts we carry from them conceptual resources serviceable in the making and understanding of many new situations and texts, and in the making of the good life. Reading literature at the level of its ethical concern (which is, for many works, the level of its justification) with empathetic understanding will not necessarily make us better people, of course, but it will *exercise our capacity for and improve our skill at moral discrimination*, provide us with concepts useful to the formation of a regulative image of the good life, and, thus, make us better equipped for right action.

## Poetics

From examining works in terms of their internal systems of justification, at the level of their motivation, functioning, and effect (that is, from meeting the responsibilities of interpretation in some rigorous fashion), we can move quite easily to *poetics*, to a consideration, that is, of formal lines of affiliation among works as *kinds*, in terms of similarities and differences in their principles of reasoning and conditions of justification. Once we have understood the principles of workingness in first this, then that, and then again another work, we can begin to establish categories of likeness/difference, aligning works, for example, which use similar *means* in similar *ways* to bring about comparable *effects* in similar *conditions of distress or perplexity*. Because we can make relevant statements about similarities in the essential features of several texts (that is, features essential to the functioning of the works), we can begin to outline the poetics of distinct forms of literature. And if we can do poetics, then we can perhaps undertake a history of forms, tracing changes and variations over time in the constructional conditions of forms and noting instances of refinement and innovation in the use of one or another kind of essential feature, as generations of writers respond to the achievements of their predecessors and the possibilities implicit in the functional features themselves. (I take up in greater detail some of the problems intrinsic to genre identification later, in Chapter 7.)

At this point, discussion can move *from* a concern with internal, constructional causes within schemes and kinds of schemes and with the changes brought about by refining and "perfecting" the possibilities inherent in the discernible and defining features of the various forms *to* a concern with any number of "preconstructional" causes of literary change in social, political, agricultural, religious, gender, musical, or other conditions. It is obvious that what is actually made of this preconstructional material, what emphases it will have and what purposes it will serve at the "constructional" level at which specific choices are made, cannot be determined by the material itself. With R. S. Crane, we affirm that though the constructional cause of elements and emphases within works "presupposes the [preconstructional causes] as their necessary substrate, the [constructional] cannot be deduced from or resolved into the [preconstructional]."[30] Here we would be especially interested in the various ways social formations of one kind or another impinge on textual interests, emphases, values, and purposes, on kinds of topics discussed, kinds of characters presented, kinds of situations depicted, kinds of dilemmas confronted, kinds of diction employed, and so on. We would be interested in, among other things, how Hobbes or Locke or landscape gardening or the Glorious Revolution or early capitalism or shifts in the nature of audiences or in means of production or distribution impacted on this or that textual feature or kind of literature.

## Criticism

These concerns with the preconstructional take us right to the territorial border of *poetics*, beyond which lies the vast wilderness of *criticism*, where works are seen in their larger artistic, social, political, ideological relations, or as subsumed by one or another domain of interest (the psychological, psychoanalytic, linguistic, anthropological, chemical, rhetorical, or other domain). Here ingenuity roams at large and can make literature relate to whatever it wants and can make literature (or anything else) whatever it wants, as long as in the making it does not refute itself or otherwise entangle itself in contradiction or absurdity. In the Big Sky Country of criticism there is room for—you name it: source and influence studies, of the traditional and anxious kind; biography, of various kinds; new or old historicist studies (though, because they are peculiarly susceptible to question begging and to finding always the same One in the Many, these are very difficult projects to manage well, as we shall see in Chapter 4); figural, image, and diction studies (at the ordinary, run of the mill, garden-variety level and at the meta-, mega-, supra-, infra-level); room for all this and, of course, much more.

Additionally, in identifying likenesses and differences among works, creating with each line of association a classification, we are not restricted, in criticism, to the deep or full classification required by poetics, which has genre identification and the elucidation of shared conditions of satisfaction among works as its objects. Any distinguishable feature, any projectible property can serve as the ground or condition of filiation. As Catherine Z. Elgin observes:

We [can] classify [works] by *subject*, as crucifixion pictures or medical bulletins [or domestic tragedies]; by *style*, as impressionist paintings or symbolist poems; [by, we might add, *manner of representation or disclosure*, as first-person or omniscient author narration]. And we classify them by *medium*, as watercolors or news reports; by *author*, as Monets or Flauberts; by *historical or cultural milieu*, as Renaissance or Victorian works.[31]

In the outback of criticism, then, there is space for an indefinite number of projects to situate themselves, including the following three, with which we will conclude our discussion. First, we can do something to refine our understanding of the peculiar features of *thought, emotion, and expression* that characterize the productions of a given writer. Something there is in various artistic works that enables us to recognize with remarkable sureness, for example, the characteristic Milton or Donne or Wordsworth quality or to determine whether a particular unidentified piece can be attributed to a particular author. Concerning such attributions, disputes rage and passions are inflamed, but there is scarcely any reader who has read much by one writer who does not feel qualified to judge the authenticity or spuriousness of a document of uncertain provenance attributed to that writer. It is perhaps reasonable to hope that the bases of this tacit understanding can be made more explicit than they currently are. And this can be accomplished by attending to the differentiable qualities of thought, emotion, and expression in the works of various writers, specifically, by reasoning back, in good Longinian fashion, from achieved effects or from the justification conditions of many works by a single author to the textually embedded, material exemplifications of mind, feeling, and style.

Second, what can be done for the writer can also be done for the writer's "age" (with age discriminated in the way all our categories are discriminated—by interest, habit, practice, and agreement, by our seeing a value in such discriminations for certain purposes). With uncanny regularity we are able to distinguish a given work as a production of a given era or period undoubtedly by bringing our accumulated knowledge and skill to bear once again on peculiarities of *thought, emotion, and expression* that we have come to recognize as characteristic of the era. Without yielding to either Zeitgeitism or historicism, old or new, we here simply acknowledge that from time to time across wide variations in a rich multiplicity of conceptual systems there are certain persistencies in questions entertained and in idioms and terms employed.

For all the manifold diversity of theoretical production in the eighteenth century, for example, there is within this mass of variety and conflict a persistent interest in a certain range of topics and a persistent reliance on a rather stable critical vocabulary. Critics of the period, however diverse and disparate their views, regularly relied on such common terms relating to *critical rules* and *literary types* as "argument," "manners," "fable," "ode," "epic," "pastoral," "thought," "invention," "expression," "arrangement," "sentiments," "middle" and "low" styles, *and* such common terms relating to *causes, effects, circumstances,* and *qualities* as "art," "nature," "the beautiful," "the pathetic," "imitation," "fancy," "judgment," "imagination," "instruction," "delight," and so on. This shared terminology silently testifies to an important and persistent fact of disputational life, namely, that a single (or widely overlapping) vocabulary can be used in support of an indefinitely large number of distinct, divergent, and even contradictory theories. (Correlatively, of course, different vocabularies can serve the interests of a single theoretical system.) Similarly, however various and different the literary productions of, say, the first thirty years of the nineteenth century are (in style, genre, topic, diction, ambition, range of concern, etc.), a considerable number of them are sufficiently distinct as a group that they are not confused with the productions of an earlier or later period. Although intertextualists and other theorists have not been reluctant to drive their Land Rovers across this perilous terrain, much remains to be done, employing categories of discrimination more generous and capacious than those currently in use, to illuminate the ground of our intuitive determinations and tacit judgments.

Finally, for purposes of illustration, where wilderness yields to jungle, there is room in criticism for commentary—largely suggestive and speculative but anchored as firmly as possible in the categories of understanding that actually inform particular works—on the social, political, ethical, ideological, religious, or cultural values implicit in literary and other artistic works. The concern here is with what the works may contribute to our understanding of ways of knowing or ways of living, of ethics, polity, epistemology, and so on. Intellectual roving in this territory is always difficult and always full of danger, because we are always working from restricted evidence to large conclusions, and because we are trying to give clarity and precision to the conceptions of the good, the true, and the beautiful that are implicit in works primarily interested in more local and mundane matters. (Despite its risks and dangers, this territory is always overcrowded with theory prospectors, largely because the dangers and risks can be safely negotiated from the comfort of a heavily padded, indeed, heavily endowed chair, largely because the "rattlers" are merely colleauges and the "coyotes" merely signs.) Underlying artistic versions (as well as all other versions) are visions or conceptions of what we can know or do or what would be good for us to know or do. If such things are difficult to discover and express, their value to and interest for us is proportionate to the difficulty of their attainment, for when it's right down to it that we get, what we most want to know something about is what's to know and how to live.

Only a preoccupation with signs and their relations, on the one hand, and with individuals as fully constructed by the ideological conditions of their existence, on the other, could have obscured from our notice that these and many other projects are possible and worth undertaking. But the key to a revival of interest in works (as distinct from "texts," sign systems, and the instability of reference and meaning in a world without transcendendal signifieds or a Foundation) begins perhaps in the recognition that we are making and understanding creatures. We make what others can understand, and we understand what others can make (otherwise, what would be the point of all our making and efforts of understanding?).

Among the many things that literature is (like anything else, it can be seen or represented under many descriptions), it is a form of behavior or action, and as such it is "rational," that is, its structure is intelligible only by reference to mental states (for example, beliefs, wishes, desires, aims, purposes, intentions). Literature has content (that is, semantic properties, such as meaning, reference, and truth conditions), and where there is content, there is rationality (assertibility or justification conditions), and the only access to the content is by means of a grasp of the rationality. Interpretation succeeds or not depending on whether the rationality is apprehended, and all the other operations that we perform with and upon literature depend on a grasp of the informing rationality, on interpretation, on reading texts within the system of their interests.

This chapter has sought not to overthrow Theory, but to reclaim much senselessly abandoned critical territory by showing that there is nothing in Theory's insights into language or culture that has rendered obsolete, meaningless, second-rate, or illusory our interests in works and authors. Indeed, it seems that practicing literary criticism without focusing on works (initially or at some level) is, finally, not possible, if desirable, and not desirable, if possible.

# Chapter 2
## The Inevitability of Professing Literature

In spite of its apparent blandness and innocuousness, the title of this chapter does not express a generally recognized homely truth, a commonly granted piece of conventional wisdom. As a matter of common fact, most critics today are not professing literature—that is, teaching it, reading it carefully with an eye to coming to some rich understanding of its meaning, integrity, and ethical force. They are instead concerned with literature as a site of deferred payment on the significance account or as a consequence or instance of preexisting power relations in the circumambient political/ideological environment. Increasingly critics produce not literary criticism or literary studies, but metacriticism, and talk not about literary works, but about writing, the free play of signifiers, or the resolution of all expressive documents into the social conditions of their making and possibility. In an article on some current trends in criticism, Catherine Gallagher notes that not one of the well-known critics participating in a lecture series held at Berkeley said anything about literature.[1]

Yet oddly, though not exactly paradoxically, literature—in a more commodious conception of the term—is also what everybody today seems determined to profess and produce. In a world without a Foundation, a world in which there is no longer a transcendent guarantor or validator of a fit between words and the way things just are, the distinction between truth and fiction is lost. All modes of expression and all forms of discourse are equally privileged (or equally disenfranchised). All modes and forms are nothing more (or less) than the *effects* of common figural or tropological maneuvers or of power plays within historically determined circumstances.

In short, all forms of writing are instances of literature. For example, as we noted in Chapter 1, Jonathan Culler, speaking for many, extols Theory as a new (or newly ascendant) literary genre.[2] Also, Richard Rorty, the proponent of his own special form of pragmatism, is everywhere discouraging interest in the sort of philosophy that seeks to gain access to truth or to resolve or take seriously the inherited problems of epistemology, ethics, metaphysics, and language, and is everywhere heralding philosophy as a kind (or as kinds) of writing or literature.[3] Not to be caught with nothing but their correspondence theories showing or to be trapped by outmoded categories, historians (some historians) have found in Hayden White—whose eclecticism brings several intellectual approaches into uneasy conjunction, including the literary criticism of Northrop Frye and the philosophical pluralism of Stephen Pepper—a highly articulate spokesman for the view that "history-writing" is a form of "emplotment." It is "the working out of the possible plots (romance, comedy, tragedy, and satire), arguments (formist, mechanistic, organicist, and contextualist), and ethical implications (anarchist, radical, conservative, and liberal) contained in tropological foundations (metaphor, metonymy, synechdoche, and irony)."[4] And, in literary criticism, Harold Bloom continues to be busily engaged in a mighty struggle of psychic wills with such precursor poets as Emerson, Blake, Stevens, Freud et al., producing such epics as *The Map of Misreading* and *The Breaking of the Vessels.*

In one sense, professing literature, then, would not seem to be a cottage industry but something approaching a cartel or a multinational, interdisciplinary enterprise. But this literature has, finally, little to do with *Moby-Dick* or *A Midsummer Night's Dream*; what we have here is Theory as literature, literature as metacommunication or metacommentary. At best, these writers are preoccupied not with what writing produces, but with what produces writing. Broadly put, they are concerned with what in the nature of language or culture (history, ideology, and so on) enables or creates writing, not with what it is for writers to produce and readers to understand sentences (and whole compositions) with determinate meanings and emphases.

From the standpoint of intellectual debate, the consequences of this liberation of Theory from handmaiden service, along with the correlative subsumption of philosophic, historical, and critical writing by literature, have not been entirely happy. Because we cannot limit the free play of the signifier or speak outside the "always already" imposed constraints of our "interpretive community," "age," "gender," or whatever, we cannot locate a common court of appeals empowered to settle different or rival claims. One lives either joyfully within the labyrinthine passages of language or despondently in the dark dungeon of an elected framework of terms and assumptions. As a naive realist or logical positivist, one can pine for centeredness, authority, and objective truth, but not from the outside of the prisonhouse of language. There's no winning for losing. Issues cannot be joined, and if some critics—E. D. Hirsch, Richard

Levin, and M. H. Abrams, among others—continue to call for debate or dialogue, they hear in return, for the most part, only the voice of silence or, worse yet, condescension.

Thus, one decidedly unfortunate side effect of much recent theorizing is that it tends to put an end, if not to all further writing, at least to fruitful debate and discussion. Moreover, to alter slightly Alexander Pope's remarks prefixed to *An Essay on Man*, the "arguments [indeed even the inquiries] of these critics have less sharpened the wits than the hearts of men against each other and have diminished the practice more than advanced the theory of criticism and interpretation." [5] Writing and debate about literature have certainly become, to many at least, low priority undertakings. To be sure, it is still possible to do a deconstruction job on a succession of works, or to conduct a survey of what can be done within the terms of the various interpretive communities, or to show how a line of poets misread their antecedents, or to track the circulation of social energy in various works and artifacts, or, finally, to disclose the ways in which countless works are complicit in political, racial, or gender oppression. Nevertheless, the disheartening fact is that once the revolutionary, theoretical thing has been said—however repugnant to earned understanding—the rest is hardly worth saying at all, since what really needs to have its say-so has had its say-so in the theoretical statement. For example, can anyone be a truly strong critic who takes Harold Bloom as his father, who imitates the father's method rather than opposes or struggles with it? Or, can I be much gratified by showing how this or that particular work internally undermines the philosophy it asserts or the hierarchical oppositions on which it relies, tracking down the rhetorical operations or the seminal tropes that produce the argumentative ground of the work according to the directives of Derrida or de Man, who truly sees into the nature of language and Western consciousness? Or, can there be much satisfaction at this point in showing with tiresome iteration that this and that work (like all the other previous works examined), despite their voluble claims to the contrary, are stooges of or apologists for repressive regimes? We have here, in short, the criticism of exhaustion; it exhausts its subject in the process of locating it.

It is not surprising that the only new industry promoted by our newer new criticism is the one Jonathan Culler specializes in: the summary of what's going on, the reader's digest of what's happening now. [6] If there is no honor intrinsic to performing the tasks implicated in the theories, there may be some in spreading the news. Ironically, in distinguishing precisely among the commitments of the various, say, deconstructionists, the writers of such synoptic works inadvertently and silently diminish the force of the commitments they successfully delineate (and in direct proportion to their success), since to do their work at all, these writers must assume, as a condition of expression, what their content denies or excoriates, namely, the determinacy of meaning, the ascertainability of embodied authorial intention, and the capacity of different expressions to convey similar meanings. We have in several of these handbooks or surveys a wonderfully vivid illustration of what Susan Hurley has called "pragmatic inconsistency." The synoptic critic's faithful account of the specific meaning of the views of various critics does not merely presuppose something inconsistent with the views elucidated; "it actually demonstrates the falsity of" those views or the "truth of something inconsistent with" them.[7] In the language of paradox much in vogue with current theorists, in being loyal and true to the determinate sense or meaning of the theorists' views, the synoptic critics are quislings to the theorists.

As a final aside on unpleasant side effects, we can note the tendency of the newer criticism to indulge in a naive kind of falsificationism, that is, to assume that because a succession of writers have scoffed at, say, intentionality and determinate meaning, such topics, like the fossilized remains of extinct species, are fit only for museums. Unless one is au courant, one is hopelessly reactionary. What we have then in the body intellectual is something analogous to an affliction of the body sexual, that is, premature articulation or adjudication, a rush to climactic judgment. As a consequence, it is becoming increasingly difficult for writers of even so-called traditional or safe articles to get a hearing, without exhibiting an awareness, if only in their notes, of the preferred terms, assumptions, or buzz words, and virtually impossible to find a place for the monograph that positively embraces "heretical" principles or to get anything but derisive reviews, if one should happen to find a place for it. In short, because of the celebrity status of certain writers and the celerity with which they acquire myrmidons, a severely restricted range of concerns and values is becoming (or threatening to become) institutionalized, thus creating conditions that preclude any challenge to those values and, ironically, lead to the bestowal of establishment credentials on the revolutionary.

The tendencies highlighted above cannot be reversed or overcome by fiat, of course, but something useful may be accomplished, first, by reminding ourselves that, despite reports to the contrary, the philosophic assumptions underlying alternative views, especially empirical, a posteriori approaches to art, have not been annihilated and, second, by considering what is entailed by one conception of language *in use*, one conception of literary art as the unique product of artistic choices determined by some principle(s) of form, some system of rationality. And as we remind ourselves of the vitality of principles and methods not consonant with those of poststructuralism in its various branches and recollect the multiple ways in which "ordinary language" philosophers and cognitive psychologists contribute to our practical grasp of how meaning is generated and comprehended, we should also remember that Derrida and company pose no genuine threat to most of the problems that come home to the business and bosoms of working critics. These are the critics who, with Michael Dummett, believe that any adequate account of language—including, of course, a literary text—must describe it as a rational activity on the part of creatures to whom can be ascribed *intention* and *purpose*, or who, with Colin McGinn recognize that "there is no such thing as meaning something by a word and it being undetermined what counts as a correct utterance [or use] of the word."[8]

As a practical tool, "deconstruction" can do a very limited sort of work, which, in the end, is not greatly unlike the rhetorical work that the ancient "new critics" (for example, W. K. Wimsatt, Cleanth Brooks, William Empson) performed. In its ludic extensions, it is preoccupied with tracing the traces of words through the labyrinth of linguistic association. In its most ludic forms (as in some of J. Hillis Miller's works),[9] it is indistinguishable from the free play of self-indulgence. And, in its most rigorous form (as in much of Paul de Man's work),[10] it discovers the tensions and the tropic or figural maneuvers that cancel (bring to aporia) the assertions within any piece of writing.

Moreover, it is important to remember that even as a program deconstruction does not presume the invalidity of other modes of inquiry, though this is not immediately apparent to anyone familiar with the vehemence and hostility with which many of the newer critics assail those whom they persistently and mistakenly identify as essentialists. Perhaps this point can be made best by appealing to an unlikely witness, Richard Rorty, who, while supporting Derrida's speculations, notes that:

There is no topic—and in particular not that of the relation between sign and signified, language and the world—on which Derrida holds a different view than [*sic*] that of any of the philosophers of language I have mentioned [Gottlob Frege, Rudolf Carnap, and Hilary Putnam most immediately]. Nor does he have any insights which complement theirs. He is not, to repeat, a philosopher of language. The closest Derrida comes to a philosophy of language is his interest in the historical question of why a view about the relation between sign and signified, the nature of representation, could ever have been thought to have been essential to our self-understanding, the starting point of the love of wisdom, first philosophy. He is interested in the connection between the "Kantian" view of philosophy and the "Kantian" view of language—in why the latest effort to cosmologize or eternalize the present should have centered on language. Here he *does* have something to say—but it is something about philosophy, not about language.[11]

The record should perhaps indicate that most philosophers in the so-called analytic tradition are not attempting to "eternalize the present"—indeed, most recognize, with W. V. Quine, that there are no facts about reference apart from those determined by our use of language—and believe, with Putnam, that Derrida employs "a systematic method that rests on a [Saussurean] philosophy of language that is very weak."[12] Nevertheless, there is one clear and useful injunction for all critics implicit in Rorty's comments, namely, to persist in the formulation, development, and testing of those hypotheses that, in prospect, hold out the best promise of fruitful results. It is only through the active encouragement of alternative ways of conceiving things that our constitutive paradigms may be strengthened, subverted, or revised. This encouragement of multiple hypotheses is not to be confused with an "anything goes" policy, for it presupposes that issues can be joined and that theories and hypotheses can be terminated or superseded. At bottom, the various alternatives are striving to displace one another or, with the less ambitious, secondary, or auxiliary hypotheses, are preparing themselves for assimilation by larger constructs.

To overcome any given theory, one can either mine from within, challenging and testing the theory on its own terms, or one can develop independent constructs that, in their entailments, cause problems for the alternative or merely different theory. Clearly then, for one writer to undermine (or improve) the theory of another, it is not necessary that the two writers share the same principles and assumptions or address the same problems. Often, the superiority of one theory is shown in its capacity to overcome or resolve problems intrinsic to rival theories or to improve upon the explanatory power of its competitors' views, doing so, moreover, in a way that earns the approval of advocates of the displaced views. Focusing on competing moral philosophies, Alasdair MacIntyre makes a similar point:

As in the case of natural science there are no general timeless standards. [Nevertheless], it is in the ability of one particular moral-philosophy-articulating-the-claims-of- a-particular-morality to identify and to transcend the limitations of its rival or rivals, limitations which can be—although they may not in fact have been—identified by the rational standards to which the protagonists of the rival morality are committed by their allegiance to it, that the rational superiority of that particular moral philosophy and that particular morality emerges.[13]

Adjudication is made possible by the commonality of the rational standards, which are not in dispute (as they are not, for example, in the heliocentric and geocentric views of planetary motion), and by the disinterestedness of those standards relative to the issue or dispute in question. On the issue of planetary motion, for example, it is clear, as John

Greenwood points out, that "the telescope observations of the stellar parallax that enabled scientists to adjudicate between geocentric and heliocentric theories were informed by the theory of the telescope, but did not presuppose the accuracy of either the geocentric or heliocentric theory." [14]

What is necessary to fruitful debate, however, is that critics give up the notion of gaining access to ultimate truth (or *the* truth about some permanently fixed relationship between words and things) and think instead in terms of truth within systems of rationality, within particular conceptual systems, since meaning and reference are intelligible only within a practice or a scheme. By doing so, some of the rancor might go out of our self-congratulation. What I am urging then is a conception of theory not as an insight into the ultimate nature of language or writing or poetry, but as a rich storehouse of various tools or practices of inquiry that are suited to a variety of distinct tasks and purposes. (Since no theory is good for all purposes, the choice of any theory should be seen as a practical decision governed by emergent interests and goals.) It would also be helpful if the theorists moderated their tendency to think of their competitors as felons or idiots and adopted, in their dealings with their less enlightened colleagues, some habits not incompatible with the justice and understanding recommended by Wayne Booth. [15]

Turning from general reminders to more specific matters, I can say that as a practicing theoretician, a classroom theorist (that is, a critic and teacher), I am interested primarily in the principles of construction, embedded in the text as products of choice (as concrete, textual particulars). Only on the assumption of these principles can I account for all the particulars of the text in their order, selection, and emphasis. As a critic/teacher I am not primarily interested in such preconstructional elements as may be derived from the study, for example, of psychology, ideology, and history, since I recognize that these elements may enter into innumerable—and often conflicting or contradictory—compositional arrangements and may provide in some sense the lexicographical substrate of many, indeed, countless discourses. General familiarity with preconstructional possibilities is a necessary but insufficient condition of textual understanding. In my efforts to understand the text, to grasp how the unfolding particulars relate to what they are determined by (that is, some controlling conception, some principle of construction, some set of justification conditions), I may guess wrong. I may misunderstand the creative intentionality underlying the work and determining the intelligibility of the parts (indeed, making them parts), but the text, in its reluctance to accommodate itself to my constitutive hypothesis, has the capacity to force me to revise my guess; my guess is tentative and corrigible, not fixed and inflexible. It inclines me to adjust all particulars to the exigencies of my hypothesis, but it is not invulnerable to the insinuations of recalcitrant material or to the hard evidence and strong arguments that my fellow critics may delightedly bring to my pained awareness.

Despite the attention I have given to "meaning" in this chapter, I use the term casually and colloquially for discursive expedience. Unlike most theorists, I certainly do not think that most of the literature we read and study is structured by theme or "ideas," though much of it clearly is so structured. Concerned as they generally are with human characters in humanly interesting situations, literary works tend to *show* and *depict* truths rather than to *express* them. In Alvin Goldman's terms, "the novelist shows what it is like to be a certain kind of person, to live in a certain era or culture. This is a commonly valued way of getting understanding of human and cultural facts; important information is somehow conveyed" about our moral lives and ethical capacities.[16] In most of our dealings with most of our literature, we are concerned with language not as meaning, theme, or propositional content, but as action. What most frequently needs to be understood is not what the words mean, but what act by what sort of person in what sort of situation the words make possible. Following this line would lead to an extended commentary on basic, inferential, and evaluative propositions,[17] on the nature and kinds of subhypotheses necessary to the full analysis of any work. But let me just say here, suggestively, that character is rarely given directly in literature; it must be inferred from its actualizations (it is the reason for or ground of the actualizations), and unless we make such inferences about character, the work has no significant effect.

Let me bring this part of the discussion to conclusion with a homely, practical maxim: as you read, strive for elegant hypotheses, for coherence and consistency, not because all works are necessarily consistent or coherent, but because you have a better chance of identifying real contradiction or inconsistency when you seek to find acceptable ways of accommodating recalcitrant material to your hypothesis than when you seek initially to find what is antithetical to or unassimilable by a coherent conception of the whole work. Nothing is easier to find than the aberrant, the contradictory, or the antithetical. Once it is found, it tends to propagate itself relentlessly, to find its *semblable* everywhere, since the "other" is always an implicit logical possibility of any isolable feature or predicate and does not have to be adjusted to a complex system of entailments.

Admittedly, the preceding discussion raises its own special problems and requires special elaboration and defense, but because this chapter is more sales pitch than treatise, full justification of its operative assumptions will have to be deferred. What I want to stress as I round the final turn and head for home can be given expeditious expression. I don't know why most people who profess literature took up an interest in professing literature, and, at bottom, I don't really know very much about the tangle of noble and ignoble causes, reasons, aims, impulses, decisions, and so forth that has conspired to make me an interested and committed teacher/scholar/critic, in short, a professor of literature. But I do know that I am not embarrassed to admit that from the beginning I have considered literary works as documents capable of giving powerful, vivid, and organized expression to an enormous range of states, conditions, attitudes, opinions, views, and perceptions that move me deeply or engage me intensely. And from the beginning I have sought to come to know and give explicit expression to the bases of my rich experience, sustained by the conviction that by deliberate and sedulous inquiry, and with a little help from my friends in history, psychology, linguistics, and philosophy, I could learn something not only about the nature and bases of art and the pleasures to be derived from it, but also about the mind, history, the creative imagination and much else besides. Throughout my professorship, as I have struggled to work through the ramifications of first this and then that hypothesis, I have been ready, as I am now, to break free of my own hermeneutical circle by (as Nelson Goodman suggests) amending a rule—a hypothesis—if it yielded an inference I was unwilling to accept or by rejecting an inference if it violated a rule I was unwilling to amend.[18]

Not for a moment, however, do I think that we should restrict our focus to interpretations or readings and provide first this and then that interpretation of first this and then that work. Quite the contrary. I see an interest in literary works leading directly to a wide range of projects, to a concern with, for example, the psychological bases of artistic effects; the differentiating characteristics of the enormously diverse texts that are grouped together rather clumsily under such broad classes as the novel, the lyric, the sonnet, and so on; the descriptive bases of sound value judgments (as well as the interdependence of facts and values and the objectivity of standards within practices, that is, within texts); the distinctive powers of the various modes of disclosing information and, hence, of controlling the reader's expectations and inferences; the history of forms; the role of character in literature; the analysis of the philosophic and psychological grounds of critical thought; the nature and function of point of view in drama; and many others.

Unfortunately, far too many critics have come to see literature as nothing more than another language, another sequence of signs caught up in the same figural maneuvers, social determinations, or differences and deferrals of meaning in which any other language (speech, writing, or écriture) is caught up. But this is no more true than that most of our friends and acquaintances are merely languages, despite assurances from some quarters that the whole fabric of existence is nothing more than a set of codes and a set of relations among the terms of those codes. (Naked science is too delicate for the purposes of life, as Samuel Johnson said; or, the beliefs that philosophy undermines are indispensable to the conduct of life, as Hume said.)

We, or some of us, have lost touch with and confidence in the human power of literature and in character, action, and thought, as exemplified or expressed in literature, because we have become convinced that, in the absence of an unmediated vision, the only basis of mediation is the system of coded relations that is always already in place. Thus, it has come to seem that the world is endlessly textual or political and that the terms of the various texts are arbitrary and without a fixed origin; they are unstable, because they belong to a system of relations and differences ceaselessly in movement or are reducible to a predetermined set of power categories. Thus, meanings are deferred and multiplied before we can grab them and hold them still, or are the predictable consequences of discriminable orders of dominance and suppression. Criticism therefore is always caught up in a chain of proliferating sense which it can neither halt nor fully comprehend or is destined to uncover with relentless persistence the same basic social mechanisms in every artifact, every form of production.

Philosophy has come to seem to be simply another variety of literature or another series of texts pervaded by the same ruses of figuration, the same tropic sleight of hand that characterizes literature. It ain't necessarily so; it ain't even close to being necessarily so, of course. Words within sentences have found rather than lost meaning and reference, and sentences within practices or languages create worlds that are not only imaginable, but inhabitable, worlds that are as true as true can be. That facts and objects, meanings and references, are term- and framework-dependent does not make them any less bump-into-able, stable, or knowable. "Why should the fact that reality cannot be described independent of our descriptions lead us to suppose that there are only descriptions?" To this question, Hilary Putnam responds: "After all, according to our descriptions themselves, the word "quark" [or "tree," "shoe," etc.] is one thing and a *quark* is quite a different thing." [19] Of course, the fact that our reality is socially constructed (how else could it be constructed?)— and our concepts, thus, are culturally relative—does not mean that society (or culture) determines the truth or falsity of what we say. As many have noted, although we certainly determine "conditions of reference" (we decide what's what, what conditions have to be met for something to be a petunia, for example), we cannot determine whether those conditions obtain. We socially construct conditions of reference, but not "reference"; we decide what a petunia is, but not whether what is right in front of us is a petunia). In the end, then, all language *in use*—and certainly all literature—is centered; otherwise, we wouldn't be able to tell the works apart or have works to separate or part. Only *différance* keeps on differentiating. That is its job, but it is not Pope's or Johnson's or Dante's or Homer's.

So, if I am not very sanguine about the prospects of immediately redirecting the attention of critics to literary works, I am willing—indeed, *inclined*—to believe that the crisis we are in has, like other crises, more apparent than real significance. And I am somewhat encouraged by the recent efforts of E. D. Hirsch, Ralph Rader, M. H. Abrams, Reed Way Dasenbrock, Paisley Livingston, Richard Levin, Wendell Harris, James Phelan, and others to ground the cure for our cultural illiteracy on a revitalized interest in our literary heritage.[20] And we can do this, of course, without subscribing to some "transmission" view of culture in the style of William Bennett or Allan Bloom and without mandating a fixed list of approved texts, while recognizing, at the same time, that there surely are texts that are uncommon artistic achievements from which we can learn to appreciate and assess human accomplishment.

# Chapter 3
# **Professionalism, Relativism, and Rationality**

For more than a few years now, the prevailing wind in literary studies—or cultural studies, as we might more fashionably and accurately say today—has been relativism, in one or another, usually extreme, form. Moreover, recent critical discussions have tended to divide the intellectual community into opposing camps, only one of which, it is repeatedly affirmed, can be credited with respectability. The worthy literary critic is a relativist rather than a naive realist; an autocrat (who determines meanings in the light of self- or community-generated categories) rather than an allocrat (who determines meanings in the light of author-initiated categories); a hermeneuticist (who recognizes that all claims are mediated) rather than an epistemologist (who seeks a grounding for truth); a non-Kantian rather than a neo-Kantian; a new historicist rather than a traditionalist; a deconstructionist rather than a foundationalist; a poststructuralist rather than a structuralist. Concurrently with this newly instituted division of labor or shuffling of social energy, the relativists/poststructuralists have taken to calling themselves *theorists*, leaving the term *critics* and the task of criticism to the less enlightened toilers in the field.[1]

The theorists are distinguished by nothing so much as their liberation from a thoroughly discredited and outmoded metaphysics and epistemology: the metaphysics of presence, of naive realism, and the epistemology of direct knowledge, of the unmediated vision. They are always distinguished from traditionalist critics—those mostly mythical beings, usually invoked for purposes of invidious comparison, who truculently persist in crediting the discredited (that is, the Transcendental Signified or the correspondence theory of meaning) and who have come to function in much criticism as the designated scapegoats. (I call these critics "mythical" because genuine, bonafide, card-carrying naive realists or essentialists have been often spotted but rarely bagged). In addition, it is generally assumed today that once things and thoughts go inside conceptual schemes, inside the language that makes them what they are, then objectivity, determinate meaning, truth, justification, and so on go by the board—along with authors, stable texts, and standards of value, which are nothing but precipitates of always-already-in-place categories and systems of meaning that shift from interpretive community to interpretive community and from period to period.

Many, if not all, modern relativists/poststructuralists, apparently believe that if there is no gold standard, no independently existing maker good and true of our assertions, if there is no solid gold (mind-independent real things) in some (metaphysical) Fort Knox to back up our paper (linguistic or merely verbal) negotiations, then no scrip(t) is better, more valuable, or more negotiable than any other scrip(t), and we can print as much of any kind of scrip(t) as we want and exchange one kind with another at will and ad infinitum. Nevertheless, while one scheme has no privilege over another, some schemes have greater authority and, hence, legitimacy than others. Authority reduces to persuasion, which reduces to power. In a world of immanent meaning, emphasis is regularly placed either on the constitutive energy of various more and less powerful paradigms, social formations, ideologies, or interpretive communities, or on the "incommensurability" of schemes, the impossibility, that is, of speaking or understanding outside the historical-ideological framework through which "reality," speakers, and all things else are spoken.

Incidentally, it is perhaps worth remarking that the issues raised by recent literary theorists are nothing other than locally differentiated instances of more general and pervasive concerns of Continental and Anglo-American philosophy. As we noted earlier (in Chapter 1), Continental philosophy is preoccupied *either* with the endless deferral of meaning, the loss of stability in signifier and signified, and the emergence of the *other* to undermine or subvert what is affirmed on the surface (what is logocentrically asserted) *or* with the determination of the speaking and the spoken, the writing and the written by social, political, cultural, ideological conditions. Anglo-American philosophy, on the other hand, devotes attention *either* to the *incommensurability of languages* (theories, conceptual schemes), the view that each language is unique and, thus, not translatable into any other language, *or* to the *indeterminacy of meaning*, the view that too many statements (theories, meanings) are compatible with the data. In the philosophical debates, as in the literary ones, the ostracized scapegoats are the same: objectivity, determinacy of meaning, stability of reference across conceptual differences, and interpretation or translation.

Two essays by Stanley Fish, "Anti-Professionalism" and "Resistance and Independence: A Reply to Gerald Graff" illuminate the sort of relativism we have in mind. They raise, in strikingly economical ways, many of the principal ideas in the current theoretical and philosophic debate: the possibility of sharing meanings and references across conceptual schemes or interpretive communities, the feasibility of adjudicating disputes by appeal to shared standards of value, and the existence of texts as systems of justification before they are read. The two essays address topics important to such philosophers and theorists as W. V. Quine, E. D. Hirsch, Richard Rorty, Stephen Greenblatt, P. D. Juhl, Wendell Harris, T. K. Seung, Michel Foucault, Hilary Putnam, Nelson Goodman, Donald Davidson, and Akeel Bilgrami, as well as to poststructuralists and new historicists generally. In taking exception to some aspects of Fish's formulations, I also hope to make available alternative and competing conceptions (especially those of Donald Davidson and Hilary Putnam) and to open up discussion to all who have an interest in such issues. In the end, my goal is not to mount an attack against a particular critic but to make a positive, albeit brief, case for translatability, interpretation, arbitration, and objective knowledge in a world without a Foundation.

## Historically Conditioned Professionalism

In "Anti-Professionalism," Fish articulates—within what he calls an "interpretivist" or "conventionalist" approach—virtually all the commonplaces of mainstream relativism. At any rate, his approach, like so many others today, is one in which "facts, values, reasons, criteria, and so on, rather than being independent of interpretive history, are the products of that history."[2] All our ideas, facts, and so on are the products of our historically conditioned interpretive practices. Moreover, all the practices prevailing at any time within any such large-scale, socially organized institution or "profession" as "literature" or "literary studies" are authorized and legitimated by the "profession" within which they have their intelligibility, since there are no ways of acting within a socially organized enterprise that are not sanctioned by the "already-in-place assumptions, stipulated definitions, and categories of understanding" of the enterprise or profession.[3] The profession determines what is and is not a professional activity. Thus, for example, the various (incommensurate) categories of understanding operative in the many interpretive communities of any period, the categories by which texts are constituted as texts (by which the "same" text is construed as "different" texts), delimit the range of the profession's interpretive concerns even as they owe the legitimacy of their own concerns to the authority of the profession.

Essentially, we are here concerned with historically conditioned, interest-determined accounts, in which facts and reasons derive from various orders of immanence, not from some order of transcendence. Fish, like almost all his "theoretical" cohorts today, sharply distinguishes his views from those of critics still committed to an "ideology of essences," to belief in the "ultimate availability of transcendent truths and values." These critics are characterized as "right-wing intellectuals."[4] And, again like others, he also distinguishes his views from those of critics who—despite their anti-foundationalism and their recognition of the "constitutive power of history,"[5] the power of history to determine and shape the thinking, the thought, and the thinkable—still cling atavistically and incoherently to the possibility of the self's making a free choice among independent values (that is, values independent of some particular scheme or partisan "professional" view). These critics he characterizes as left-wing antiprofessionals, but because of their unextinguished faith in free choice, he considers them closet essentialists and, hence, closet right-wing intellectuals as well.

From the perspective of professionalism (or what Richard Rorty might call "group solidarity"), then, right and left wing are ultimately distinctions without much of a difference. It is impossible to be in a profession and not be a professional, since even one's antiprofessionalism, even one's apostasy and one's denunciations of the profession are made possible by and are intelligible (if intelligible at all) within the profession. Indeed, antiprofessionalism is professionalism in its sincerest form: "A professional must find a way to operate in the context of purposes, motivations, and possibilities that precede and even define him and yet maintain the conviction that he is 'essentially the proprietor of his own person and capacities.' *The way he finds is anti-professionalism.*"[6] Since acting in some way that is independent of the profession—of the categories, purposes, interests of the profession—is impossible (attack, denial, critique, and so on are themselves inextricably bound up with the assumptions and aims of the profession), it matters little whether the profession is "advocated" or "derided." It is supported and maintained in either case.

Nevertheless, even though we cannot avoid operating in institutionally sponsored and sanctioned ways, real opposition or dispute is possible, because, it is affirmed, one can always argue that some institutional ways are better than others. Hence we can understand the antiprofessional as someone who is "looking around (with institution-informed eyes) to see conditions (institutionally established) that are unjust or merely inefficient (with justice and efficiency institutionally defined) and proposing remedies and changes that will improve the situation."[7]

In summary, neither professionals nor, of course, antiprofessionals can transcend the conditions of their own intellectual being. The one thing "a historically conditioned consciousness cannot do" is scrutinize its own beliefs, conduct a rational examination of its own convictions . . . for in order to begin such a scrutiny, it would first have to escape the grounds of its own possibility, and it could do that only if it were not historically conditioned and were instead an acontextual or unsituated entity of the kind that is rendered unavailable by the first principle of the interpretivist or conventionalist view.[8]

Thus, we are inescapably confined to the prisonhouse of our own categories, bound by the conventions we are chosen by.

To say that everything is professional or is conceived within the space already defined by professional interests is no more enlightening than to say (as Fish also does, more and less explicitly) that everything is historically or culturally conditioned. The trouble, of course, is that while everything we think and feel and know is made possible by or is grounded in something already in place, there are always just too many things in place, too many different, conflicting, contradictory, irreconcilable things in place or possible. Given our imaginative capacities and the enormously rich stock of conceptual possibilities available to us from past and present uses of language, we are always able both to create and understand innumerable new cognitive frameworks and conceptual schemes, however diverse, conflicting, and contradictory they may be.

Working within the historically cumulative—or even within the more narrowly conceived, culturally conditioned—conceptual availabilities, we can generate and comprehend limitless schemes, patterns, and structures. Our capacity to create, imagine, and understand new structures and patterns is captured in Steven Winter's notion of *transperspectivity*, which is "the ability of a physically, historically, socially, and culturally situated self to reflect critically on its own construction of a world, and to imagine other possible worlds that might be constructed." Focusing on one aspect of transperspectivity, Winter observes that "Although we may be situated in a web of belief, there is nothing that prevents us from making those beliefs translucent and, thus, amenable to reflection. . . . [Also], situated self-consciousness involves the ability to imagine how the world might be constructed differently."[9] Moreover, even when we narrow our focus to a particular community of interest, we invariably find an indefinite number of incompatible, mutually exclusive, conflicting, or different ways of talking that are consistent with our peculiar background assumptions or with the theoretical and practical constraints on our practice. Otherwise, differences would never arise and change never occur.

The assumptions and categories of understanding determined by and loosely definitive of our community of interest (our interpretive community) are not monolithic; they do not, that is, determine the details of any particular strategy in use. Thus, if the "community" is Marxist, then there is room for x-tuple exemplifications. If it is Leninist-Marxist, then there is still room for x-tuple exemplifications—and so on through ever so many refinements, because, as George Lakoff has reminded us, there are many different and even conflicting and contradictory ways "within a single conceptual system and a single language of conceptualizing a domain" of interest.[10] Indeed, it is the very denseness or indeterminacy of our terms and concepts—considered apart from some local context of use, some informing principle of rationality or system of justification—that makes it possible for them to serve an indefinite number of hypotheses, theories, and views, and for even the same referents to contribute to different meanings (as they do in many ambiguous sentences, such as the one discussed in Chapter 1, "Alphonse likes exciting sheep"). A conditioner that supplies conditions for all manner of conditions is not much of a conditioner of anything in particular, especially when it also has no means of ruling out possibilities. We have here, then, inescapable and ineradicable problems of indefeasibility.[11]

A more devastating critique of the position expressed here by Fish and echoed by many others (that is, the view that we cannot scrutinize our own beliefs) can be found, at least implicitly, in recent analyses of "radical interpretation," especially those of Donald Davidson. In "radical interpretation," the interpreter confronts radically different, indeed, "alien," categories and, hence, meanings and cognitive values. Speaker and interpreter are assumed to have fundamentally different categories, beliefs, and historical conditionings: The urban *homme moyen sensuel*, for example, confronts the linguistic behavior of the Martian, the Samoan, or, if one prefers, the distinctly other. By successfully meeting the harder challenge of at once scrutinizing and understanding categories and systems of beliefs that we do not and cannot by our historical conditioning possibly share, radical interpretation shows us that the modern theorist's easier task—scrutinizing a rich variety of beliefs expressed in our native language—is not the labor of a full work week. The hugely successful and tediously iterative interpretive experience of countless field linguists confirms the possibility of radical interpretation. Indeed, so successful is the practice that we find nothing peculiar in Davidson's conviction that anything said in one language can be translated understandably into another language. For Davidson, the idea of a *conceptual* scheme that is totally inaccessible to our understanding is an unintelligible and incoherent notion.

The philosophical case in defense of the common practice is a long one with many codicils and whereases, but an abstract will have to serve our present needs. In brief, the case (in Davidson's version) assumes and depends upon a holistic theory of meaning and a semantic, truth-conditional theory of truth, as distinct from a correspondence or metaphysical theory of truth. Meaning is holistic in that local units depend for their meaning on their place and role in the language (and, analogously, in the framework or conceptual scheme). Just as knowing what words mean depends upon grasping how they are used in sentences (sentence meaning is prior to word meaning), so knowing what sentences (and, hence, words) mean is a matter of knowing how they function in and serve the total structure of which they are a part. The semantic theory of truth is truth-conditional in the sense that it is based on a progressively less tentative specification of relations between language use and the "world"—that is, on establishing a progressively more secure understanding of the equivalence conditions being "satisfied" in particular cases of linguistic behavior, in particular word-"world" correlations.

In other words, as W. V. Quine has noted, Davidson has recognized "Tarski's theory of truth" (that is, the disquotational theory in which truth in the object language is "verified" by satisfying equivalence conditions in the metalanguage, as in " 'snow is white is true' if and only if snow is white") "as the very structure of a theory of meaning." [12] In this scheme, words and objects are coeval; they come into existence together. Thus, it is possible to say what matches what, even what corresponds to what (correspondence is "real" correlation). Truth or satisfaction is a matter of categorical fit within the language. And, hence, it is ineluctably true that the only evidence for the truth of one sentence is another sentence or other sentences.

Davidson argues against the relativism that Fish and others today endorse and that Karl Popper has identified with the "myth of the framework," the idea that we are prisoners of the conceptual system that we are enabled by, trapped in the prisonhouse of a particular conceptual scheme. Davidson observes, "Of course, the truth of sentences remains relative to language, but that is as objective as can be." The only test of truth value, then, is fit, coherence within the language, for, as he also notes,

nothing [else] makes sentences and theories true: not experience, not [as Quine would insist] surface irritations, not the world. . . . *That* experience takes a certain course, that our skin is warmed or punctured . . . these facts, if we like to talk that way make sentences and theories true. But the point is better made without the mention of facts. The sentence "my skin is warm" is true if and only if my skin is warm. Hence, there is no reference to a fact, a world, an an experience or a piece of evidence. [13]

"Warm skin" is a fact within a description, a true fact within that description, but the description is neither unique nor necessary; it is not warranted by the way things just are independently of conceptual choice. Skin, of course, is not warm or cold apart from our interests and categories (it has no *semantic* preferences), but its being warm or cold is a fact—and a true fact about our skin—within our temperature-of-the-skin interests. Warm skin is not simply (or simply is not) a matter of language or of community consensus.

In addition to being coherentist, holistic, and truth-conditional, Davidson's approach is intentionalist and agential in that the whole point of interpretation is to provide a reasonable account, by our standards (what other standards could we recognize or employ?), of the behavior of others. Assuming a belief-desire model of linguistic (and other) behavior, Davidson observes:

If we cannot find a way to interpret the utterances and other behavior of a creature as revealing a set of beliefs [a set of ways of relating words and thoughts to the world; a set of intentions, in other words] largely consistent and true by our standards, we have no reason to count that creature as rational, as having beliefs, or as saying anything at all.[14]

In other words, actions, as distinct from mere motions or movements, derive their meaning and intelligibility from the relations among the mental states—for example, belief and desire—that are the reasons and, hence, causes of them. (Simply, I lift the mug to my mouth because I *want* a drink and *believe* that by so doing I will satisfy my want, get what I want.) From the perspective of radical interpretation, it is impossible to reach the point where we can confidently assert that we do not or cannot understand this *other language*, since to say so much is already to know more than is compatible with incapacity to understand.

The argument in defense of radical interpretation is useful to our present business, because it evinces that even under the most extreme or severe circumstances it is quite possible to scrutinize and understand beliefs (and actions) which we do not ourselves believe and which we indeed may find downright unbelievable or repugnant. For our quotidian needs as critics and scholars, we are not obliged to practice radical interpretation (though we certainly could do so if we wished or if we deliberately set about to be real good at playing real dumb for the nonce). As inveterate speakers of English and the various dialects of our profession (and countless other local, getting-on-in-the-world dialects as well), we bring to our encounters with one another a vast array of common beliefs and shared assumptions about what goes with what, what fits, coheres with, or belongs to what. We share many references and concepts and, consequently, do not have to start from the ground floor every time we hope to rise to shared understanding or communication. We have no trouble passing with referential ease from the Hamlet in Denmark to the hamlet in Vermont or determining whether Stephen Greenblatt circulates his linguistic energy in a way that satisfies the internal justification conditions of his discourse or whether Fredric Jameson satisfies the conditions determined by the needs of his own practice. Nor, for that matter, do we ordinarily have any trouble determining whether this or that assertion or argument is more nearly consonant with what we consider acceptable or reasonable or whether this or that evaluative or methodological criterion, this or that makeshift, flexible but more or less durable regulative ideal is applicable and authoritative under these particular circumstances. At any rate, scrutinizing the beliefs at work in the various articles and books written in our native language and familiar dialects is certainly common enough and easy enough, much easier at least than the difficult but doable job of scrutinizing alien beliefs.

Finally on this matter, it is worth noting that Kurt Gödel's reflections on our mathematical capacity work against the linguistic relativism of so many of our theoreticians. His idea, in its least elaborate incarnation, is that it is impossible to formalize our mathematical capacity fully, because it is always within the capacity of that capacity to go beyond whatever it can formalize. Hilary Putnam has extended Gödel's insight to justification and rationality in general, showing that "reason can go beyond whatever reason can formalize." [15] What is true of our mathematical capacity is equally true, it would seem, of our conceptualizing capacity. In full exfoliation, the Gödelian insight reaches undoubtedly into the everyday world of common psychological events, as in our experiences of reflexive reflection: I know that you know that I know that you know, and so on, *ad capacitum* (that is, to the limits of our capacity for regressive reflection). Thus, we witness the capacity of our awareness to be always one awareness ahead of our "present" awareness. What we can do in the awareness line with our awarenesses we can similarly do in the scrutiny line with our beliefs. We can always talk *about* what we think (and talk) *with*, can always go "meta-" on our discourse, and, thus, we have additional reasons for believing that we are incapable of being permanently confined to the prisonhouse of any particular language (though, of course, so long as our thoughts have rich conceptual content there's no escaping some language system).

Curiously and not uninterestingly, the view that all our ideas are historically or professionally conditioned is itself not historically or professionally conditioned. Thus, if the historically conditioned view is true, then, it is false—because it is self-refuting; its articulation is denied by what it articulates, and, as we might say, it "escapes the grounds of its own possibility." What is expressed in history is not necessarily conditioned expressly by the (larger) historical conditions in which it is expressed, except in the most trivial sense in which any expression occurs at some time in a form possible to that time. Of course, "mum" is History's (or Culture's) favorite—and, alas, *only*—word; and because, as I noted above, so diversely much is sayable at any time and in any culture, actual sayings cannot easily be resolved into or deduced from the voice of circumambient History (or Culture). History, in short, says nothing at all or too much. Also, if the view is true, then the contrary view, namely, that our "ideas are *not* historically conditioned," must also be historically conditioned and, of course, true, *if it is expressed.* Indeed, this latter view seems to be embraced by Fish (saying "no" to professionalism is one of professionalism's most respected ways of saying its say). But if *everything* we say is historically/professionally conditioned, even the negate of our assertion about historical/professional conditioning, then the view is empty, as well as self-refuting.[16]

It seems clear that Fish is doing in his essay what he claims cannot be done, and doing it in the very act of denying its possibility. That is, he is apparently scrutinizing the nature and conditioning conditions of professionalism, conducting a rational examination of the convictions underlying and supporting professionalism. Thus he escapes the grounds of professionalism's possibility and, more interestingly still, makes available what is "rendered unavailable" (that is, the situation professionalism is situated in) "by the first principle of the interpretivist or conventionalist view," or at least of the view of the interpretivist or conventionalist who is also a historicist. In short, what he is saying does not appear to be historically conditioned in that, among other things, it applies generally, across periods and professions. What he says about professionalism's situatedness is, well, "true" in the *sub specie aeternitatis* sense and, thus, untrue, by definition. He has come up with a conception of professionalism that excludes the very professionalism it was devised to define.[17] If it applies generally to this and that profession, in this period and that, then it is neither historically nor professionally conditioned, except in the broadest sense, the sense in which all talk of any kind begins from what is in place, from some inherited categories or values.

It is worth remarking that it is still possible to use for some local purpose (for example, antiquarian study or categorical play) categories and conceptual schemes that we no longer believe in or credit. Knowing what I know about the categories and argumentative logic of an outmoded conceptual system (for example, the Ptolemaic or the Thomas Rymerian system), I can discuss, within the terms of the system, any number of things that were unavailable for discussion in the historical period in which the system prevailed. Working from Thomas Rymer's critical principles and assumptions and relying throughout on his lexical resources and preferences, for instance, I can supply my local newspaper with a review of Madonna's latest concert. Similarly, we never have any trouble understanding current views that we disagree with, that are inconsistent or incompatible with those that in our personal and private capacities we believe to be true. In sum, by operating from within our present historical conditioning, we can understand and use many outmoded systems, conditioned by enormously diverse historical conditions, and we can understand and use in many ways and for many purposes the many conflicting systems currently in use and conditioned by the present historical conditions. To perform either of these tasks we must be able, as we are, to give good accounts of these systems as systems; that is, we must be able to say *what* they explain and *how* they go about the job of explanation. For example, though we do not believe in a Ptolemaic cosmology, we can give a good account of what it explains and how it goes about explaining what it explains, as we can of Kenneth Burke's dramatistic symbology and Harold Bloom's revisionism; of phlogiston, fact-value distinctions, the categorical imperative; of *Tom Jones, Othello,* and so on.

What our view does not permit, however, is discussion of the nature and functioning of a theory (perspective, scheme, system of rationality) from within the theory. Similarly, a principle cannot be a principle of itself—the sentences of an essay, for example, cannot supply the principle of their own arrangement and emphasis—and the elements of a lower level cannot determine the boundary conditions of their operation or functioning at a higher level. The terms of the lower level are rich in possibility or potentiality but poor in determination. (Our familiar, everyday observation and reference terms are, as we say, "dense," that is, capable of serving or functioning in a wide variety of conceptual systems or schemes.) Thus, just as the system of rules governing both the values (meanings) of chess pieces and the relations into which they may enter does not and cannot determine the strategy of any particular game,[18] so the "rules" of language, considered as a relational system of possible meanings and possible combinations and substitutions, cannot determine the satisfaction or justification conditions of any particular work or conceptual scheme. The game cannot be played outside the rules, but the rules cannot organize a strategy; there can be no algorithm for invention or for the organization of meanings. Within the theory, terms and categories of understanding are *used*, not *discussed*. But nothing prevents us from not only discussing but also comparing and judging the relative value of radically different theories in a language that is *fair to both but partial to neither.*

For rival theories to be compared, for example, they need only have some references in common and concatenate propositions according to some recognizable system of inference and derivation.[19] When these conditions obtain, we can describe *what* both theories are trying to explain and *how* they go about the business of explanation, doing so in a language that is intelligible to the proponents of both theories. Our commitment to one or another view or our "impartiality" relative to both does not prevent us from understanding, for instance, the views of the Copernican and the Ptolemaist, the Marxist and the Lacanian. And, in describing their differences, we can easily avoid expressions that presuppose the utility or validity of either, *though not expressions with no presuppositions of their own*, or without any presuppositions at all. No description or theory expresses the way things just are. Nature or reality has no language of its own, no preferred categories, no semantic favorites. As Nelson Goodman observes, "no organization into units is unique or mandatory."[20]

For a homely, and professional, example of "impartiality," we can turn to a not-so-ancient critical rivalry. Both the New Critics and the so-called Chicago critics were identified as "formalists." Certainly both were interested in and used the term *form*, yet they developed different, largely incompatible theoretical positions. For the New Critics, "form" made a pair with and found its antithesis in "content," and this binary unit found a complementary pair in "style and content" or "the poetic and the discursive." On the other hand, for the Chicago critics, "form," in fine Aristotelian fashion, was what gave "matter" its structure and function, and a text was a regulated, hierarchical sequence of "form-matter" relationships, with the "form" of one level becoming the "matter" of the next higher level, all the way up to the synthesizing principle of form for the whole text. As many historians of criticism have demonstrated, it is possible to describe, without resorting to language partial to either position, how these critics variously used the "same" terms, what they sought to explain, and how they went about their explanations. Indeed, I have just provided such a description, albeit a sketchy one. By judiciously applying the loose, changing, but relatively stable methodological criteria by which we continue unregenerately to evaluate our theories and assertions—for example, scope, plausibility, coherence, efficiency—we manage to supply "rational" grounds for preferring this theory on this occasion (or relative to this task) and another theory on another occasion. There is no way to formalize all this practical activity, no way to play our various games consistently by the rules, but we do get decisively on in ways that are, for us and for now, rational.

Whatever professionalism is, it cannot define or delimit what reason is or what is reasonable, because it presupposes rather than defines reason, as does its negate, antiprofessionalism. Because professionalism and antiprofessionalism have different and contesting assumptions about what reason and the reasonable mean, professionalism cannot subsume its negate. What is reasonable or reason within one system is not reasonable or reason within the other. Nevertheless, despite their differences the two may share a *conception of reasonableness* and come to talk, if not to agree perfectly, with one another. They can talk usefully because, in addition to sharing some references and concepts, they share a methodological criterion, a regulative ideal, of *reasonableness* in this case.

To the extent that professionalism is not one practice but many practices, as it necessarily is—its practices are as numerous as its interpretive communities—it is also not one system of reason but many systems. And if it is many systems of reason, professionalism (the subsumptive heading for the various practices of a profession) cannot define or typify what reason is for the profession. The various reasons cannot be combined with one another, arranged in a system of subordination, or relativized to some common denominator. Yet professionalism may sponsor *methodological criteria*, including standards and tests of reasonableness, that apply across particular arguments. But because these criteria are broad and flexible, applying to many schemes, and because they have relevance to schemes outside the profession, there is no way to confine them to a given profession.

Such criteria, we inevitably find, are not only transparadigmatic but also transprofessional in their value and efficacy. The notion of the transparadigmatic should not be particularly shocking or troubling, since critique and judgment always oblige us to take a view from the balcony. To say, for example, that two views or theories are incommensurable or that something is "true" within a language game or "true" relative to a conceptual scheme is to stand outside—and not to speak within—the schemes or scheme discussed, though not, of course, outside some system of intentionality. Thus, many of the profession's standards (plausibility, coherence, consistency, economy, beauty) are standards for many other "professions" as well. Also, as Ruth Anna Putnam notes, because "critics and literary theorists belong to [many] communities other than communities of critics," other than those making up a given profession, "it is possible from time to time for a critic to create a radically new interpretation, to make use of an old text in radically new ways." [21] And, incidentally, it is worth noting that the radically new theory or interpretation would have to be expressed in a language accessible to readers from many communities, a language relying on shared, commonly intelligible meanings, references, concepts, and so forth. Otherwise, the new theory or interpretation would be unintelligible not only to others but also to its proponent. And what was intelligible across community divides would be persuasive only to the extent that it paid obeisance to transprofessional methodological criteria and transparadigmatic standards.

We should now be able to see what is particularly troubling even about the apparently innocuous, plain-faced claim that professionals talk to other professionals about what they are interested in, in the sorts of ways that interest them, even when those ways amount to attacks upon the profession itself or challenges to the prevailing notions of the profession. (The opposition counts as opposition to the extent that it opposes a professionally defined set of goals, aims, options, and interests, and, thus, it is enabled by the interests it opposes.) What makes the antiprofessional as much a professional as the professional, we are told, is that his seeing and talking is also institutionally informed. That is, he looks around with "institution informed eyes" to see "institutionally established" conditions that are "unjust or merely inefficient" (with justice and efficiency institutionally defined) and proposes "remedies . . . that will improve the situation." The whole procedure, we are assured, is "underwritten" by the profession. But the problem is that the profession both "*under*writes" professional activity, in that it determines no scheme in its particularity, and "*over*writes" it, in that it accommodates too many different and conflicting schemes.

Also, there is in this description of the professionalism of the antiprofessional a kind of verbal equivalent to the optical illusion, and it is, curiously, precisely the kind of illusion that the linguistic relativist is elsewhere diligent to expose. Despite their being enrolled under the same rubric, their being identified as members of the same guild, syndicate, or sodality, the professional and antiprofessional simply are not enabled by the *same* "already-in-place assumptions, stipulated definitions, and categories of understanding" of the *same* profession. The two are working from *different* conceptions of the profession. The profession is not a shared middle term. Each is trying to establish the norms of the profession, to determine what the nature and aims of the "profession" are. And, as we have seen, the efficiency and justice for which, or in the name of which, they argue are transinstitutional, transprofessional norms or regulative ideals. If they were norms of the institution or profession, as differently defined by each party, they would be assumed within each argument and would hence be incapable of adjudicating claims.

The claims of the professional and antiprofessional are simply not compatible: professionals wisely *know* that they operate in the "context of purposes, motivations, and possibilities that precede and even define" them, whereas antiprofessionals operate under the delusion that they are free agents choosing freely among options uncontaminated by professional restrictions. But this way of framing the difference presents us with another "verbal illusion." There are no antiprofessionals in this description; antiprofessionals are defined by the way professionals perceive them. Their condition is delusional according to the "professional" view of it. The actual "antiprofessionals" do not see themselves as operating *outside* already-in-place systems of value or categories of understanding, of course, though they do see themselves as concerned with something other than the "profession" that Fish here and elsewhere has in mind. They are, of course, unprepared and unwilling to allow their concerns about the profession to be tricked into subordinating themselves to Fish's "Profession." The contest over defining the profession is not to be finessed out of existence by announcing, "Hey, what's the beef, we're all professionals here and what we're having, whatever else it may be, is, you know, a professional dispute." What we have here in fact is an instance of methodological solipsism. The "other" of the case at hand is always the other as seen by someone else, and the "you" is always the "you according to me." What this opposition should tell us is that when the issue (even if only in part) is about *what the profession is*, what its values and categories of understanding are, we cannot settle it by denominating it a "professional" dispute, a matter of "professionalism" either way.[22]

Nothing but incoherence is served by electing to assign one of the opponents—in this case, the antiprofessional—the function of "regulative ideal," as Fish later does: "Thus while an antiprofessional stance is certainly possible, it will itself be enabled by the interests to which it is (polemically) opposed. In short, anti-professionalism is itself a component of professionalism, and while it can function as a regulative ideal, it is an ideal the profession itself nominates."[23] Here we have a real nifty move of the "heads I win, tails you lose" variety. But, of course, antiprofessionalism cannot function as a "regulative ideal" *within its opposition* to "professionalism" or *within* "professionalism." Antiprofessionalism, in its capacity as an alternative to or an opponent of professionalism, is not a value or goal projectible from (and, hence, it cannot be regulative of) the interests to which it is opposed. To suggest otherwise, to give the antiprofessionalism stance a regulative function, is to remove its power in an act of investiture. It is to contain, marginalize, and trivialize the stance while appearing to accommodate and dignify it. Antiprofessionalism can serve the role of an ideal regulating (professional) practice only by giving up its role as a challenger to that practice. (The old political word for this sort of accommodation, of course, is *co-optation*.)

Sometimes this and that so-and-so are members of the "same" profession, and sometimes such-and-such arguments can be said to deal with the interests of a particular profession. Sometimes, however, the profession itself is at stake, its nature and the nature of its rationality. Discussion at this level obviously depends on a conception of acceptability broader than that implicit in either professionalism or antiprofessionalism; otherwise, discussion would be impossible. Sometimes Fish talks about one thing (matters internal to the profession), sometimes about another (disputes about the *nature* of the profession itself), often confusedly.[24] Our differences, as outlined here, are not merely professional.

## Communities and Totalitarianism

In response to Gerald Graff's comments on the antiprofessional essay, Fish expresses the fundamental conviction underlying his conventionalist or interpretivist position as follows:

> The question of whether or not a text invites a particular interpretation (or range of interpretations) only becomes urgent within the assumption that at some level texts exist prior to interpretation; but if one rejects that assumption, as I do, then the question becomes at once unaskable and trivial.[25]

Notably, this statement is his response to a point made by Graff, a point that we too understand perfectly well and recognize as actually having been made by Graff. If we take Fish seriously and at his word, then, we cannot take him seriously at his word, because Fish is *responding* to a view of his view which he (along with you and me and countless others) recognizes as different from, inconsonant with, and, thus, not generated by his view. In short, Graff's view is perfectly intelligible to him (and to me and you), even though it is transported to us in a linguistic vehicle for which allocations were not provided in the budget of Fish's community. And if, to some, this is an easy objection, it is not, for all its ease, an undeep one.

The text that Fish and we understand exists as a version of things or as a system of justification prior to or at least independent of any individual's particular reading of it. The *intelligibility* of the view that "meanings are given or produced by interpreters" is inconsistent with (indeed, establishes the falsity of) the *content* of the view, to the extent that the view is intelligible; understanding amounts to refutation of the view. Objects, references, concepts, and so on may not exist (that is, as those objects, references, concepts, and so on) apart from some conceptual and interpretive system, but this "truth" does not preclude an understanding of someone else's system as a system of conceptual entailments. Much confusion has been caused, it seems, by a false analogy, namely, that just as there is no Transcendental Signified, no one, objectively discernible, mind-independent reality authorizing and validating our statements about the world, so, likewise, there is no *meaning in the text* validating or authorizing our interpretations. Or, just as there is no one epistemological correspondence between words and things, so there is no hermeneutical correspondence between an interpretation and the intentional meaning of the text, the meaning answerable to the intentional states that are responsible for it. The analogy is false because the lack of any direct or unique correlation between our words and things as they are in themselves imposes no restrictions on our ability to understand *versions* of the relations of words and things. There is no reason, given the inaccessibility of "reality" apart from versions or conceptual schemes, that we cannot understand versions other than our own, since even our own favorite or preferred system (we always work with many systems, of course) allows for multiple extensions, refinements, revisions, and extrapolations. Otherwise, we would never be able to recognize different systems or a difference between systems.

My remarks on radical interpretation above apply with special force to the radical linguistic relativism articulated here. Without rehearsing former arguments or Davidson's views, we can at least recall that knowing what the words in a language system mean depends on understanding how they are used; that use is holistic; that meaning is not a linguistic or ontological but a truth-conditional matter; that from the agent perspective, the aim of interpretation is to come to some understanding of another's (linguistic) behavior; and, consequently, that interpretive practice obliges us, as a condition of its satisfaction, to attribute true beliefs and reasonable desires to speakers and writers, to rationalize linguistic action. If we are not engaged in such attribution, we are not engaged in interpretation. Nevertheless, following Hilary Putnam, who in part follows Quine and Davidson, we should bear in mind that "there is no criterion of sameness of meaning except actual interpretive practice," that "the only 'handle' we actually have on the notion of 'same belief' is interpretive practice." To insist "that two words have the same meaning [or the 'same reference'] is just to say that it is good interpretive practice to equate their meaning"—and, collaterally, that it would be bad interpretive practice not to so equate them.[26]

Fish's rejection of Graff's view implies that no text exists prior to Fish's interpretation (or, at the stretch, "his community's" interpretation), a suggestion that precipitates the regressive slide of solipsism again. From my perspective, the rejection introduces rather than drives away the trivial and makes askable such odd but necessary questions as these: How, on the one hand, could readers *know* that no *text* exists prior to interpretation? (That is, what would readers have to know—about texts, about how to recognize or identify texts, say—in order to *know* this?) How, on the other hand, could readers know that what they had *made* was an "interpretation," as distinct from some other kind of verbal construct? Why, furthermore, would readers be obliged to issue such a rejection of textual priority in the first place, and to whom would they issue it?

Again, the rejection denies the very activity of interpretation, since for us the text is already—or, perhaps, always already—a self-satisfied, self-justified version (that is, already an interpretation), and, as Davidson observes, the whole point and justification of any interpretive activity is to make sense of somebody else's justified activity.[27] A text presupposes and depends on some system of justification that is not of our own making, though we may find the system agreeable or disagreeable, even repulsive, to our interests, values, beliefs.

We take the *agent*, not the *patient* or *spectator*, view of things and assume that persons with desires not unlike our own behave in ways that are, if not our ways exactly, intelligible and rational to us. If they in fact do not behave so, we either do not understand them or do not know that we do not. With Davidson and others we agree that interpretive practice always requires us "to attribute to the speaker [or writer] a substantial number of true beliefs and reasonable desires." Action, as opposed to mere motion, is always grounded in true beliefs and desires. For us (as for Davidson and others), then, "an interpreted conceptual scheme will necessarily turn out to be for the most part like our own, however violently it may contradict our own in its higher reaches"—that is, in what it affirms or expresses.[28] Interpretation, as distinct from "reading," is always a matter of finding a fit or a fittingness that works in some justification system, some system of rationality that is not our own, though it is like one or the kind of one we would make.

For the linguistic relativist, in contrast, interpretation is always a matter of reading within the interests of one or another interpretive community. It does not involve reading within the interests of texts or reading within the systems of rationality from which texts derive their meanings and to which they owe their meaningful structure of internal fittingness. Fish observes, for example, that "while the interpreter will certainly have desires, the desires he can have will have been specified by the enterprise in which he has accepted membership."[29] By "enterprise," Fish means the profession itself, not a special subcommunity within the vague, collective entity called the "profession." The desires specified by the culture, however broadly or narrowly it is defined, are indispensable, since all our thinking begins with something already in place in our culture (or, more accurately, our cultures). But these desires are also incapacitating rather than enabling, since they are various, contradictory, inconsistent, and unstable, when considered outside the constraints of *local* functions and purposes. As noted earlier, the culture both over- and underwrites our desires.

Despite Fish's apparent desire for discussion, debate, and change within the enterprise, one inescapable consequence of his rejection of what we might call the internal interests, desires, and satisfactions of texts is a form of total relativism. He talks about views being in opposition to one another, about one interpretation "working against [the] resistance" of another interpretation, about the "resistance offered by one interpretively produced shape to the production of another interpretively produced shape." [30] But, clearly, from within his position, the shape resisted must always be the one shaped by the interests of the shape doing the resisting. There is always at work what Hilary Putnam has called an "asymmetry" of cultures, or of interpretively produced shapes in this case, since the "other" is always constructed from within our interests. Fish argues, for instance, that "while everyone will see [a given text] as a particular text and therefore as one that invites a particular interpretation, everyone's particular text will not be the same." [31] This view is deeply troubled, in large part because we cannot figure out the vantage point from which it is being stated. How can the interpretations be seen as different? Or, if they are, how can the difference amount to more than "different according to me or my view," given the asymmetry and thus the inequality of the interpretations? And, finally, what interpretive view underwrites this view of interpretive views? So long as the possibility of arriving at some "objective" knowledge of someone else's discourse at the level of its interest and belief is ruled out, the position advocated by our linguistic relativists will be susceptible to rust—to erosion from within, or self-refutation.

But that possibility, it would seem, is the one thing that these critics are determined not to rule in, because to do so would be tantamount to placing Nobodaddy back on the ontological throne, to sacrificing the interest-relativity of discourse on the altar of foundationalism. Fish, for example, persistently differentiates his interpretivist or conventionalist view from its despised and thoroughly discredited antagonist, "objectivity," the child and natural heir of essentialism. On one side there is the interpretivist, whereas on the other side there are the foundationalists, essentialists, right-wing intellectuals, and naive realists clinging desperately to Bedrock. Of course, nothing separates my position more sharply from that of these relativists than my endorsement of "objectivity," an objectivity with many foundations, but no single foundation; it is an objectivity that in giving up on the Transcendent Signified has not been obliged to find its only comfort in the frigid embrace of skepticism or in the cloying chumminess of this or that interpretive group, in the consensus judgments of linguistic cellmates.

Fish sets out in an acceptably wise direction when he notes that "no text has an existence independent of the categories of understanding within which it is seen as this rather than that." [32] But, of course, he gets off an exit or two too soon by denying the possibility of finding the categories of understanding that fit the interests of the text before him and that make it work in its own best interests. And because, like so many of his contemporaries, he has trouble resisting the impulse to swell a handsome lizard to a frightening dragon's bulk—to enlarge a modest, limited, and irrefragable claim to its utmost, absolutist limits, thereby destroying its comeliness and authority—we are regularly forced to weep when most we would applaud.

Meanings, concepts, references, values, emphases, standards of rationality are indeed context-sensitive and interest-relative. They are relative to conceptual scheme, as Fish says (or to language, as Davidson says), but for us the consequence of this scheme- and mind-dependent variability of things and worlds is not the view that "all discourse" is "essentially rhetorical." [33] Where nothing is (absolutely) true, so the argument goes, then what prevails prevails not because of its truth, but because of its (persuasive) power; but when disputants can appeal to no recognized tribunal of adjudication, persuasion is merely the name the powerful give to the weapon by which their preeminence is secured. In Fish's apparently more benign terms:

In a world where value is inconceivable apart from interest, any rationality will be interested—inseparable from some political vision or agenda—and therefore the triumph of a rationality, its installation as a point of resistance against partisan appeal, will be the triumph of a partisan appeal whose force has become so great that it seems to be independent.[34]

Putting aside the ostensibly gratuitous (but very modish) equation of every system of rationality with a political agenda or vision (as though a particular *system* of rationality could not—and did not—support many diverse, even conflicting political agendas, or as though a given political agenda or vision could—and did—prohibit the production of diverse systems of rationality),[35] we witness here systems of rationality as ignorant armies clashing by night, with triumph going not to the true, the good, and the beautiful but to the most rhetorical, most "persuasive." Interestingly, with the equation of system of rationality with particular political agenda, Fish comes dangerously close to finding the foundation he would evade; such a politics is a ground and "maker true" of assertions, against which claims can be tested and by which they can be adjudicated.

The wise theorist is not a "mere" rhetorician, for he knows that what is fitting and right and appropriate within a system is not something to be determined by community agreement. Sometimes members of the community get things wrong; sometimes they get them right. Certainly, those in the same community often disagree and, more important, often come to agreement. What is right or wrong in any given case is not something to be settled by appealing to the facts of the case, as independently established by the nature of things in the preexistent world, or by appealing to the consensus view of some interpretive community. How fast the car is going is a matter of fact according to each (conventional) system of measurement, and it is a matter of fact to all "readers," regardless of whether they belong to the miles-per-hour or kilometers-per-hour community. Whether such and such is right and fitting is certainly a meaningless issue outside of some conceptual scheme, but within the scheme it is definitely right and fitting or definitely wrong and ill fitting.

Finally, although our schemes are always interest-relative and mind-dependent—and although our regulative ideals, our methodological criteria, change over the years (we make and weigh our criteria as well as our schemes)—we are never incapable of making or understanding fitting versions or of choosing among good and bad, right and wrong versions. The standards we apply are standards we have devised, but they are standards in the local and particular circumstances of mutual intelligibility and shared methodological criteria, standards to which persuasion may appeal and from which it may reasonably expect a fair hearing. As Fish himself might impishly say, if you argue with, dispute, or wish to criticize my view, then you must agree with and accept it to do so; otherwise, you won't be able to formulate, and I will not be able to understand, your disagreement.

# Chapter 4
# Ideology, Textual Practice, and Bakhtin

No kind of critical writing is more pervasive and influential today than that which is ideological, in some sense of the term, that is concerned, in one way or another, with patterns of power relations in all the cultural and institutional products of an era, with "the historicity of texts" and the "textuality of history," as Louis Montrose's catchy jingle has it.[1] Wherever your turn, you find critics and theorists preoccupied with the ways in which all the isolable features, institutions, and products of a particular historical period—including authors, readers, texts—reflect, promote, enforce, or otherwise maintain the power differentials of authority and impotence, domination and subordination definitive of that period. They are concerned with the ways various culturally shaped institutions, products, and power formations reciprocally influence one another and negotiate power transactions on the cultural-energy exchange. These approaches betray their own historical origins in their adherence to what for convenience can be called "postmodern eclecticism," that unstable compound of post-Saussurean linguistics, post-Althusserian Marxism, post-Foucauldian sociology, and post-Lacanian psychoanalysis, a compound that is distinguished by nothing so much as its preoccupation with some structure of differential relations (usually binary relations) underlying all manifestations of human cultural activity from governmental policy to family relationships to popular entertainments and the production of artifacts of all kinds.

In all studies of the kind considered here, meaning and reference in cultural products derive not from the creative choices of individuals in the process of constructing systems of intentionality, but from the dynamics of extrapersonal forces. Authors, texts, and readers are subordinated (at best) to the operations of the impersonal mechanisms of which they are the product, and literary works (like all cultural products, that is, like all else) have interest not as unified wholes, as ethically valuable, emotionally powerful, intellectually engaging systems of satisfaction or rationality, but as reflections of deeper political and social conditions. In short, all that is central to this book is antithetical to the interests and assumptions of these approaches. Indeed, the prevailing view is that the theory of language and meaning that underwrites this book is complicit with the essentialist metaphysics, bourgeois capitalism, and colonialist oppression that "historicist" criticism is peculiarly designed to expose and transcend.

In what follows the basic aims are to consider the limitations (and, incidentally, the powers) of one way of talking about the inherence of power relations in literary works (the Bakhtinian way) and, by this means, to illuminate some of the weaknesses (and strengths) of "historicist" approaches generally. At the outset, however, it is necessary to re- mind ourselves that if we are not going to look at such cultural products as literary works as unified structures whose parts are determined by and functional relative to specific justification conditions, to systems of inten- tionality created by human agents, then we must look outside human agency for the conditions endowing the parts with meaning and signifi- cance, since there is no meaning, emphasis, or value whatsoever apart from some system of relationships, some pattern of use. Moreover, it is important to remember that in the "historicist" approaches the parts are not understood in terms of their contribution to the workingness of the whole (system of intentionality); rather, each part is emblematic in some way of the the extra-artifactual social tensions or circumstances that they exemplify or, in some cases, influence or alter. In short, the parts are not subordinated to some end in view, from which they derive their empha- sis, value, meaning, or significance; instead, they are signs, causes, con- sequences, or instances of preexisting conditions. Constraint is exerted externally, not internally, and, thus, specific content is based on a prior analysis of the social conditions—otherwise, it would be impossible to know what textual elements had clout or had meaningful content.

Because every differentiable aspect of a text may be the subject of independent inquiry, because every discriminable element may have predicates of quality or value attached to it, and because there is no way to determine merely by looking hard at a text which elements are essen- tial and which incidental, it is not surprising that meaningful units have been found at virtually every level of discrimination (for example, word, image, trope, proposition). It is certainly possible to focus attention on the thematic significance of subsentential items, of, for example, itera- tive words and phrases. More expansively, it is possible to focus on the possible thematic relations among recurrent terms, "ideas," and "propositions" as these are variously determined by the rhetorical interests of one or another reader (as "New Critics" frequently did); on the "canceling" or "retreating" meaning of some salient (though often hidden or obscured) tropological or figural device (as de Man frequently did); or on the diverse and usually conflicting or contradictory "meanings" that a text calls into play by shifting among styles of "discourse" (as many Bakhtinians do). At this level of structural concern (the level that dominates critical theory and practice in and out of the "historicist" mode in our period, where orders—and disorders—of meaning and significance emerge from an examination of relations among terms, modes of diction, tropes, propositions, and styles of discourse), many things may be said about texts which all will find interesting and many stunningly insightful. Especially insightful will such things be if one is predisposed to grant the "truth" of the prior assumptions about "language" or "social reality" upon which discussion is founded and to which each text brings support or confirmation, since the "units" have been selected in the interests of the prior social analysis or the prior understanding of the way "language" undoes itself or evokes its opposite.

If all reading is "hypothetical," in the sense that "meaning" and "reference" are not givens but takens—determined by some system of interest in agents or in culture, history, ideology, or language—reading at this level is peculiarly hypothetical. The inherence in the texts of the special features almost invariably depends on a habit or reading determined by the hypothesis about language or "reality" one is attempting to establish. The critic finds what he knows is "always already" there, what his dialectic requires: the players may suit up in marvelously diverse outfits, but they always play the same game; the many are always one, however cunningly they may disguise their appearances; and, of course, depending on controlling interest, the one has many names—aporia, colonialism, capitalism, and so on.

More often than not, analysis at this level carries us to the very bowels of our governing category, to the very infrastructure of language or historical becoming, to being and nothingness (or to the traces of nothingness in beingness itself). Moreover, criticism or discursive practice here valorizes the divided line. It is, in other words, "antithetical," concerned with binary features, with opposition or conflict in various pairs of "tropemes" or "ideomemes." Thus, discussion focuses on tension, irony, paradox, or ambiguity; on oppositions (speech/writing, containment/subversion, male/female, power/resistance, nature/culture, and so on); on the absence of presence and the presence of absence (and consequently on those devices which enable us to proclaim that "it's there *because* it's *missing*, namely, suppression, displacement, and substitution);

on cancellations, the dialogic struggle of "ideologemes," the emergence of the repressed from within the expressed content, the insubordination of the element subordinated in traditional orders of value, and so on.

As a matter of necessity, explanation at this level is largely indifferent to all that has prominence at the psychological/intentional level, to what we might call the intentional, emotional, affective structure of texts. By way of clarification, I would count as "psychological" all explanations that account for purposeful behavior in terms of mental contents. Basically, to paraphrase one of Donald Davidson's most frequent formulations, such explanations assume that actions—whether those of writers in composing or of characters in works—are events that are intentional under some description, the description under which they are rationalized by the contents of the mental states that are the reasons or justification conditions for them. Hence, in these analyses, the conventional literary categories through which psychological talk (that is, talk relating to the intentional and affective grounds of "meaning") is filtered—such as plot, act, character, thought, scene, and motive—are disregarded, neglected, or treated, if acknowledged at all, as necessary incidentals. They become lines on which to hang what has our primary interest or so many surface mechanisms by which to disguise or obscure the unresolved tensions in class, gender, race, power, and so on that inform the text at the deeper level. Of course, there is nothing sacrosanct about psychological categories, and no special privilege attaches to psychological talk or to the kinds of generalizations that such talk makes possible. Nevertheless, it is important to remember that in a world where all meanings are relative to cognitive frameworks, no special privileges can be granted to "historicist" or other ways of talking in the "antithetical mode" either.

It is worth recognizing that if it has no special privileges, psychological talk nevertheless has special powers and virtues. For example, if, like the pragmatic pluralist, you are interested in coming to know how the parts, as Nelson Goodman says, contribute to the functioning of the work as a symbol, then the statements that psychological talk (that is, talk about conditions of satisfaction within systems of justification) makes possible are especially valuable. It is to such statements that we must appeal if we would understand, cognitively and emotionally, what it "means" for such a man as Lear, both king and father, to say in such and such circumstances of abuse that he is "more sinned against than sinning" and if we would understand, retrospectively, why such a "truth," no less true for being more than half made up of pride and self-pity, pales in emotional and moral significance when placed beside his later desire to "expose" himself "to feel what wretches feel" so that he may "shake the superflux to them" and "show the heavens more just" (III.iv). What out of Lear's mouth moves us to pity would out of Goneril's move us to contempt, and it is psychological, intentional talk that enables us to understand this.

Only by some empathetic grasp (again made possible by our ordinary psychological ways of rationalizing—that is, understanding—behavior) of the kind of suffering that is worn and borne by the kind of man Lear is can we understand what it "means" to say what he says and be moved by his saying it. From our encounters with literature, as from our encounters with everyday events, we gain principles of reasoning—what Davidson calls principles of charity: those commonsense "rules" or intuitions we rely on when we attempt to make sense of the behavior of others. We enlarge and validate our principles in proportion to our experience, to our grasp of the "meaning" of new practices.[2] By virtue of our participation in various social practices and situations, we learn the "truth" conditions that endow sentences and whole works with these rather than those meanings and references; we learn to recognize, say, what a "pitiful scene" is and to understand that the "meaning" of a sentence expressed in such a scene is conditioned by psychological states (aims, wishes, desires, feelings, beliefs).

Further, explanations at the psychological level are transportable or "functional." They apply across material differences, enabling us to see within new contexts the operations of the "same" intentions or truth conditions, of the "Lear-like" in the materially un-Lear-like. The pity that is evoked in one situation of undeserved misfortune will be evoked in another completely different situation of the same kind (in Mary's case as well as in John's case).

## Ideologemic Explanations: The Example of Bakhtin

Historicist or what, following Bakhtin, I shall call ideologemic explanations clearly have capacities that psychological explanations do not have, simply because no good system of explanation is good for all purposes and because there are, as I have maintained elsewhere, no uniquely good cognitive processes. When scrupulously and rigorously exercised, ideologemic explanations have the capacity, for example, to expose salient trends of representation in a given era. Such explanations, however, also have limitations and, in their application, are fraught with difficulties, to some of which I shall now turn, taking prominent aspects of Bakhtin's "ideological" explanations as my points of departure. The ultimate purpose of this analysis is not only to expose what I take to be inherent weaknesses in ideology-based criticism but also to suggest why psychological explanations might on certain occasions and for certain purposes be more interesting and more intellectually secure than ideological explanations.

Initially, it is important to understand that while each system of explanation may acknowledge the interests of the other system, what has center stage in one system has at best only a walk-on role in the other. If for certain kinds of works, action and character are central to explanations at the psychological level (because "meaning" and "reference" are relative to the intentional states of persons of distinctive character in specific circumstances), they are relatively insignificant to "ideological" explanations. On the other hand, if the "ideologeme" (a unit of discourse embedded in another discourse that expresses a "particular way of viewing the world, one that strives for a social significance") is to Bakhtin the chief "object of representation" in a novel, it is to the "psychologist," if it is recognized as a discrete unit of "meaning" at all, a material component (in much the way phonemic, morphemic, and syntactic units are material components) whose "meaning" is relativized to the interest in which it is embedded. Its meaning, in other words, is determined by some psychological condition or some mental state (for example, anger or jealousy).[3] From the psychological perspective, at any rate, the ideologeme is not an *independent object of representation*, a differentiable unit whose "meaning" is isolable from the circumstantial intentionality from which it derives its specific content.

For Bakhtinians and historicists generally, a character—as well as the author and the narrator—is interesting to the extent that his discourse is "ideologemic," expressive directly or implicitly of a view with a certain social significance. The author's primary task is a "stylistic" one (that is, finding ways to represent artistically "images" of language, ideologemes). In this scheme, then, "Individual character and individual fates—and the individual discourse that is determined by these and these only—are in themselves of no concern for the novel." The "internal" moral relevance of particular speeches and expressions that are, in the psychological scheme, determined by the "thought" of ethically discriminable persons in specific situations of perplexity and choice is not important to analysis at the ideologemic level. What is "distinctive" in such discourse (significantly, language is always "discourse," not speech or utterance, in these analyses) "strives" for a "certain social significance," and when such discourse achieves what it strives for, it becomes a "language," an "image of a language," in short, an "ideologeme." Characters, of course, act as well as speak, but their action is significant relative to and is "always highlighted by ideology." Further, their action "is associated with an ideological motif and occupies a definite ideological position." More specifically, "The action and individual act of a character in a novel are essential in order to expose—as well as to test—his ideological position, his discourse."[4]

At bottom, the novel is "an artistically organized system for bringing different languages" (that is, ideologies, or different "social significances" within an overarching ideology) "in contact with one another."[5] As a consequence, "the plot itself is subordinated to the task of coordinating and exposing languages to each other"; hence the "primary stylistic project of the novel as a genre is to create images of languages" for the sake of highlighting their *contradictions* and "sharpening our perception of socio-linguistic differentiations."[6]

The kind of unity the novel realizes is, we are assured, an open-ended one, one in which the "dialogic" contradictions are not resolved but shown for what they are. The work as a whole expresses what ordinary discourse and experience normally conceal, the very *conflicts* underlying the sociohistorical reality in which the work has its being.[7] For many historicists, of course, the "closure" of the plot, along with the pleasure that accompanies it, is a device by which the author or, most commonly, the dominant culture, working through the conventions of its cultural products, contains the subversive elements whose "voices" have been allowed some expression in the plot. Indeed, the subversive "voices" or "languages" of the oppressed or victimized have been allowed for the sake of their ultimate suppression, a suppression which we will come to see, if the dominant energies are doing their job, as *good* and *natural*. If ordinary speech in the Bakhtinian scheme is a heteroglossic mixture of potential ideologemes, novelistic speech is dialogic, still a series of speeches within other speeches, but one in which the ideological potentialities within the mixture are actualized. The unity achieved by the novel is a unity only in the sense that the work is a "concrete" imaging of the dialogic diversity actually constituting a particular stage of "historical becoming."

Ordinary speech and conversation hide what the novelist succeeds in disclosing. We are always involved in speaking somebody else's speech in somebody else's language. More than half of what we say, according to Bakhtin, belongs to others—of course, in some sense of "belongs," a full 100 percent belongs to others, if we discount a few odd neologisms popping up here and there. But the novelist, through such devices as parody and hybridization, manages to capture the ideologemic in the heteroglossic languages of his narrators and characters and, thus, to get beyond the confused, surface diversity to the ideological unity, or core, of historical diversity. Bakhtin says:

Novelistic dialogue is pregnant with an endless multitude of dialogic confrontations, which do not and cannot resolve it, and which, as it were, only locally (as one out of many possible dialogues) illustrate this endless, deep-lying dialogue of languages; novel dialogue is determined by the very socio-ideological evolution of languages and society. A dialogue of languages is a dialogue of social forces perceived not only in their static co-existence, but also as a dialogue of different times, epochs and days, a dialogue that is forever dying, living, being born: co-existence and becoming are here fused into an indissoluble concrete unity that is contradictory, multi-speeched and heterogeneous; . . . from this dialogue of languages these [ideologemes] take their openendedness, their inability to say anything once and for all or to think anything through to its end, they take from it their lifelike concreteness, their "naturalistic quality."[8]

As documents reflecting states of "historical becoming" (and, implicitly, valuable to the extent that they are explicable in ideological terms), novels are, of necessity, open-ended.

In this system of analysis (though not in most "historicist" systems), the *author* is crucial to the realization of ideologemic conflicts, which are brought into open conflict only by his conscious and conscientious effort, but he is himself, finally, subordinated to the dialogic contradictions that he exhibits, since his inability to resolve conflicts is directly proportional to his success in exhibiting them (in representing, that is, the salient ideological features of "historical becoming"). To resolve in any way any of the displayed contradictions, he would have to be what he is not, that is, history itself, which tells its complex, multivoiced, and as yet unresolved metastory in its own way. He is subsumed by the forces he inscribes and is himself a mediated mediator. Of course, he could speak with "one" voice—a nondialogic heteroglossia—but not without losing himself as a novelist. He can end his plot (a matter of small moment), but not his dialogue. The plot is not the thing wherein to catch the conscience (or consciousness) of the race; it is a paltry stick on which the golden birds (ideologemes) sing of what is past, passing, and striving to become. Speaking of whole works, with special reference to those by Dostoevsky, Bakhtin says:

[the novels] in their entirety, taken as utterances of their *author*, are the same never-ending, internally unresolved dialogues among characters (seen as embodied points of view) and between the author himself and his characters; the characters' discourse is never entirely subsumed and remains free and open (as does the discourse of the author himself). In Dostoevsky's novels, the life experience of the characters and their discourse may be resolved as far as the plot is concerned, but internally they remain incomplete and unresolved.[9]

To present Bakhtin's views in such a summary fashion is to do not a little violence, if not to the fundamentals of the argument, at least to the richness, subtlety, and (sometimes) compelling power of those arguments. No one who reads Bakhtin can fail to be impressed by the range of his mind or by his more than occasional incisiveness, especially when he focuses on specific literary works and identifies distinguishable types of discourse concealed within, say, the author's (or the narrator's or a character's) discourse. If, then, I have done less than full justice to *his* discourse, I have, nevertheless, fairly exposed what in this mode of analysis is relevant to our discussion (and to our broader consideration of "ideological" modes of analysis and explanation), namely, its subordination of the "psychological" to the "ideologemic."

No pragmatic pluralist would suppose that a "true" account of some things could not be made from a properly and delicately managed use of the "historicist" method or from the materials of this method of analysis or assume that for some purposes its explanations (provided they actually explained something rather than merely correlated terms in some algebraic way or derived them in some algorithmic way) would not be preferable to those supplied by an analysis conducted at the psychological level. After all, adequacy and utility are relative to our interests and purposes. On the other hand, if such an approach began to claim special privileges, insisting that it was peculiarly suited to the task of explaining, say, novels—because it made available to contemplation or awareness the only interests or forces actually constitutive of experience and production—then the pragmatic pluralist would be obliged to ask it to temper its arrogance with a little modesty. Still, after granting the possible explanatory strength of certain aspects of this historicist way of talking about power or ideological relations within texts (and, implicitly, other cultural products), the pragmatic pluralist—the pluralist as psychologist, at any rate—would in an interval of sobriety be bothered by what could be seen as certain inherent and, hence, inescapable limitations in the approach and would have trouble acceding to many of its claims and to several of the assumptions underlying them.

For one thing, the whole approach seems to be focused on too narrow a band of units in the sociohistorical continuum that is the register of "historical becoming" (whatever that is exactly). More important, the approach seems to be based on a *prior analysis of the conflictual forces*. Indeed, if it were not so based, the "ideologemic" could not be identified as ideologemic; the embedded discourse could not be singled out as a bearer of a peculiar social significance. A word, phrase, or term, considered apart from some mental component, some intentionality, has, like nature, no semantic preferences. Moreover, as I have consistently stated, all words are like Wittgenstein's rabbit-duck, in the sense that every word can be understood in many ways. For anything to be taken as given in a certain way (and nothing can be seen or understood unless it is taken in some way), it has to be seen as given in the way it is taken. Beyond chiastic cuteness, the point is simply that to take something in a certain way is already to be involved in a system of entailments, that system in which the taken is functional relative to.

Moreover, if the reader simply *identifies* what the author by conscious effort has made ideologemic in the heteroglossic, then the problem is not removed but compounded, for now both author and reader/theorist are implicated in prior analysis and prior restraint. What the author deliberately highlights as significant must be recognized by the reader as having such highlighting and such significance. Of course, in some modes of this form of analysis, the author is the unconscious transmitter of meanings ghostwritten by history or the political unconscious that the "historicist" critic, by dint of superior cognitive predispositions, is peculiarly qualified to discern. Still, the problem remains, for if there is no thought or content apart from structure or system, the system must be in place or intuitively grasped if the content is to emerge. To be in a position, then, to spot the "ideologemic" in the heteroglossic, one must, in a sense, be *in* socially differentiated time but not *of* it (since, if for no other reason, we cannot talk about or discuss a cognitive system or theory about power relations from within the theory). We must, in some sense, already know the contradictions of which one (or the text) is constituted. It would be reasonable to inquire about the world view within the historicist view that makes possible the discrimination of socially significant world views in texts.

We may be able to put aside this inquiry and assume that it is possible to work, as some are inclined to say, at the *margins* of discourse, to be where we can *see our seeing* (being), see the eye seeing its seeing as it sees. (Of course, in talking from the margins about what is "true" or a "fact" in a given language game or a given culture, we speak from "outside" the language game or the culture, and, thus, our speaking is an "appropriation" of the "other" from a different culturally determined perspective, as some "historicists" are obliged to admit.) But if we put all this aside, we are back to the narrowness problem, for we can immediately see that the band of "meaningful units" observed by this approach, focused as it is on units of what is vaguely called "social significance," is too narrow. The band is too narrow precisely because *virtually everything* we say is made up of other people's saying. Our speech is compounded of elements already in verbal circulation emanating from an enormous range of practices that have a social significance of some kind when viewed from one angle or another. Our plenty makes us poor, it would seem. The band, as distinguished by Bakhtin, is too narrow *precisely because* the world is so heteroglossic, so multilanguaged, so full of discourses belonging to a rich diversity of "social" interests, each discourse having a social significance to the extent that it is accessible to and used by more than one person. Too narrow, furthermore, because words and things (the *same* words and things, mind you), with no semantic preferences of their own, are so willing to participate in so many orders of significance.

We make our verbal pots by gluing together the shards of discourse available to us. We inherit a language already "-phemed" (morphemed, graphemed, and so on), vocabularized, and syntaxed. We learn the various uses to which this "rule-laden" (and, of course, "use-laden") language can be put and the various meanings it can bear in the process of using it to meet both our predictable and our emergent needs in the various circumstances in which we find ourselves and in the process of understanding the practices of others, of grasping, that is, the circumstantial and motivational conditions that would justify the attribution of one rather than another kind of interest relativity to the sentences we encounter in the various enterprises in which we participate from day to day. In using it and understanding its uses, we make and gain access to innumerable kinds of social significance. Outside some practice, there are no social significances, and every sentence can serve many practices. As Hilary Putnam observes, "the assertibility conditions of an arbitrary sentence are not surveyable," in that every sentence can be made functional within many systems of justification. But if "the assertibility conditions are not surveyable how do we learn them? We learn them" (in just the way Michael Dummett has suggested) "by acquiring a practice." [10]

Of course, all our practices are "sociohistoric" in the broad sense (that is, they emerge and subsist in sociohistoric time). Nevertheless, not all such practices are specifically "ideological," in the narrow sense singled out by Bakhtin, who counts as "interesting" only those language units within practices (textually embodied as "ideologemes") which have a certain predetermined "social significance," a kind of significance that the practices of, say, genetics, horticulture, sailing, or geometry presumably do not have (at least not in their "technical" aspects), though, since so much depends on the predeterminations and inclinations of the theorist, there's no telling where a socially significant unit will come from.

Some historicists, to be sure, affirm that all discourses—indeed, all components of all discourses—are constrained in their meaning and significance by the *social* conditions of their production. Surely this must be wrong, since every day we see the "same" components serving different practices or serving the same practices in contradictory ways. At any rate, much in the ways of talking of genetics, horticulture and so on is not determined by or contingent upon some particular social formation in Bakhtin's narrow sense. At least Bakhtin seems to think so, for if he did not, then everything, every bit of every discourse, would be ideologemic.

To the pragmatic pluralist, then, Bakhtin gives emphasis to a small group of "-emes" embedded in texts. Without his help, however, the members of this group could not be identified as having in themselves any particular significance at all, because, as we have noted more than once, such units have in themselves no *semantic* preferences. Units of language have no specific content, no particular meaning or reference, apart from use, apart from particular mental states. Abstracted from contexts of use, Bakhtin's units have no significance. Only as language "tokens," not as language "types," do units have specific significance. Tokens, as bearers of specific content, are not "iterable." Speaking broadly, we can say that whereas "dog," "cat," and "boat" are types that identify all members of the class, "Fido," "Fluffy," and "Intrepid" are tokens that identify particular members of or instances within the class. This point is regularly made by philosophers of thought and language, but by none more forcibly than Davidson, who reminds us that

There would be no saying what language a sentence belonged to if there were not actual utterances or writings. . . . So in the end the sole source of linguistic meaning is the intentional production of tokens of sentences. If such acts did not have meanings, nothing would. There is no harm in assigning meanings to sentences, but this must always be a meaning derived from concrete occasions on which sentences are put to work.[11]

But we are getting ahead of our argument. For the time being, it is necessary to stick to the narrowness problem. From the pluralist perspective, there are within easy reach many worlds of practices available for incorporation into our discursive practices of everyday life, our familiar, familial, ordinary sayings and writings (the practices of sailing, home maintenance, gardening, and so on). To the extent that a portion of any of these worlds of practice could be isolated and treated as epitomizing the "world view" from which it was extracted, that "epitome" so isolated could then be embedded in another discourse and presumably identified by an alert reader as belonging to (or as having a natural alliance with) a distinguishable world of "meaning" (the world of martial arts, gardening, accounting, home maintenance, or pottery, for instance). In this way, then, we isolate and embed a unit of discourse that strives for something other than social significance in the Bakhtinian sense; it strives for and presumably exhibits some other kind of significance (for example, practical or technical significance) in some "world view" other than the narrowly social. If every isolable, "world"-illuminating unit of discourse is understood to strive in one way or another for "social significance," then the force of the ideologemic is lost, and the *social* is trivialized.

What we can do with one such epitome we can do with many; that is, in one discourse we can embed many discourses, creating in the end a patchwork of practices that is, in a sense, emblematic of the concrete variety of "experience" itself in this "era." Note, however, that in our revised scheme of artistic quilting, there is no reason to assume that the worlds brought together will be in conflict with one another. (Contradiction is one of the historicists' essentialist abstractions, a dialectical—in more than one sense—necessity.) Indeed, though formerly sailors, gardeners, and so on they now function *cooperatively* as contributors to the functioning of their new enterprise.

Although we have anticipated our argument somewhat, at this point the Bakhtinian, to compensate for lack of thoroughness (by our lights), is only enjoined to add variety to diversity, to cross-fertilize "ideologemes" with other "-emes," so that in the end the harvest (the representation of experienced reality in this or that era) will be more plentiful (that is, more accurate). As of now, the Bakhtinian reaps what the novelist (artist) sows in very limited fields of "reality." In short, the pragmatic pluralist sees no reason why any special privileges should be granted to "images" of language that betoken "sociolinguistic differentiations," especially when such "images" (as conceived) rather impose limits on than define the range of socially significant "realities" experienced in any era and exhibited in, for example, any novel.

Unfortunately, once we move beyond narrowness, we encounter graver difficulties. Even if the pragmatic pluralist granted special privileges to the "ideologemic" units, he would still be perplexed because, for another and much more important reason, the "ideologemic" unit would itself seem to be heteroglossic, compounded, that is, of elements (words) deriving from or capable of entering into a multiplicity of reference relations. Any deconstructionist or anyone influenced by the philosophy of language informing deconstructionism (that is, any postmodern theorist) only half committed to the job could show, for example, how each of the particles making up the ideologeme was itself the bearer of many traces of signification, could show that the stability of the ideologeme was illusory. Since, however, the pragmatic pluralist is no deconstructionist (though, like one, recognizing that the "reference" of arbitrary words cannot be fixed), he or she would wonder why the intentional circumstantiality of the context of which the ideologeme is a part would not do unto the ideologeme what the ideologeme does unto the words comprising it: that is, fix the interest relativity, fix the meaning. Unlike the deconstructionist (and others), the pragmatic pluralist recognizes that reference and meaning can be fixed and fixed for good within a system of intentionality.

It would seem to the pragmatic pluralist (as psychologist) that just as the *words* function in the service of the "ideologeme" (have their reference fixed by the ideologeme), so the *ideologeme* functions in the service of that "intentionality" in which it is embedded. The assertibility conditions of ideologemes—no more than those of arbitrary phonemes, morphemes, words, and sentences—cannot be conveniently delimited. Ideologemes, like these other potentially meaningful units, cannot determine their own boundary conditions. One of the covering maxims here is: To recognize that a phrase, taken as given in a certain way in one context, satisfies a certain justification condition is also to be aware that it does not satisfy that condition when it is taken as given in another context. To treat these ideologemes as though they preserved in their new context the meanings they carried in the context from which they were taken would be to favor them as no other "-emes" are favored, to favor them in a way that the Freudian "-emes" and Emersonian "-emes" are not favored when they are used to advance an original argument, as they are, for example, in Harold Bloom's writings. The Freudian "-emes" undergo a sea change as they change contexts and are incorporated first into Bloom's and then into Norman Holland's discourse. And clearly these "-emes" belong to "images" of significance as surely as do the ideologemes singled out for notice by Bakhtinians.

Analogously, we could say that treating these ideologemes as irreducible nuggets of meaningful social significance is comparable to treating the "world" from which any given metaphor derives its terms or categories of comparison as an independently significant world of meaning. Thus, when a character is at the "zenith" of her career, she is astronomically significant; when a beloved is like a red, red rose, she is horticulturally meaningful and—in addition to being lovely, fresh, or mortal—inescapably implicated in whatever it is that rose plants do to keep themselves from the doldrums in the world in which they have their significance. Even so, it is perhaps worth noting that if our character were discovered by such a habit of reading to be living now in the heavens—at the zenith—and now in the garden—as a rose—we would not also be obliged to conclude that she lived in conflict or in contradictory worlds.

A further wrinkle here is that while we could not know what anyone meant when a beloved was called a rose unless we knew what a rose was, the nature of the rose, as a rose, is no part of the current meaning of the term. I agree with Michael Dummett when he says that, though the meaning "of an expression determines its reference, inasmuch as reference follows from its sense" (meaning), the "reference is not part of the meaning—it is not part of whatever is known by anyone who understands the expression."[12] For example, consider Lear's "Pray, you, undo this button" from the conclusion to *King Lear*; the meaning of this remark in context determines the reference of "button." It is the button on a shirt or cloak, not the button that turns a piece of machinery on or the button on the top of a cap, but the meaning of the sentence has to do with the nature of Lear's request or the condition of humility from which it is made. It has to do with what it means for such a man to make such a request at such a time in such circumstances of suffering and loss. The sense or meaning is not about buttons. So, in the case of "ideologemes," the new contexts in which they appear are not about the "ideologemes" that are referentially signaled in the sentences. A similar point is made by Akeel Bilgrami; he observes that "reference has nothing to do with the meaning of terms or with content. . . . Though external things are involved in their determination, the meanings of terms are specified not by specifying their mediated reference but simply by specifying an agent's beliefs." [13] It is at the local level, the level of specific intentionality, that meanings are determined.

Now, if ideologemes could be identified as readily and as easily as metaphoric vehicles, we would willingly pay unto the studies conducted in their behalf all the respect that we pay unto imagery studies, but, as we have seen, such "-emes" have a tendency to lose their specific social significations in the process of becoming functional in new contexts. Moreover, even in the world in which an ideologeme can have a social significance (let us for convenience say that the "ideologeme" before us belongs squarely in the world of commerce or labor relations or parliamentary proceedings), it is capable of serving as a carrier of various kinds of "social significance" within that world of interest, depending on whether, for example, it expresses the "truth" honored by this faction or the one honored by that faction within the social community from which it is taken. Also, how it is "honored" (that is, understood or meant) in its present context may be something quite apart from how it has ever been honored before. The ideologeme, so to speak, is a generalization to a class (commerce, parliamentary proceeding, or whatever), but *it does not apply directly or immediately to any cases in the class*, inasmuch as it only has specific meaning *within a case*. It is a type, not a token. The ideologemic, wherever found, always has an interest-relative meaning, if it has any meaning at all; it does not belong to any specific world—it has no specific content—independently of some interest relation, some justification conditions.

To think otherwise is to realize the sort of essentialism on which the term reification is not wasted. Different *ideologues* use the same "ideologemes" in different ways. The ideologeme is not transparently and unmistakably a distinct "world view," but only potentially one. An ideologeme, like a general term such as "tree," may have a more or less definite default meaning (or a range of meanings), but it has no specific content apart from a context, a content-fixing system of intentionality. The point I am making here is comparable to one made by Bilgrami when he distinguishes between a *concept* or a *theory of meaning* (what in my context is an "ideologeme") and a *content* (what I call a context-determined meaning). We need to make a distinction, he says, between two levels, "the level of a theory of meaning" (the level of concepts, of "ideologemes") "on the one hand and the level of contents at which behavior is (commonsensically) explained [and specific meaning determined] on the other. I describe the former as 'aggregative' and the latter as 'local.'" Moreover, "the point of the distinction is to mark the fact that explanations [and meanings] are always in a locality and that meaning theories which specify concepts [or, in my case, "ideologemes"] in general have no *direct* relevance to particular localities." [14]

Thus, we are back to prior analysis and prior restraint, a prior understanding of the peculiar and durable social significance of the ideologemic possessed by the social theorist or historicist. What is said of the ideologeme is largely true of the metaphoric vehicle, except that if we have said enough to carry on with imagery study when by consensus we agree that this or that vehicle is horticultural or navigational in origin, we have not said enough to carry on with "ideologemic" study when we agree that this or that ideologeme derives from the world of romance, or satire, or commerce, or parliamentary proceedings. To be truly ideologemic, the ideologeme must have a specific, fixed social significance in the world in which it is a world view (which it does not and cannot have) and must be capable of supporting that specific significance in each new context to which it is brought (which it cannot do).

If we put all this aside and assume that social practice has imposed severe constraints on the social significance or the "world"-meaning that the ideologeme can bear, the pragmatic pluralist-psychologist would still wonder why the critic would be essentially indifferent to the reference relations in which the ideologemic entered as a result of being functional in this or that context of plot concern, or of author, narrator, or character concern, especially since the number of reference relations into which it can enter—even assuming its integrity as a meaningful unit—is virtually infinite and since its meaningfulness as a unit is not unaffected by the circumstantial intentionality in which it finds itself. But to wonder why, if the words can be adjusted to the interest of the ideologeme, the ideologeme cannot be adjusted to the interest of that in which it is embedded and which it subserves is to succumb, I suppose, to creeping Henry Higginsism, that is, to wonder why the "ideologemist" is not more like a psychologist.

In the end, however, notwithstanding many reservations about ideologemic study, particularly about the theory of language or of thought which underlies it, the pluralist-psychologist recognizes that in practice such study (like image studies), especially when undertaken cautiously and with a sensitivity alert to subtle shifts in style (as it frequently is by Bakhtin), is often quite interesting and illuminating. Moreover, no reader would deny that it is peculiarly adept at detecting modes of discourse within discourse or varieties of distinguishable elements of which our language in use is compounded. Such study can indeed bring to awareness broad classes of "speech," and by isolating and focusing on these speech classes, considered apart from their specific functional value and emphasis within their local context of intentionality, we can undoubtedly learn in a general way something not uninteresting about the social (and other) "realities" that inform our texts. Like image patterns, these "speech" or, in other historicist and "global" approaches, "verbal" patterns may tell us something valuable—depending on the interests of the theorist—about mind, culture, gender, power relations, and so on.

It is always possible for a critic or theorist to locate nonintentional patterns or recurrences in literary works and to align them with patterns or recurrences elsewhere in the cultural productions of an era, according to some system of analogy, but this enterprise is always a tricky and dangerous business, because, as we have noted on several occasions, regularities (or similarities) are where you find them. As Nelson Goodman insists, you can find them anywhere once the master categories—from politics, race, mind, or power relations—of one's analogical scheme are in place, or once the scheme for translating between manifest and latent content, for seeing how this is really that, is in place.[15] Still, most will agree that some regularities are worth knowing about and are really there to be found or uncovered, provided one has delicate and flexible enough cognitive instruments to work with, not simply self-confirming hypotheses.

That such ideologemic study will also lead to a clear understanding of any particular stage of historical becoming seems unlikely, however, in part because the notion of "historical becoming" is itself highly problematic—indeed insupportable: It is dependent on historicist assumptions about the shaping influence, in every period, of some reified "historical forces" or of one world view or one culture (the "dominant culture") on all cognitive processes and all "social" and imaginative productions, which, as I have argued, can be constructed to satisfy an indefinite number of meaning and reference conditions no matter how severe the restrictions imposed on our imaginative and practical activity by the political or cognitive regime in which we find ourselves.[16] The argument here is not directed against the notion of dominant or prominent trends in any particular era, but against the extent of their control and influence over the possibilities of imaginative construction. For the most part, the subsumptive or controlling conditions are usually defined very broadly and abstractly in terms of such things, for example, as means of production, capitalism, colonialism, the commodification of values, in terms of abstractions that are from the point of view of actual practices cognitive non-starters. Separated from their immediate contexts, the objects or phrases to which the controlling or shaping conditions are applied are almost infinitely malleable, are willing to accommodate themselves to the directives of an unlimited assortment of prior political, cultural, and psychological categories. In their application the dominant conditions (or categories) always lead to the same results—the exemplification of what is implicated in the categories themselves. Finally, and correlatively, the application of such categories is unlikely to lead to any clear understanding of "historical becoming," because, in every period (however denominated), as we extend our survey of cases—our survey of texts and other cultural products—we discover not only myriad productions but also diversity and discord and multiplicity within the "dominant system" that we have been willing to treat as constitutive of the historical stage to which we assumed we had privileged access.

At any rate, whatever the value of imagery studies and of "ideologemic" (and other such) studies, it should be clear that nothing in them precludes discussion at the psychological level, as many historicists and other "postmodern" theorists have assumed. If imagists and ideologemists, as well as a host of other recent theorists, recognize but neglect, say, character and action for the sake of exploring their interests in relations among images and ideologemes, we are not justified in assuming from such practice that the categories of interest to the psychologist are either unimportant or uninteresting (or, as some theorists seem fond of proclaiming, illegitimate or second-rate). In generous moments, the psychologist would say to all those who would subordinate (at best) his or her interests to theirs: If you are interested in coming to understand the text as a coordinated system of meaning and reference not of your own devising, you would be well advised to put off your own kind of felicity a while and subordinate your interest to mine. (Of course, if you have no such interests—for example, interests in action, character, moral choice—at least have the courtesy to refrain from saying that such interests are either impossible or uninteresting.)

More expansively, the psychologist would suggest that, since at the psychological level we are concerned with the assertibility conditions endowing the language we use with specific meaning and reference, explanations at this level are generally very useful and interesting to feeling and thinking creatures, to those interacting with other feeling and thinking creatures. This is so because in general we are quite likely to confront situations from day to day in which we are interested in knowing if and why someone is angry or jealous or ironic, in knowing whether in some circumstances this or that remark or response is appropriate, or what a remark "means" when said by a particular person in a certain frame of mind, and so on. Such situations are much more likely to occur than those in which it is pressingly important to know something about the kinds of socially—that is, ideologically—significant discourse embedded in the angry speech directed to us or about the derivational base of the imagery in such a speech. And speaking generally, the psychologist can confidently say that language is important to us because it represents how things are (to us) and what we think, believe, hope, feel, intend to do about them.[17] Moreover, generalizations at the psychological level apply to an enormous number of materially different but humanly salient cases, retaining their explanatory power across huge differences in mental contents and "external" circumstances. To size up a situation as one in which jealousy is "warranted" and a remark as one designed to give the jealous speaker a measure of mean gratification is not only to grasp the "truth-conditions" or justification conditions determining the "meaning" of what is said, but also to gain access to a conceptual (psychological) resource not exhausted in its local embodiment but permanently available as a possible conditioner of meaning in a variety of comparable but materially different circumstances. By means of psychological reading, as from experience, we gain what Samuel Johnson called "principles of reasoning."

If all "meanings" in all texts are interest-relative, and if "meanings" not our own can be retrospectively constructed by grasping the assertibility or justification conditions of their expression, then anyone interested in the interest relativity of "meanings" will not be indifferent to explanations at the psychological level, since these explanations are preeminently concerned with *interests*. (We cannot know what Bakhtin's, Greenblatt's, Foucault's, or anybody's text "means" without knowing its interests, and we cannot even know what is being referred to in a sentence or text without knowing what system of intentionality governs expression.) To be engaged at all by a literary text—at least the kind of text that attracts, say, Bakhtin's or Greenblatt's attention, in which plot and character figure prominently—we are obliged to figure out, for example, what purpose (or belief, wish, aim, desire, fear, and so on) would induce a particular person to act or speak as he or she does in a particular situation, or we are obliged to ask what way of sizing up the situation would render intelligible what so-and-so says and does to so-and-so. In short, we are obliged to *explain* behavior. For beings like us, such explanation requires us to find some way of rationalizing actions. Our way is to explain or rationalize actions in terms of the mental contents (beliefs, desires, and so on through the intentional repertoire) that are the *reasons* for or causes of them. More specifically, we are obliged to consider what "thin likelihoods of modern seeming" would induce a noble Othello to treat a faultless Desdemona as he does.

As we read a text, we size up the conditions conditioning the way the characters we have sized up in a particular way size up the situations they are in; we imagine vividly—and apart from immediate self-interest—the moral and emotional determinants of specific "meaning" in humanly interesting situations. All "-phemes," words, sentences, images, or ideologemes, no matter how interesting in themselves as elements in (formal) systems of structural relations, are material bases or components of the interests that they are informed by at the psychological level. Moreover, the situations are humanly interesting because *their intelligibility depends precisely upon the same kind of moral reasoning that we are forced to employ in the world of everyday experience.* There is, then, a powerful, nontrivial sense to the notion that literature provides us with "equipment for living." It (or some parts of it) enlarges the stock of concepts and references on which we can draw when the business before us is to make some kind of sense of what we say and do and of what is said to and done unto us, when we are impelled to find a fit between what is said or done and what is "meant" (is it a threat? can it be taken seriously? is she speaking figuratively? ironically?, and so on). Some texts, then, are interesting precisely because they are systems of moral reasoning, systems exhibiting moral reasoning (in characters) and requiring moral reasoning (in the reader). In schooling ourselves in their ways of moral reasoning, we learn something relevant to the moral reasoning we must employ whenever we leave the garret and start bumping into folks who insist on being attended to.

Given the historicists' interests, as determined by the systems of rationality informing their productions, there is no reason why literature should hold any more of their attention than any other manifestation of cultural energy, and I certainly would not wish at this stage to accuse them of having any interest in literature as literature, that is, as unique products of art, which in some cases achieve an uncommon excellence of structural integrity and moral significance. Still, the psychologist's dark suspicion is that the vast majority of literary texts that generations of readers have found interesting would interest us hardly at all if they were not systems of moral reasoning, intentional systems of moral and intellectual concern about how to live and what to believe (and, thus, susceptible to explanations at what we have been calling the psychological level). If such a suspicion were not unfounded, no one, then, would blame the psychologist for preferring, on some occasions, psychological explanations to a host of other kinds of explanations. If the psychologist insists that we cannot do without psychological talk (intentional, epistemic talk), there is no one who can legitimately gainsay his view without giving up reference and meaning altogether, without giving up the pleasures of having attitudes about contents.

# Chapter 5
# Criticism: The More It Changes, the More It Is the Same Thing

Despite the many transformations criticism has undergone over the last sixty years or so, as one "-ism" has yielded pride of place to another in fairly rapid succession or as groups of contenders have jockeyed for prominence while other groups have pushed forward to notice, argumentative method in criticism has remained relatively stable. However different their ground terms and the privileged bases of analogical reference, virtually all new approaches have given prominence to binary oppositions or antithetical categories, shown how the many participate in, exhibit, or reflect the one, and stressed the importance of the divided line separating the manifest from the latent, the overt from the covert, the surface from the deep meaning. Moreover, the method is peculiarly adept at finding what it is looking for, since its findings are invariably implications of the terminology and method by means of which the investigation is conducted. The differences in the different views are in the materials moved about, not in the manners of moving about the materials, and while the method employed was not invented in our period, its current hegemony perhaps deserves the attention of social historians.

In this mode of argumentation, the first task is to find some preeminent derivational base of "knowledge" or "truth," a base complete with "god-terms" (in Kenneth Burke's happy phrase) and a mechanism ("many in one," "divided line," or both) for choreographing their movements. The derivational base supplies the common cause or ground of all literary (in narrow versions) or cultural (in broader, more comprehensive versions) productions. Of the many bases available, critics and theorists in our period have appealed most frequently to history, mind, power relations, language, and, more specifically, to myth, ritual, Saussurean linguistics, anthropology, and psychoanalysis, among others, favoring for the most part explanatory models originating in the social rather than the nomothetic sciences. In short, cultural products of all kinds have such and such features and qualities in such and such relation because language, mind, history, or whatever has just this character. Once selected, the explanatory model (which supplies the common cause of all production) is sent forward to put questions—for which it necessarily already has answers—to all the discourses which we have wittingly and unwittingly inscribed or by which we have been inscribed.

Not surprisingly, the method works, for wherever we look, we find the localized manifestation (or hidden expression) of precisely those features that the model "explains" as it identifies. Inhering in all "texts" (which includes all systems of organization and all behavior) are exactly those traits the model would require if it were, as it is assumed to be, a special conditioner of "meaning." If literary discourse is distinguished *by* special features of language, by, say, "irony" or "paradox" (in addition to being distinguished *from* "logical structure" or "univocal meaning"), then analysis discloses in this and that and the next work the inherence of irony; if all discourse is characterized by *différance*, then . . . , and so on.

Moreover, the explanatory power of the model is best seen when the material to which it is applied seems most resistant to its authority, when what the material *seems* to "mean" directly contradicts what the model would have the material "mean." It is here that the operations made familiar by psychoanalysis—namely, suppression, displacement, substitution, and so on—come in handy. If the surest sign of presence is absence, and of absence, presence, or if the saying of this indicates the suppression of that, or if one thing is really only a sign of its contrary or opposite, then the way is cleared for the invention of the Procrustean bed; then no hypothesis should starve for lack of evidential nutrition. Indeed, the more counterintuitive the claim, the more antithetical it seems to hard-won, experienced-on-the-pulses, seen-with-my-own-eyes knowledge, sense, or wisdom, the better. In such circumstances the very "perversity" of the explanation serves as a powerful "proof" of its validity (it must be true, since it violates everything I formerly knew or believed). No one likes to be taken in by mere appearances (and everyone perhaps harbors the deep suspicion that nothing is really as it seems), and thus nothing delights quite so much as the knowledge that things are other than we had thought them to be or, better yet, worse than we had guessed or, best, just the reverse of what we had innocently suspected them of being—and that this is so of necessity, because language, history, or mind is, make no mistake about it, the way it is. Satan is Milton's hero, and Hamlet, not Claudius, is the play's villain. There are no authors, only texts and intertexts. There is nothing outside the text. All texts are—indeed, everything is—political or ideological.

Although generally recognized as one of the chief stooges or apologists for the Elizabethan reign of terror, Shakespeare is, in fact, the primary arsonist or instigator of revolution in the period (here, of course, we have one startingly original view seeking to supplant its predecessor in startling originality). Long suspected of being the poet of the inner condition, of the individual mind, Wordsworth is *really* the most political of poets, and this we know because of his suppression of the political in his most distinctive or characteristic poems. As Marjorie Levinson observes, "Given the sort of issues raised by 'Tintern Abbey' 's occasion, it follows that the primary poetic action is the suppression of the social. . . . 'Tintern Abbey' 's suppression of historical consciousness is exactly what makes it so Romantic a poem." [1] And so on.

The ultimate authority of the model, however, derives from our concessions to the "truth" of its claims about the "real nature" of, say, history, mind, or language. If language or mind, for example, works this way or that way, then it follows that, regardless of what they seem individually to be saying or to be about, all "texts" or "coded" systems of behavior—whether great or small, popular or elite, spontaneous or contrived, whether taking the form of dreams, jokes, epic poetry, lyric poetry, editorials, State Department memoranda—are acting in more or less open complicity with the categorical directives by which the scope of their activity is always already determined. To prove the bare existence of such modes of reasoning in literary studies would be an exercise in supererogation, inasmuch as such a proof is already available to every reader for whom literary studies is not a mere string of vocables. Nevertheless, a quick overview of the mode in two of its more popular incarnations—New Criticism and deconstruction—would perhaps not be criminally superfluous, especially since New Criticism is a methodological precursor of deconstruction and since the theory of language underlying deconstruction continues to exert its influence on virtually every mode of critical inquiry currently in vogue.

## Foreknowledge: The Example of New Criticism

The New Critics begin inquiry not from some general conception of the nature of language as such (as the deconstructionists and others do), but from a dialectical distinction between poetic and nonpoetic language or discourse. They sharply distinguish between "scientific," "logical," "practical," or "discursive" language and "poetic" language and discourse; between, in John Crowe Ransom's characteristic formulation, "logical structure" and "irrelevant local texture"; between "idea" (a domesticated thing fit for dull, practical, appropriative tasks) and "image" (a generous, free-spirited thing inclined to embrace experience in all its rich complexity and ambiguous particularity); between "denotative" and "connotative" language; and so on. Plot, character, and thought, say, belong to the world of "logical structure." They are, if you will, necessary incidentals, the "discursive" ropes on which what is most important—the recurrent images, metaphors, themes—can be hung. From this initial arrangement of dialectical opposites all subsequent reasoning follows.

To anticipate our argument slightly, we can see here, in their innocent, unrefined form the crucial dialectical elements of Paul de Man's deconstructive criticism. (They are unrefined in the sense of being uninformed by a superior understanding of the capacity of language, as such, to disseminate significations, to generate an indefinite number of conflicting significations, a plethora of meanings while eliminating any means of choosing among them.) These dialectical elements are "grammar" (the tame rules and conventions of language) and "rhetoric" (the play of figures and tropes); or, in combination with the preceding dialectical opposites, the "constative" and the "performative" functions of language, the latter functions undoing what the former assert or say. "Grammar" seeks determinate referentiality and meaning, whereas "rhetoric" discloses the naivete of "grammar's" illusionary hopes by tracking the instability and self-immolating character of all apparent fixities. Thus, de Man performs close reading with a vengeance, but by his practices he betrays his kinship relations.[2]

What distinguishes literature from other "ways of knowing" in the New Critical scheme is traceable ultimately to the peculiar characteristics of its medium of expression (its language). Literary or poetic language is polysemous, faithful to the rich diversity of experience, and hence especially suited to expressing and exposing by means of paradox, irony, and ambiguity the dynamic tensions or the tensional oppositions that underlie our encounters with the world and our attempts to know. To the young Turks who replaced them, the New Critics labored under the illusion that works, though self-conflicted, were distinct entities with organic unity, indeed, that they owed their unity to the peculiar but finite set of meanings they held in tensional balance. Moreover, their polysemeity allowed only a fixed set of conflicting meanings to be operative in any given work. The *arrivistes*, on the other hand, know that polysemeity is just another envelope to be emptied of its bounded contents.

Where irony, paradox, and ambiguity can be found, there too—and there only—is literature. (The cynic might wonder where they could *not* be found, since, as Alexander Pope observes, all looks yellow to the jaundiced eye.) The critic's task is to show how various texts variously realize their peculiarly "tensed meaning" as a result of maintaining some dynamic equilibrium between opposites or countervailing tendencies. The text is a structure of meanings determined by tensions between, for example, denotations and connotations, between the meaning of one term, phrase, idea, or pattern of imagery and that of another. Like the aspiring actor who wishes to be just like Marlon Brando, but in his own way, each text exhibits the same thing, but in its own way, with its own set of contraries or balanced oppositions. In general, once the basic opposition has been located, the forces it holds in gyroscopic balance can be found at work throughout the text in greater and lesser textual units, in terms, phrases, images, verse paragraphs, scenes, and so on, each unit thus serving as the metonymic epitome of the whole work.

Because the only appropriate vehicle for the expression of the text's "meaning" is the text itself, the linear, propositional reasoning employed in analysis, description, or paraphrase can at best only suggest or approximate what the text embodies. That is, *readings* of texts are not satisfactory substitutes for the internal *meanings* of texts, but they are the only simulacra academics can offer the journals and one another. By means of such "readings," these critics could perhaps suggest, albeit in propositional, "unpoetic" form, the "meanings" that transcended the propositional (or what would later become the logocentric). Like their legitimate heirs, the deconstructionists, they made do with the logocentrism that they canceled or derided. In practice this approach results in thematic readings of texts, in readings that for the most part disclose the dynamic interaction of such general ideas, themes, or binary pairs as love and reason, wit and witchcraft, the individual and society, death-in-life and life-in-death, and so on.

And if each text exhibits a unique complex of meaning, all texts go about the business of meaning in the same way—inevitably so, since by prior commitment we know what poetic language is like and consequently what poetic structure must be if poetic language is as we assume it to be. As Samuel Johnson once remarked, the whole "system seems to be established on a concession which if it be refused cannot be extorted." [3] And what applies with signal force to the "great chain of being" (the topic occasioning Johnson's comment) applies no less aptly to the language assumptions of New Criticism and, as we shall now see, deconstruction.

## Losing Ground: The Example of Deconstruction

Although deconstruction now has gray in its beard and is no longer walking the halls of Academe with a spring in its step, its conception of language has left its mark on virtually every current critical theory or intellectual position. Especially durable are deconstruction's assumptions about the dispersal and "undecidability" of meanings as a consequence of there being for language no external ground of stability or centeredness in either human intentionality or ontological presence and of the uncontrollable play of signifiers in the language system, and its corollary hypothesis that all texts subvert or undermine their own ostensible or surface meanings or assertions. It has come to be known by one and all that everything is discourse or textual. As such, everything reflects the truth of Saussurean linguistics as filtered through Derridean philosophy of language.

If the New Critic begins inquiry with a distinction between "scientific" discourse and "poetic" discourse, a distinction based on a conception of the rich, playful, ironic, polysemous nature of poetic language, the deconstructionist begins with assumptions about the general nature of language or sign systems. He begins more particularly with a denial of the "metaphysics of presence," the belief in some ground outside of language, which anchors our signifiers to some presence, which delimits the bounds of reference and fixes the meaning of our speeches and inscriptions, the way words are anchored to "reality" by the things to which they correspond in the correspondence theory of truth. But for Derrida and others there is no Transcendental Signified authorizing and legitimating our attributions (whether in God, Reason, or authorial intent); there is only the play of signifiers (the elements of language) and signifieds (the conceptual units, the meanings) in the system of language.

In brief, language at all levels, from the phoneme or grapheme on up, is a system of differences; no element is positively present because whatever seeming "presence" it has depends on the traces of the system of differences of which it is a part. Presence is always caught up in self-deferral, since "positive" terms can never be validated or substantiated by anything outside the system of differences; they can never stand apart from or appear independently of the system that makes them possible. Such terms exist *nowhere* apart from a system of differences. Whatever seeming determinacy of meaning or stability of reference a term may have is an "effect" of all the *nonpresent* meanings of the other terms in the system which by their difference from the focal term make possible the term's having its current, albeit shaky and unanchored, significance. It is an "effect" of the "trace" of the others (the other meanings, in relation to which the term's difference is marked) on the present term, giving it an aura of determinacy. Such an "effect" is necessary, of course, if we are ever to get on with talking about this or that. The play of signifiers produces "effects" of determinacy, but because there is no warrant for anything said in any given text outside of or independent of the system of signs, the stability of meaning is illusory. It is always open to dispersal or "dissemination" by the play of forces that brought the stability into being in the first place.

No phone or word or concept or whatever can escape the chain of referral or signification, since it is only relative to this chain that its difference is marked; differences are marked in a system of differences. Thus, the "c" of *cap* and "t" of *tap* are in a sense mutually implicative in that the functioning of the one is impossible without the functioning of the other and both are functional within a class of sound differences. As noted above, what is "true" at the level of sound is "true" at the higher levels of "signification," for as Derrida asserts, "no element can function as a sign without referring to another element which itself is not simply present. This interweaving results in each 'element' . . . being constituted on the basis of the trace within it of the other elements of the chain or system." Thus, "nothing, neither among the elements nor within the system, is anywhere ever simply present or absent. There are only, everywhere, differences and traces of traces." [4]

Deconstructionists are not content to work with sounds (or "graphs") or words in isolation from the larger contexts in which these linguistic elements find themselves, despite the fact that there would seem to be no easy way to maintain contact with the principles upon which the system is based while extending the range of concern to larger units of "meaning," inasmuch as "presence" is never and nowhere to be found. That is, analysis would never get off the ground, if, for example, the "-phemes" of the larger units to be deconstructed were not at least temporarily capable of "seeming" to achieve enough presence to subserve the interests (in, for example, words, phrases, themes) that the critic is interested in deconstructing. In short, deconstructionists do not restrict their attention to the smallest differentiable elements of language. In practice, analysis always begins where traditional criticism leaves off. For "traditional criticism" the reader could, without impropriety read New Criticism, though any deconstructionist worthy of her epaulets could begin the process of deconstruction with any conventional reading whatsoever, any reading that imposed determinate meaning on sentences, since any apparently fixed meaning is by inner necessity—a necessity deriving from the nature of language—unstable. Every text is in the business of self-subversion, of undermining from within every illusory fortress of determinate meaning upon which it seems to be built, but for critics operating in the deconstructive mode, analysis always begins with readings that emphasize themes or binary oppositions.

No writer, no matter how doggedly he or she sets about it, can commit full logocentrism, can really operate outside the limits limiting writing. Less darkly, writers, regardless of how valiantly they attempt to come to a point, to express a view, to articulate a philosophy, to defend a position, will inevitably subvert or undermine the positive "present" meaning they would establish in the process of establishing it. The "other" that they would suppress is a necessary condition of the something they aim to express; it is part of the system of differences upon which the positive depends. And this we know, because we know that nothing can signify without referring (implicitly but necessarily) to other elements in a system of differences. What is true at the phonemic or graphemic level is also true at the sentential or conceptual level. As a consequence, of course, writers are powerless to delimit the range of meanings they would express, inasmuch as reference and meaning are, ultimately, floating features of systems always in flux.

If a text tries to give priority to one of the terms suspended in binary opposition (to reason, not imagination; nature, not nurture; speech, not writing; male, not female; truth, not fiction; the individual, not the state, and so on), the critic, knowing full well that the "system" is a horizontal rather than a vertical one (that is, hierarchy is illusory), can easily turn the tables on the text by claiming, (1) that since the primary or dominant term is positioned as primary by the secondary, the secondary is primary, and (2) that the mutual dependence makes the notion of primacy or priority a species of arrant nonsense. If, for purposes of deconstructive analysis, some term, rhetorical figure, concept, or statement can be considered as epitomizing the concerns of the text (no matter how marginally important it may have seemed to prior investigators, no matter how subservient to local interests it may have formerly seemed), then unto that figure or statement (and what it apparently "signifies") we can do what we can always do unto any besotted signifier that has delusions of fixing a reference or meaning: We can make it a party to the subversion of what it would affirm. For example, if "parasite" is our principal metaphor (or figural centerpiece), then by an easy conversion we can make a guest of our host and a host of our guest, revealing thereby the deep-down deferentiality of referentiality to the economics of exchange.

There is, of course, the danger that discussion could wander off in any direction at all (a danger not at all bothersome to the fearless critics practicing or influenced by deconstruction), since there is no limit to the number of relations in which one thing, trope, or idea may stand to another. If, as Nelson Goodman observes, "regularities are where you find them, and you can find them anywhere," the same is true of irregularities or differences: you can find irregularities (or contradictions) anywhere. And what, according to Hilary Putnam, is true of similarities is true also of dissimilarities: "the number of similarities [or dissimilarities] you can find between any two objects is limited only by ingenuity and time."[5] Even "identical" objects can be differentiated from one another in an unlimited number of ways.

There is no end to what "is said" can imply, if any "other-than-said" can be shown to exist in some relation to what is said, as it always can, for some condition of relation always obtains between one thing and another. And if binary opposites are always mutually implicative, then the surest sign of being for something is to oppose it, of being in favor of colonialism, say, is to speak against it. In fact, "the-absence-is-presence, presence-is-absence" argument is a staple of contemporary critical discourse (see, for example, the remarks on Wordsworth's "Tintern Abbey" above).

Once beyond simple grammatical units (though even here there are difficulties), once we reach semantic units (words, sentences), it is virtually impossible to determine what system of differences serve to mark significance, since the units can participate in innumerable systems of difference. "There are lots of dogs in South Providence," for example, can be marked as significant for many Providentials in relation to an extremely rich number of semantic background assumptions or relations, all of which are entailed by the conception of language endorsed by deconstruction. In other words, not only will the many different people who share the thought that "there are lots of dogs in South Providence" undoubtedly realize the thought in different brain states (that is, it is neither necessary nor likely that this thought requires all its thinkers to be in the same brain state, to have identical neuronal activity), but they will also have the thought in relation to a variable network of other beliefs, as the thought is held by, say, the dogcatcher, the dog fancier, the parent, the chef, or by a single individual at different times or in different moods. Analogously, though Sam and the Boston Strangler are, as it turns out, one and the same person, the line of thought associated with Sam and the line associated with the Strangler are strikingly different. The network of beliefs and assumptions from which Sam and the Strangler derive their functional content are massively different, and, as a consequence, we would not hesitate to accept a lift home from one but not the other.[6] Of course, aporia, the endless regress, or the generation of endless relationships of signification is not a dreadful prospect to be shunned by the theoretically temerious. Still, when anything one might say is as good as anything else one might say, the better part of wisdom might be silence.

The pragmatic pluralist, of course, avoids the danger by hanging onto objectivity and determinate meaning while giving up the "metaphysics of presence." For this theorist, "truth" is not a heavyweight ontological notion implying some especially strong relation between words, thoughts, and things, such that a fixed relation exists—a strict correspondence exists—between a word and some independently existent transcendent object; truth is a semantic issue, having to do with meaning, reference, and truth-conditions within systems of intentionality. Truth, along with facts and meanings, is content-dependent, and where there is content there is intentionality; and where there is intentionality there are conditions of satisfaction. If the conditions are met, then beliefs are true, desires are met, intentions are realized, and so on.

Talk of truth or reference or meaning apart from some conceptual scheme or system of rationality is, as W. V. Quine and many others have shown, nonsense, and there are no facts about reference distinct from those *fixed* by our use of language. But facts so fixed are indeed fixed as those facts. Outside the scheme there are no facts, only floating signifiers; but inside the scheme, the facts have relation to their intentionality and nothing else. For example, words as *types* (general abstract notions such as "song," "dog," "boat," and so forth) can form limitless associations, but words as *tokens* (concrete particulars such as "Fido," "Rhode Island redhead from Pawtucket," and so on) are tied by bonds of connubial obligation and satisfaction to their spousal intendeds. There are many "presences," though no "ultimate referent" that can serve as the guarantor for all or any of them. No way of describing things is unique or mandatory (as Nelson Goodman says), but some descriptions are true and some are not, some things should be believed and some should not. Otherwise, we would fall down and hurt ourselves, again and again. Belief depends on the possibility of error, and both belief and disbelief have consequences, sometimes painful ones.

Of course, in one way of talking, differential relations do mark differences and, thus, permit distinctions, but what is relational becomes categorical when it is put to some use. Nelson Goodman uses "integers" to make the point. Every integer is (strangely and paradoxically, some might be inclined to say) both an immediate predecessor and an immediate successor. The integer 5, say, is trapped in aporia, caught up in an endless conflict between internal counterforces or in an undecidable struggle of self-conflicting significations. And what is true of 5 is true of every number in the differential sequence or system of number relations. Yet, with 5 as base or origin, we all know with certainty what the immediate successor to 4 or the immediate predecessor of 6 is, our friend 5. "Adoption of a stance," Goodman observes, "turns a relational term into a categorical one." Although all integers are both immediate predecessors and immediate successors at one and the same time, 5 is absolutely, make no mistake about, as a matter of unshakeable fact, the immediate successor and absolutely not the immediate predecessor to 4. This is a stable fact, and like all stable facts (and all stable meanings), which owe their stability to a system of use and intentionality, it does not depend on any "metaphysics of presence" to achieve its objective facthood.[7]

What meanings are true or false, good or bad, right or wrong, better or worse, and so on depends, of course, on purpose and local situational context, and under these situational conditions and relative to this purpose what is right or wrong or better or worse is not a matter of opinion or of consensus. It is a matter of, well, *fact.* According to the principle of meaning-holism, meanings do not come in single trucks, but in convoys; that is, the meaning of one sentence is tied up with a whole host of beliefs and background assumptions (most of which are unexpressed though absolutely necessary to the specific sense of the sentence). Thus, sentences in use cannot participate in any other system of meaning possibilities without losing contact with that which gives them their specific content (that is, meaning). But we digress. We shall consider some further differences between the theory of language that underlies most contemporary critical enterprises and that underlying the pragmatic pluralists' efforts later. For now, we must resume our discussion of deconstruction and take up some practical matters.

Summing up matters to this point, we can say that as a practical activity, deconstruction, like New Criticism and Bakhtinian dialogism (as well as some forms of feminism, Marxism, New Historicism, and Cultural Materialism), is concerned chiefly not with what determines "meaning" at the intentional or psychological level (that is, aims, wishes, beliefs, fears, purposes, hopes, mental contents, and circumstantial conditions), but with themes, views, key terms, concepts, tropes, images, and so on, considered relationally in systematic and largely abstract terms. What these critics know before inquiry begins is that all "texts" are sites of their own undoing, are up to something more and other than they show on the surface. All texts are self-undermining regardless of how determined they are to "mean" this and not that, of how skillfully and diversely they arrange the ruses of figuration to trap this and not that sense, and of how deviously they deploy their rhetorical strategies to catch this rather than that view in its unsupplemented present presence. And since culture, history, and everything else is textual, all artistic and cultural products exhibit the common features of signification. A postmodern critic may abandon the sort of "close reading" characteristic of deconstruction in its practical mode, but he or she cannot give up the insights into language that deconstruction, via Saussurean linguistics, has made available, for if it is unwise, as some wag has put it, to neglect the historicity of texts, it is folly to deny the textuality of history.[8] As an "always already" mode of reasoning, this criticism always finds what it seeks, and it shields itself from surprise by digging only where it has already filled the explanatory space with treasure; the ways of texts may be many, but the ways of language are one.

The danger within deconstruction of drifting aimlessly, of sanctioning any kind of babble whatsoever, is one recognized by Derrida, and that in part is why he begins inquiry with the "effects" of determinate meaning at the level of conventional reading, with the apparent, the logocentric meanings of texts. The instability and undecidability of texts can only be seen against the background of apparent determinacy or stability of meaning. As believers in immanent rather than transcendent meanings, Derrida and all others who have adopted or unquestioningly assumed the value and legitimacy of the theory of language undergirding deconstruction (that is, virtually all postmodern theorists) are certainly willing to grant that within this but not that conceptual scheme or language game (apparently) determinate reference is made to "shortstops," "martinis," "class warfare," the "French Revolution," "congenital weakness of will," and so on, and that sentences mean what we conventionally take them to mean. Indeed, it is just this or that attribution of immanent and determinate meaning upon which the deconstructive enterprise depends. It (and all its cohorts) has a vested interest in the preservation of what it undoes, since the *undoing* lives and has its being only in parasitic or symbiotic relationship with the *doing* (as does fiction with truth, writing with speech, nurture with nature, yin with yang, slave with master, and so on). For in both linguistic (deconstructive) and political (most other contemporary) studies the dialectical relations reduce to or reflect the working of language *as such*.

This criticism seeks not to replace "ordinary," "conventional," or "traditional" readings but to accompany and supplement them. (As beings trapped in logocentrism we cannot help but write and read logocentrically, at least initially.) In her introduction to Derrida's *Of Grammatology*, Gayatri Spivak assures us that the deconstructionist's first task is to read "in the traditional way." [9] Despite the manifest diversity of critical readings—and, hence, the diversity of traditions—a traditional way, silently equated more often than not with the New Critical way, is assumed. Of course, the process can begin from any more or less plausible reading, since any postulated meaning is only a first step to what really matters anyway, the undecidable conflict within. Derrida shrewdly notes that without "all the instruments of traditional criticism . . . critical production would risk developing in any direction at all and authorize itself to say almost anything. But this indispensable guardrail has always only *protected*, it has never *opened*, a reading." [10]

Reading first in the "traditional" way, the deconstructive reader eventually tries to locate, as Spivak says, the "text's 'navel,' as it were, the moment that is undecidable in terms of the text's apparent system of meaning, the moment in the text that seems to transgress its own system of values." [11] It is never a question of *whether* a text at some point violates or abuses itself but of *when* or *where* self-abuse makes its nasty appearance, since appear it must given the nature of language.

This moment of textual civil war or textual undoing is a natural and inevitable consequence of the differential, dialectical, relational nature of language. History or politics is dialectical in part because history is textual, and texts obey the differential, relational laws of language, in which what is missing is more than partly definitive of what is "present." As another proponent would have it, this undoing, "made necessary by the 'trace,' and so by the duplicitous quality of words and texts, must not be confused with the simple locating of [just any] moment of [surface] ambiguity or irony . . . rather, it is the moment that threatens the collapse of [the] entire system." [12] In these remarks on ordinary or surface irony and ambiguity we can see one of the ways in which deconstruction seeks to go beyond New Criticism. Of course, the New Critics would not think of themselves as looking for any old surface irony or ambiguity, for they were after the peculiarly contradictory quality of "reality" or the "immediacy" of complex experience in texts, the experience of holding antithetical meaning or feeling in balance that could not be captured by any purely discursive practice or by the "heresy of paraphrase." Given what we know of language, the "navel" or the moment of impending collapse could be found at almost any point in the text, since "navels," like "regularities" (or similarities/dissimilarities) are where you find them, and you can find them anywhere. In a radical sense, then, every text is all and nothing but navel, is navel all the way down. Thus, even when beginning from a "traditional reading" (whatever that is exactly) this system continues to "risk developing in any direction at all." All efforts at fixation—all logocentric assertions or affirmations—are unstable and self-demolishing, incapable of excluding the "other" in the system of language or reference to which the affirmations belong. They owe whatever authority or "naturalness" they have, so the political theorists would affirm, to fluctuations in the ongoing social dynamics of power and oppression, as predetermined by our "political" assumptions.

In summary, the position maintains that "traditional reading" is necessary because without it deconstructive reading could authorize itself to say almost anything; that every text has a navel, a moment of self-transgression (this, of course, is an assumption that, like many others in this criticism, cannot be extorted, if it be not granted); and that this moment is unavoidable because language is as it is, because language has no center, no ultimate, authorizing, external warrant and just is a differential system of relations, a network of differences and deferrals, in which there can be found only the traces of actual presences.

As noted earlier, however, it is clear that in principle there is no reason why analysis could not begin anywhere. There is no reason to privilege or even to adopt the "traditional" reading as a starting point (even assuming for the nonce that there is *a* traditional reading, as distinct from many, many "traditional" readings). And there is no reason to rule out any "reading" or line of inquiry, since deconstruction, like most political or cultural materialist approaches to texts, does not and *cannot* provide any test of acceptability or any defeasibility criteria that would enable us to rule a reading in or out. So long as a relation can be shown to subsist between this sign and that, the discussion has all the warrant it needs. Discussion can begin anywhere and go anywhere—go wherever a line of relation can be shown, wherever ingenuity can show a relation (and when has ingenuity ever been at a loss to show a relation?).

In contrast, the kind of pragmatic pluralism that we have endorsed earlier (and throughout this book) is extraordinarily rich in defeasibility criteria for each and every local case. To be "right" is to be "true," and to be "true" is to be "justified" under certain knowable conditions. Acceptability is determined by right categorization and fit within a system of rationality and intentionality, and when the parts fail to mesh, the system fails to satisfy the conditions of its own making. But fitting is not simply a matter of formal coherence; it is a matter of workingness and of being acceptable to our ongoing and established network of beliefs and understandings about the world, about what feelings, motives, responses, and so on are appropriate in certain specifiable and identifiable conditions of human and social interaction. The criteria are flexible and context relative, to be sure, but in each case of interest there are recognizable internal goods that are more and less valuable to us as experiencing and thinking beings.

The difference between the views of many modern theorists influenced by the deconstructionist philosophy of language—one concerned with relations among signs and not with right assertibility within systems of intentionality—and those of the pragmatic pluralist can be partially illuminated perhaps by Wittgenstein's argument against "private language." For Wittgenstein, "any meaningful use of language must take place against the context of a rule-governed situation in which there are recognizable proper and improper 'moves.'" Both writer and reader (speaker and hearer) must be able to determine "when the rules are being followed or violated. Without such rules no expression has the kind of *use* that makes it possible to employ it to say something meaningful." [13] The rules, the right moves, derive from the practice or the "form of life" in which linguistic choices have their function. As Donald Davidson repeatedly notes, it is only against the background of a practice, a structure, a set of justification conditions that we can identify thoughts and determine their rightness or appropriateness. For the words to be right and fixed in their rightness they must fit the conditions of assertibility that are the reasons for them.

In short, the system of intentionality supplies the conditions of defeasibility, and there is no reason to think that in the process of performing the successive acts of choice that make up the writing of the text, the writer will inevitably fall into a navel or violate the intentionality of the system by which his choices are governed. Of course, mistake and inadvertency are always possible (perhaps even highly probable), but there is no inevitability about mistake; indeed, it seems likely that the dictates of intentionality would become stronger and easier to recognize and satisfy as the work progressed. And I see no reason why writers are less well equipped than critics to recognize a misfit when they see one. Unlike the deconstructionist, the pragmatic-pluralist critic (and writer) is not a stranger to defeasibility criteria.

Whatever may be true in principle, deconstructionists in fact are unwilling to credit all readings or to begin with any reading whatsoever. They embark from some "traditional" reading or any reading that has won a hearing because, presumably, it reflects or captures the prevailing "logocentric" interests or prejudices. Nevertheless, despite the manifold differences in the surface meanings of texts, upon all logocentric preoccupations they perform essentially the same operation. They disclose the alien Other lurking within the familiar and privileged favorite or the way in which the preferred member of the culture-defining antithesis (be it speech/writing, male/female, truth/fiction, master/slave, or some other antithesis) is dependent upon or subordinate to what it dominates, oppresses, suppresses, or conceals. Although some friends of deconstruction *and* political activism have tried to show that deconstruction has leftist political leanings, a moment's reflection on its fundamental commitments informs us that it is primarily and for the most part an apolitical independent, an equal-opportunity debunker of the claims of logocentricity.[14] Still, it has bequeathed to historicist and political theorists the benefits of "double reading," that is, of reading from the surface meaning to the hidden ideological structure, of finding the absent Other in the present emblem, of exposing the gears of the ideological machine within the duplicitous facade of apparent meaning. All this is possible because history, mind, politics and so forth are themselves systems of relational differences, because they function the way language functions. It is commonplace today to talk about the demise of deconstruction as a force in literary theory, but in fact its authority over argumentation is pervasive.

From my perspective, the philosophy of language on which the currently popular form of critical reasoning is based is weak, counterintuitive, unsatisfying, and, more important, offensive to our hard-won achievements as makers and readers of meanings. Moreover, the criticism to which it leads seems at once monolithic, in that for all its fondness for diversity it relies on a one-size-fits-all method, and reductionistic, in that all interests are finally reduced to "syntactic" interests, to relations among signs,[15] to, more specifically, the relations among terms, ideas, tropes, figures, paradoxes, antitheses and so on. And, in its "political" varieties, the interests are reduced to the (ideological) positions, claims, assertions that these relations make or imply, considered apart from any human intentionality, any system of rationality, only relative to which, we affirm, can content and meaning emerge. This last point reminds us that, while the New Critics were interested in elucidating the internal structures of works produced by *authors*, they also brought us, with their focus on the autotelic nature of literary art (on literature as a self-intelligible structure of "meanings") and their attacks against authorial intention, a long way toward the author-depleted and sign-relational view of art in the post-Barthesian, post-Foucauldian, post-Derridean, the, in a word, "postmodern" era.

In the interests of clarity and for purposes of qualification, one final comment on this criticism is perhaps in order. Throughout this chapter, I have not attempted to show that deconstruction betrays any special indebtedness to or descends in any directly lineal way from New Criticism or to suggest that studies focusing on salient features of texts considered apart from some system of intentionality may not tell us much that is interesting and important (indeed, startlingly "true") about the workings of mind, politics, history, ideology, race, gender, and much else in a given era (or generally, for that matter). Rather, I have directed attention to what I take to be the pervasiveness of divided-line thinking and of circular reasoning in most contemporary criticism and theory (nothing can show up that is not already a permutational possibility of the conception of language from which inquiry springs) as well as to what I take to be the inherent weaknesses in the conception of language underlying modern critical theory and practice of both the deconstructionist and "political" kind.[16]

## Last Words: A Few Notes on Different Worlds and Worlds of Difference

With deconstructionists and other postmodern theorists, we have abandoned belief in the correspondence theory of truth (at least in the correspondence theory that privileges one language), in the Transcendental Signified, in the metaphysics of presence, in some ultimate ground or warrant for our ascriptions, and so on. But, unlike our fellow theorists, we have not given up on all correspondences between words and things, on real presences in real worlds, or on true explanations of the objective facts in systems of intentionality. As we have repeatedly affirmed, to give up on these would be to give up on all contents, facts, objects, linguistic meanings, experiences, understandings, and so on, which we cannot do without first undergoing a brainectomy (but, of course, at that point "giving up" will not be an option for us). If there is no unique description of the real, there are limitless good, right, and true descriptions of the real that depend on our various systems of intentionality and our various ways of "seeing-as." In short, we recognize that there are no facts or meanings apart from systems of rationality or intentionality; facts and meaning are fixed relative to use. In this view words, sentences, beliefs, and so on have meaning, not relative to systems of differences, but relative to their coherence with other elements in a network of intentionality. Thus, unlike deconstructionists and others, who tolerate many schemes of immanent meaning while insisting that no scheme can hold, can avoid self-cancellation or the evocation of the Other it would suppress, we insist that *every right scheme will hold* (indeed, must hold, if it is to be right and true)—not for all purposes, to be sure, but for those for which it was designed to hold.

Furthermore, from our point of view, the focus in much contemporary theory on "relations of terms," or on what Hume would call "relations of ideas"—along with the concomitant removal of interest in agents either as authors or fictional persons and, consequently, in the motives and purposes of characters in situations requiring choice and action—has severely reduced the kinds of questions and explanations we can be interested in. Indeed, not to put too fine a point on it, the focus has determined that many of these questions and interests are intellectually bankrupt, because they are sponsored by an outmoded metaphysics and tied to a discredited epistemology.

By giving attention to meanings, values, and emphases within systems of intentionality, we can do something to return if not to prominence at least to respectability certain explanations that have been proscribed or neglected in recent critical studies. These include, perhaps especially, all those explanations that start from the internal interest of literary works and involve considerations of character and motivation. For example, what, at times, has our interest and excites an explanation is Othello's treatment of Desdemona or his readiness to respond so immediately and powerfully to Iago's suggestions. Our full understanding of the text depends on grasping the contents of the mental states that are the reasons for the behavior. What we want here is an explanation of jealousy in terms of character and of belief and desire, not one in terms of propositional, lexical, or grammatological systems of relation. As readers, we are most often concerned with something other than "relations of ideas"; we are concerned with emotions, feelings, beliefs, with what gives action and behavior intelligibility.

Whatever the interests of literary texts—and such interests are as manifold and various and numerous as texts themselves—explanations at the level of their interest, in terms of the justification conditions that they are obliged to satisfy if they hope to make anything of themselves, are certainly possible. There is nothing in the nature of language that prohibits us from taking an interest in the interests of texts, in the intentional conditions of their possibility. And because texts, not unlike academics, tend to act in their own selfish interests, they make deliberate and determined efforts to avoid life-threatening behavior. Further, because all structures of meaning take place within a network of assumptions and beliefs that are not expressed but nevertheless necessary to specific meaning (meaning-holism), they are not much inclined to self-cancellation. (For example, my belief that there is a fly in my soup and your understanding that I believe there is a fly in my soup entail a whole host of unexpressed but necessary further beliefs about soup, insects, food, flying, floating, and so on.) Texts, of course, may be self-destructive, but they certainly aren't so because of some inner necessity; as always, breaking up is hard to do (though, admittedly, harder for some than for others).

In the end, I see no reason why we should allow the skeptics or the know-it-alls (of course, these are not mutually exclusive categories) among us to assert without challenge that breaches of contract are just part of the natural order of things, that self-cancellation is universally true. No, that is to go too far. Indeed, as it turns out, to believe that *that* is true is to know that *that* is false, since if it is true, then it is by inner necessity false.

# Chapter 6
# Philosophical Pluralism, Elder Olson, and Postanalytic Philosophy

This essay began life as a review article focusing on the achievements of Elder Olson as a critic and theoretician, occasioned by the publication in 1976 of his *On Value Judgments in the Arts and Other Essays,* a collection representing more than forty years of serious and thoughtful concern with the theory and practice of criticism, with problems relating to the construction, interpretation, and judgment of literature. In what follows I have preserved much of the original piece, but I have also subordinated its original emphases to the concerns of this book. I have drawn out the parallels between Olson's thought and that of some of the most prominent and influential philosophers working in what has been called the post-Carnapian or postanalytic tradition—especially W. V. Quine, Donald Davidson, Michael Dummett, and Hilary Putnam—and highlighted those aspects of the review that clarify or illuminate issues raised throughout this volume. The broad aim of this redirecting of emphases is to show that the kind of philosophical pluralism that underlies and informs the intellectual practices of Olson and the other so-called "Chicago" or "Neo-Aristotelian" critics (R. S. Crane, Bernard Weinberg, Norman Maclean, and Richard McKeon) belongs to a strong intellectual tradition that continues not only to thrive but to set the agenda of theoretical discussion in the Academy (though, alas, not in literary studies). Further, I intend to indicate briefly and roughly how Olson's agent- and intention-based approaches to meaning and interpretation are fully consonant with the predominant views in recent work in the philosophy of thought and language (which are also agent- and intention based, unlike the post-Saussurean, system-based, agent-deprived or diminished views of poststructuralist theorists).[1]

It is perhaps fair to say that the views of no modern critics have undergone more misrepresentation, distortion, or oversimplification at the hands of commentators than those of the Chicago or, as they are sometimes with equal inappropriateness called, the Neo-Aristotelian critics, despite the fact that few critics have done more than they to articulate their views clearly, precisely, and fully, to define exactly the philosophic and theoretical bases of their positions, and to delineate carefully what aspects of the subject under discussion legitimately fall within the range of their concern and the competence of their elected modes of discourse (believing, quite sensibly, that we can only think about and, hence, refer to only so much of any topic as comes within the semantic range of our system of representation and intentionality). Typically, the commentator isolates a doctrine from its context and from the principles and assumptions only in relation to which it has determinate meaning and then delivers a blistering attack against the simplemindedness of maintaining, say (as Olson does), that the words are one of the least important elements in works of literature, or any verbal work, for that matter. Such a view of words is anathema to those critics whose analyses depend upon spinning out the implications of words, phrases, tropes, ideologemes, and figural devices considered apart from any role they may have in the overall textual structure. These are the critics for whom the center or "navel" of the work, as some Derrideans might insist, is in the "Otherness" necessarily implicated in these crucial elements or in the larger social significance they have in a broader economy of power relations.

But from an agential and intentional view of language, Olson's judgment is as inevitable as it is wise. Words are clearly less important than their functions, less important than that for the sake of which they are present at all, than that only in relation to which they have reference or specific content. Indeed, words have no content or meaning whatsoever apart from their function within a system of relationships, a system of justification conditions. We cannot learn the meaning or function of words by attending to the proclivities of words (they have an indefinite number of such proclivities); the meaning of words and concepts is determined by justification conditions in a context of use. More particularly, as Davidson insists, "just as words have meaning only in the context of a sentence, a sentence has meaning only in the context of *use*, as part, in some sense, of a particular language," a particular structure of intentional entailments.[2] In Olson's terms, "the words must be explained in terms of something else, not the poem [that is, any work] in terms of the words, and, further, a principle must be a principle of something other than itself; hence the words cannot be a principle of their own arrangements."[3] The words cannot subsume what they subserve (or what's a functional relationship for?). The relation is a one-way, lower-to-higher relation. The justification conditions endow the limitless verbal possibilities with determinate meaning. To revise Olson slightly, words are the cause (the material cause, in Aristotelian terms) of *our coming to know* a meaning, but meaning is the *cause of* (the final cause of) the words in their selection, arrangement, emphasis, and semantic determinacy.

The dismaying fact is that too many critics today, waiting on the docks for the latest word from France or watching for critical pronouncements written in neon-tubing, are too ready to assume, on the basis of ignorance or misunderstanding, that the Chicago critics write in black letter. (For convenience I continue to identify these critics as "Chicago critics," even though they are more properly designated pragmatic pluralists or pluralistic pragmatists.) No sooner has a Chicago critic begun to answer a question about, say, a stick—noting, for example, that it is a wooden object with two ends and that there are really many kinds of sticks of various lengths composed of various materials and serving a variety of functions—than he is shouted down by the *one endians, no endians, endless-deferral-of-ends endians.* Or he may be obliged to contend with those who, with more than a hint of condescension, proclaim, "Well, yes, but all that is nothing to the point, for a stick is really a male talisman, a phallic—indeed a logophallic—symbol; or a sign of tribal or feudal or capitalist power; or a club; or *the* club which the primitive son applied with more than slight force to the head of the primitive papa when he heard the primitive bedsprings squeaking at the primal scene; or, since a stick is really inert and incidental matter considered independently of "sticker" and "stickee," a sign both of stickwielder (colonial oppressor) and stick-feeler (oppressed native); and so on.

To these and so many other critics who wish to find the one and only stick or the anagogic key to stickness as such, to reduce the many to one, to treat unique products of artistic choice only as signs, instances, or consequences of something else (something more comprehensive and inclusive, such as power, ideology, the nature of language), to pursue only the othernesses or aporias in the endlessly wandering stick tracings, or to identify the social energy being circulated by the stick in late capitalism, when authority and all other values are debased and commodified—to all these critics or theorists the so-called Chicago critics can offer only a discouraging word, which, as we all know, is seldom heard. But to all those who are interested in pursuing such knowledge of art as it can yield, when considered deliberately and rigorously under each of its various divisions of existence (ethics, logic, rhetoric, psychology, poetics), and when considered in its own terms, in each of its manifestations, as an imaginatively vivid, morally significant, or thematically interesting composite of justified parts—to all these people the so-called Chicago critics have much to say. It is only necessary to keep in mind Samuel Johnson's more-durable-than-brass reminder: sound and wise critics can provide *reasons*, but they cannot provide *understandings*.

With the possible exception of Richard McKeon and R. S. Crane, none of the these critics has written more extensively on the theoretical foundations of critical systems, on the principled bases of practical criticism, and on particular literary works than Elder Olson. Thus, if what misrepresentation or misunderstanding may have fostered and ignorance or prejudice may have sustained can be undermined, then Olson's writings are admirably suited to the task of demolition. If "Chicago criticism" is to be neglected or abused, it should be so treated because of what it is, not because of what it is mistakenly represented to be, and no book, it seems to me, is better qualified to disabuse readers of misprision or misapprehension than *On Value Judgments in the Arts*, to read which is to meet Kant's challenge, *sapere aude*.

Olson's book is more than a collection of disparate essays; it is a *book* of essays dealing essentially with principles of critical and philosophic reasoning and with the three primary branches of literary inquiry: hermeneutics, poetics, and criticism. His writing may cause the reader some difficulty, but what he says of Marianne Moore's poetry applies equally well to his own writing: Olson, like Moore, is a difficult writer, but not an obscure one; on the contrary, he is extremely clear, and our difficulty comes primarily from his insistence that we think and think well at every point in his essays. Because he takes up difficult issues and deals with them in all their complexity, he is under an obligation, if he has any regard for his subject and his reader, to speak perspicuously. Given the prevailing flocculence of the prose in critical and theoretical studies today, one is inclined to think that there is an inverse correlation between clarity of expression and difficulty of thought, because we usually get three bagsful of wool for every pouch of sense. Olson, on the other hand, adheres to Quine's maxim: "It is a basic maxim for serious thought that whatever there is to be said can, through perseverance, be said clearly. Something that persistently resists clear expression, far from meriting reverence for its profundity, merits suspicion."[4] Except in the practical criticism section, Olson is throughout concerned as much with what critics think *with* as with what they think *about*; that is, he is interested not only in the critic's subject matter, but in the mode of reasoning employed in dealing with that subject matter.

Each essay explores thoroughly and systematically the problem with which it engages, but the book is also a whole book in the sense that it reflects a unified and coherent system of entailments. The various essays, written over a long span of time and addressed to discrete problems, both imply and are implied by a unified system of principles. Olson's philosophic system, like that embodied in Sir Joshua Reynold's *Discourses*, "derives its unity, not from the time of its utterance but from the compendency of its parts" (112).

The capstone of the book is the last essay, "The Dialectical Foundations of Critical Pluralism." The philosophic orientation of the whole book (and of "Chicago criticism" generally) can be found in this essay, which is a detailed investigation of the nature and causes of variation in philosophic and critical discourse. Underlying the essay and the book as a whole is a conception of the legitimacy and validity of many different critical principles and methods. The essence of pragmatic pluralism is in this recognition of many valid approaches. As Crane observes:

> The pluralistic critic . . . [takes] the view that the basic principles and methods of any distinguishable mode of criticism are tools of inquiry and interpretation rather than formulations of the "real" nature of things and that the choice of any special "language," among the many possible for the study of [literature], is a practical decision to be justified solely in terms of the kind of knowledge the critic wants to attain.[5]

Echoing or reaffirming Olson's view, Crane here expresses a conception of cognitive processes that reflects the pragmatist tradition. As Stephen Stich has noted, cognitive processes for pragmatists are not thought of principally as mechanisms for producing truths, but rather as things "akin to tools, technologies, or practices that can be used more or less successfully in achieving a variety of goals." There is no uniquely good or metaphysically justified (justified, that is, by the way things really are in themselves independent of our interests and goals) conceptual scheme or system of cognitive processes. For the pragmatist, as for the Chicago critics, "the system to be preferred is the one that would be most likely to achieve those things that are intrinsically valued by the person whose interests are relevant to the purposes of the evaluation."[6]

Olson, Crane, and the others concur not only with the pragmatists's explicit and implicit conceptions of the relativity of meaning, reference, and truth value to frameworks but also with, for example, Quine's and Rudolf Carnap's view that the acceptability of a particular framework is, to a large extent, a "practical matter,"[7] dependent on interests and purposes. Thus, with Catherine Elgin, the Chicago critics agree that "the acceptability of any particular scheme depends on the truths it enables us to state, the methods it permits [us] to employ, the projects it furthers, and the values it promotes. . . . And a failure of the components to mesh undermines the system, preventing it from doing what it ought to do."[8]

A brief caveat or note is perhaps necessary here. None of the philosophers cited above, including the Chicago critics, endorses relativism. Reference is meaningless outside a conceptual system, to be sure, but some systems are better than others, if only because some are more directly and perfectly answerable to our needs and interests or more felicitously consonant with existing states of affairs; and within systems there is such a thing as getting it right or getting it wrong. Moreover, getting it right or wrong is not up to us or a matter of consensus; it's a matter of fitting-ness and right categorization, of having the parts fit or, as Elgin says, mesh. Finally, a framework or conception is never right merely because it is justified, because it is an internally self-justifying system; the justified system must be appropriate to the operative interests and goals.[9]

What strikes us most forcibly today is the timeliness of "The Dialectical Foundations of Critical Pluralism," its relevance to current philosophic debate and inquiry. Its pragmatic pluralism is instinct with what are presently the most important and influential lines of thought in the philosophy of mind and language. Like so many in the forefront of philosophic debate (Davidson, Putnam, Quine, Dummett, Goodman, and many others), the Chicago critics, as pragmatic pluralists, distinguish themselves from dogmatists, skeptics, eclectics, and relativists—especially perhaps from skeptics and relativists. Olson's opposition to relativism is apparent throughout this essay, but perhaps the strongest "Chicago" case against it is put by Crane. He notes not only the self-refuting character of all statements of the doctrine (if all truth is relative, so too is this truth; thus, if relativism is true, it is false), but also the failure of relativism to meet the "common experience" test:

the matter is simpler than that [shown by the self-refutation argument], for if there were indeed any fixed causal relation between the languages which critics have used and the social and cultural conditions of their times, the very diversity of critical languages [including conflicting and contradictory languages] which confronts us in every period or civilization in which criticism has flourished would have been impossible, and the coexistence in classical Greece of Plato and Aristotle [or, in the modern period, of Foucault and M. H. Abrams] would be a miraculous event.[10]

In the philosophical literature, we encounter innumerable variations on the self-refutation argument. Focusing on the core of Hilary Putnam's many refutations of "relativism and allied heresies," Michael Dummett writes: "any attempt to state the general thesis must run foul of that actual practice which it claims to be the source of necessity and truth, and hence be self-refuting; it is an attempt to view our language and our thought from that external vantage-point which it declares to be inaccessible."[11] In his own voice, Putnam, thinking of philosophical debates, addresses the kind of relativism that, in literary criticism, finds perhaps its most articulate spokesperson in Stanley Fish: "the radical view that interpretations are simply the inventions of the interpreter is just the old self-refuting relativism in its latest guise,"[12] for, again, the articulation of the view invalidates its own content. The skeptic about the determinacy of language (including language in *use* presumably) falls,

like the Fishean relativist, in the slough of self-refutation and necessarily into what Susan Hurley calls "pragmatic inconsistency," which
involves the speaker in doing things which are inconsistent with his view.
Thus, the skeptic's *expression* of his view is inconsistent with the content
of that view. The "skeptic's expression of his thesis does not merely presuppose something inconsistent with his thesis; it actually demonstrates
the falsity of it." [13] The pluralist position articulated by Olson in this essay, including its subsidiary defenses of determinate meaning and attacks against relativism, now requires our attention and, in the following
pages, will be briefly outlined.

The basic tenets of the pluralist system are quickly stated, but no
readers should substitute this overview for direct perusal of the argument
in its fully developed and tightly argued form. Briefly, then, pluralism
maintains that "any philosophic problem must be relative to its formulation; and since any solution to a problem is also relative to the problem,
the solution must also be relative to that formulation. But that
formulation . . . must be finite." This is so because of the selective and
restrictive nature of language: we can only discuss so much of a subject
matter as falls within the semantic and logical range of our terms as used;
or, as Quine has repeatedly noted, there are no facts about reference
beyond those fixed by our use of language on specific occasions for spe-
cificpurposes.[14] For Olson,

It follows that there can be no single philosophic system embracing all truth; and
by the same token, no method which is the only right method. . . . [Philosophic
variation] is a function of two things: first, the fundamental dialectic of the system
[its system of inference and reasoning; its way of concatenating propositions];
second, the subject matter on which the dialectic is exerted [those aspects of the
subject that the justification conditions pick out as objects of attention and interest, since we cannot think about anything except in some particular way[15]]. (300)

Olson expresses here what are by now commonplaces of philosophic
thought, if not of literary theory. The basic principle—that "no theory
or description is good for all purposes," as Putnam says—is one that the
Chicago critics share with all philosophical pluralists. Moreover, just as
no object can be completely described (all descriptions are from some
point of view, or all objects are offered to us in some particular way), so
no problem can be completely formulated (all problems are the problems of their formulation and are, thus, accountable to some but not
other questions). To think about anything in some particular way—and
this is the only way we can think about it—is also to see it as belonging to
or fitting with some other things. But there is nothing subjective about
any of this; the fitting and belonging are as objective as objective gets.

Olson distinguishes between dialectic and subject matter as grounds of variation in discourse more fully in "An Outline of Poetic Theory":

> It is impossible within the scope of this essay to discuss all the factors in the foundations of philosophies and criticisms; but perhaps a rough and partial statement may serve for illustration. I propose that the number of possible critical positions is relative to the number of possible philosophic positions and that the latter is determined by two principal considerations: (1) the number of aspects of a subject which can be brought into discussion, as constituting its *subject matter*; (2) the kinds of basic dialectic which may be exerted upon that subject matter. I draw this distinction between the subject and the subject matter: the subject is what is talked about; the subject matter is that subject in so far as it is represented or implied in the discussion. Philosophers do not discuss *subjects themselves*; they can discuss only so much as the terms or materials of the discussion permit; and that is the subject matter. We cannot discuss what we cannot first of all mention, or what we cannot bring to mind. In other words, any discussion of a "subject" is relative to its formulation. But, further, any discursive reasoning must employ some method of reasoning or inference; and, since there are various possible systems of inference, we may say that a given discussion is a function of its subject matter and of the dialectic, i.e., system of inference exerted upon that subject matter. (269–70)

To be in a position to discuss anything you have to be able to think about it and to refer to it, and we cannot think about anything except in some particular way. That is what it is to be conscious of something; that is what constitutes intentionality—thinking about or referring to something in a particular way. And where there is intentionality, there are conditions of satisfaction, such that if they are met the intentional system of which the local intentions are a part is justified (truth is the condition justifying a belief, and satisfaction the condition answerable to desire). This is the case because our intentions are always part of a network of commitments or beliefs, of a holistic structure of entailments, and the system stands or falls as a system. Justification is holistic in that, as we have seen, the words have meaning relative to the sentence and the sentences relative to their satisfaction of the justification conditions of the practice or argument of which they are a necessary and integral part. Akeel Bilgrami gives a crisper version of this view, when he notes that "any given content is what it is because of the other contents it is inferentially and conceptually related with." [16] And, of course, if all *thinking of* is thinking of in a certain way, [17] then all intentional states "represent their conditions of satisfaction only under certain aspects," [18] the aspects that are important or interesting to those states.

It is by attending to the aspectual nature of intentionality and the holistic character of its entailments that Olson, along with the other Chicago critics, hopes to disclose the power and limitations of the many valid approaches to critical problems and particular texts. To Olson, only when we recognize that much of what appears to be conflict or contradiction in critical discourse is really *difference*, occasioned by the systematic operations of different assumptions and methods on different problems, can we begin to identify what is durably valuable in the past and to contribute to the stock of critical knowledge.

The consequences following from the pluralistic stance are everywhere apparent in *On Value Judgments*, but especially in sections 3 and 4, on "Critics" and "Critical Theory." When we examine critical documents, it is absolutely essential, from the pluralistic point of view, that we consider both the doctrines and methods of that criticism; that we examine the works in the light of the peculiar problems, assumptions, and principles of reasoning determining their specific content; and that we avoid the tendency either to associate or to distinguish critical systems simply on the basis of some ostensible (or superficially real) similarity or disparity in the nature of the particular statements or doctrines expressed in those systems. Often, such verbal or doctrinal similarities conceal deep differences in intentional systems, in those conditions in relation to which the terms and doctrines have specific meaning and reference. Things and "ideas" taken one way may not be the same things and "ideas" when taken another way, when justified by another scheme of relationships. Expressing an analogous point, Catherine Elgin reminds us that "A single domain can be organized in a multitude of ways, while different schematizations may employ a single vocabulary." [19] And, as Olson goes on to note, "When any philosophic or critical method is reduced to statement, the most opposite philosophers or critics can be brought to coincide, and the most similar to disagree" (108). Considered apart from their reference-setting purposes, any two systems, it is fair to say, can be seen as similar (in some respects at least). Or, as Putnam somewhere says, "The number of similarities one can find between any two things is limited only by time and ingenuity." [20]

A striking illustration of the tendency to establish critical similarity or affiliation on the basis of ostensible compatibility (or identity) of doctrine is offered in "Longinus and Reynolds." There Olson, after isolating a number of remarkable doctrinal correspondences between *On the Sublime* and the *Discourses*, trenchantly demonstrates that, while both critics concentrate on qualities rather than species of art and share an interest in the faculties of the artist and the emotional effects of art, they are as critics "not only dissimilar, but quite unrelated to each other. They do not deal with the same critical problem; they make different assumptions; and they pursue different methods of argument. Longinus views the products of several arts in terms of a single effect; Reynolds views all the effects of a single art" (116).

Again, for Olson and other pluralists there are many valid approaches to art as well, of course, as many invalid or deficient approaches. With Stich and others, Olson regularly emphasizes the point that there are no uniquely good cognitive systems. Still, as always, only the good systems are good. In composing an argument, as in producing a novel, a play, a poem, there are many ways of going wrong and few ways of going right. Martha Nussbaum, arguing a similar case, notes that "there are many ways of wrecking a ship in a storm, and very few ways of sailing it well." [21] To this Aristotelian point we need to add the appropriate codicil: the one is easy (arguing ineptly or writing poorly), and the other is very difficult (writing well). If, according to Aristotle, the answer to the fundamental ethical question "how should a human being live?" is, "in accordance with all the forms of good functioning that make up a complete human life," then Olson's answer to "how should a literary text live?" or to "how should a critical or philosophical argument live?" is, "in accordance with all the forms of good functioning that make up a complete (satisfied, justified) text or argument."

What the analysis and recovery of the principles underlying and informing various critical systems leads to in Olson is a healthy respect for the explanatory powers of diverse critical approaches and a finely tuned, earned awareness of the limitations necessarily implicated in or associated with the powers of those systems:

Recognition of the methodological differences between systems of criticism, and of their consequent respective powers and limitations quickly establishes the fact that twenty-five centuries of inquiry have not been spent in vain. On the contrary, the partial systems supplement one another, the comprehensive intertranslate, to form a vast body of poetic knowledge; and contemporary theorists, instead of constantly seeking new bases for criticism, would do better to examine the bases of such criticism as we have and so avail themselves of that knowledge. Many a modern theory of criticism would have died a-borning, had its author done a little more reading as he thought, or thinking as he read. (274)

If we are ever to get out of the fashion business in criticism and out of the habit of looking for the key to *all* useful critical deliberation in, say, politics, ideology, power relations, and so on (that is, in all those enterprises that owe their current preeminence to our full and unexamined faith in the doctrine of the social construction of reality, to our unwavering belief only in realities constructed and shaped by social forces acting independently of human interests and actions), we critics must take advantage of the available valid approaches, extending their methods into new areas of investigation and applying sound and established principles to materials and problems not previously investigated. Moreover, much reclamation work is necessary to undo the baleful effects that much recent criticism and theory has had upon literary studies. For it is sadly true that perhaps as many as two generations of graduate students have now come of age as critics and especially as theorists, believing, for example, in the death of authors, in there being nothing outside the text, in the creation of "self" or "privacy" or whatever in the late eighteenth century, and so on, through the whole dreadful catechism of sanctioned shibboleths. Unlike the theorists who now dominate literary studies, but quite like the philosophers who continue to work in the pragmatic-pluralist tradition, Olson actively and persistently encourages "the development of every valid approach" (305), recognizing that "any philosophic method worthy of the name is not one which produces merely passive results, but one through which we may actively inquire, prove, and know" (197).

Of the many valid approaches available for extension and refinement, Olson concentrates on two comprehensive systems, the Aristotelian and the Platonic. Despite the tag "Neo-Aristotelian," Olson is no more fully dedicated to the development of an Aristotelian theory of art than to the development of a Platonic or Longinian one, as the volume repeatedly evinces. Consequently, the reader should bear in mind that when Olson (along with other pluralist critics) works as an Aristotelian, he is engaging in only one of many useful critical ventures and using the method to address only those problems which it is inherently capable of resolving. Like Alvin Goldman and others, he recognizes the epistemic utility of Aristotle's division of questions into the theoretical, the practical, and the productive, with the productive—concerned with the reasoning implicit in the making of any product—being a species of practical questions.

Although a species of the practical, productive science has its own peculiar concerns, relating principally not to a change of belief or behavior, but to the best realization of a distinct product. As Goldman insists, "it is worth highlighting the fact that creative, artistic, and technical activities generate [their own distinct] problems and solution-seeking activities" as a consequence of their special focus on making.[22] And poetics, as a productive enterprise, focuses on the principles of artistic reasoning, on the justification conditions responsible for the experientially registered and distinctly realized differences in the structures and effects of different literary works. The task, then, of the "Aristotelian critic," broadly conceived, is to disclose the principles, precepts, or conditions implicit in specific artistic practices. In "matching the poetry with a poetics," as Kenneth Burke says, "the critic seeks to make these implicit principles explicit."[23]

As a productive science focusing on the reasoning implicit in the structure of artistic products, Aristotelian poetics cannot deal directly with, for example, the artistic faculties or processes, or the nature of audiences, or the political or social functions or causes of art (with what

Crane has on various occasions called the preconstructional or postconstructional causes of art, as distinct from the constructional causes, which are the focus of poetics). Rather, an Aristotelian poetics takes

for its starting point, or principle, the artistic whole which is to be produced and [proceeds] through the various parts of the various kinds to be assembled. The reasoning is hypothetical because it is based on hypotheses: if such and such a work, which is a whole, is to be produced, then the parts must be of such and such a kind and quality. The reasoning is regressive because it works backward from the whole, which is to exist, to the parts which must have existence previous to that of the whole. Since the reasoning is based upon a definition of a certain whole as its principle and since that definition must be arrived at in some fashion, any productive science must consist of two main parts: inductive reasoning toward its principle, and deductive reasoning from its principle. One part must make possible the formulation of the whole; the other must determine the parts according to that formulation. (191)

There is undoubtedly much in this passage that is not congenial to our current ways of thinking: its apparent commitment to an arid inductive-deductive, Millian, scientific methodology, its traces of what some might call a naive faith in "positivism," and its adherence to an outmoded formalism cut off from the political and ideological conditions of all contentful expressions. In essence, however, Olson is here simply articulating, albeit in rather abstract terminology, what our common practice is when, in the everyday affairs of the world, we try to understand the conversation or to read the behavior of others. Indeed, what Olson says here squares perfectly, I think, with what Donald Davidson says about "actions," namely, that they are "events which are intentional under some description, the description under which they are rationalized by the contents of the mental states which are the reasons for them."[24] Since writing is a form of activity, a series of actions, it is subject to the same conditions of rationality that inform all actions. For behavior to be an action, it must be rational relative to, for example, such and such beliefs and desires. To explain behavior we must rationalize it, for it is meaningless apart from some system of rationality.

Understanding the dynamics of a piece of literature is a form of understanding action. And if, as we have discovered earlier (with Frege, Davidson, Dummett, and others), words have meaning only relative to sentences, and sentences have meaning only relative to *use* within some structure or system of rationality, then texts, as a system of choices, are meaningful relative to what Olson calls a hypothesis. In our ordinary day-to-day dealings we know that a person with such and such beliefs and desires will very likely speak or behave in such and such way; or that a person acting or speaking in such and such way would in all likelihood have to believe and desire such and such. Olson in this passage brings to writing and interpretation the same habits of rationalization that we bring to everyday action events. And just as justification conditions guide the production of sentences and texts, so understanding is impossible apart from a grasp of justification conditions, or what Olson calls "hypotheses." (Indeed, our intentional states get their whole point from their role in determining content and in explaining behavior.) Whether this family likeness between Olson's procedure and that of many present-day philosophers will do much to enhance Olson's reputation and influence, I cannot say, but it should at least give pause to those inclined to dismiss his views out of hand. The case before Olson calls for an analysis of practical reason, and that is what he provides. And, as Frederick Schmitt usefully reminds us, "practical reason [involves reasoning] from a belief and desire to an action." [25]

We can clearly see what working with Aristotelian (or, as we have seen, Davidsonian) principles means in practical terms by turning briefly to "'Sailing to Byzantium': A Prolegomena to a Poetics of the Lyric," in which, before examining Yeats's poem in detail, Olson notes that the central task is

to discover some principle in the work which is the principle of its unity and order—a principle which, it goes without saying, will have to be a purely poetic principle, i.e., a formal principle of the poem, and not something extrinsic to it such as the differentiation either of authors, audiences, subject matters, or orders of diction would afford [these four, in various and manifold permutations, supply the first- order categories for most critical approaches, even to this very moment]. Since in a formal consideration the form is the end, and since the end renders everything else intelligible, a mark of the discovery of the formal principle would be that everything else in the poem would be found to be explicable in terms of it. (5)

As we have seen above, what Olson delivers in the argot of Aristotelianism could, without impoverishment (or enhancement, for that matter) of sense, be presented in Davidsonian or Dummettian or Putnamian terms. Speaking in a Davidsonian idiom, John Heil notes that "the recovery of sense, interpretation, is a matter of bringing to bear a theory of truth [a principle of form, according to Olson]. A theory of truth provides a systematic, projectable mapping of sentences uttered onto sentences understood. You understand my utterances only if you possess a theory of truth." [26] As an Aristotelian critic, and only as an Aristotelian critic, Olson is concerned with synthesizing principles of form (that is, justification conditions or a theory of truth), with those formal principles of works which govern the functions of the parts and in relation to which the parts have their functions (that is, with the principles that are the conditions of the possibility of those functions).

Whether he is dealing with mimetic or didactic works, Olson, along with the other Chicago critics, is interested in discovering the intrinsic causes of their artistic (or intentional) integrity and, hence, of their emotional and moral power and significance. The interest, finally, is not in formal integrity as such—valuable and interesting as that is—but in what the satisfaction of formal conditions enables us to experience and know, the whole enterprise guided by the not unwarranted assumption that the most impressive products of imaginative activity are not, by and large, the result of what in the philosophical literature is called "weakness of will," of, that is, our propensity for irrationality. For the most part, literary works attempt to convey truths of feeling and experience by "showing or depicting them. The novelist, [for example], shows what it is like to be a certain kind of person, to live in a certain era or culture. [And] this is a commonly valued way of getting understanding of human and cultural facts." [27] These ends are best accomplished when writers satisfy the conditions of the systems of intentionality that they manufacture.

To those critics who accuse the Chicago critics of constructing prescriptive definitions of artistic forms and, then, of pronouncing works good or bad, great or small, on the basis of the extent to which they correspond, point for point, to the generic ideal, they can only say again what they have said again and again: the critic does not and cannot legislate to the artist, and the artist, as Olson says, "is properly bound by no law but the dictates of the individual work" (68). To these critics, each work is a unique particular, and, on the issue of the particular and the species, Olson sharply discriminates between natural and artificial objects: natural things (horses, trees, bi-valves, and so on) have such and such characteristics because they belong to a class, whereas artificial things belong to a class (a class constructed by our interests) because they have such and such characteristics. In other words, the materials of "nature" (or "natural kinds") are, as Olson says, "programmed," in a manner of speaking, to be what they are, whereas the materials of art (of "artifactual kinds")—wood, stone, words, and so on—are not naturally disposed to assume any particular form. Apart from a system of intentionality, stones and words, for instance, are not inclined to become "Parliament House" or *Pride and Prejudice*. Artifact kinds are produced by human beings to accomplish a particular function, the one determined by the locally operative system of intentionality. Like mental kinds generally, "artifact kinds [as distinct from natural kinds] are tied to our ways of treating things, not to what the things are independently of being so treated." [28]

Once a particular work has been formed, as a result of an artist's imposing some form upon some material in some manner for some purpose, however, the realized or achieved work can be discussed in relation to other works that are similarly formed by similiar means in similar ways for similar purposes and, hence, can be formally associated with those works or *construed* as a representative of a distinguishable class of works. And all this can be done without affecting the unique particularity of the individual work. Furthermore, a theory of forms can be developed which provides a complete causal account of the possibility of formal achievement in the various kinds. Of course, those critics not interested in grouping works in terms of productive causes (that is, of grouping them in "poetic" terms) may continue to categorize along any lines of resemblance that are, for the occasion or moment, useful or desirable. The discrimination of forms in terms of productive causes that are adjusted or functional relative to some informing intentionality is, for the Chicago critics, preferred, not mandatory (and preferred because it makes possible a history of forms in terms of artistic choices, in terms of constructional causes of actually realized effects).[29]

With one more example of consonance between the views of the Chicago critics and those of postanalytic, pragmatic-pluralist philsophers I can conclude this chapter. Both critics and philosophers tend to collapse or eliminate the fact-value distinction, to insist, more exactly, that facts and values emerge together, that the good of a fact or detail is a matter of its supporting a function or of its fitting the system of intentionality of which it is a part. Value is something integral to structure. Olson's fullest statement of this position is expressed in "On Value Judgments in the Arts," and what he says there about the objectivity of value within structural systems is in perfect accord with much current thinking in philosophy. A detail of a text is good to the extent that it contributes, as Nelson Goodman says, "to the functioning of the work as a symbol" (that is, as a work).[30] What is good is fitting, is appropriate to the system of intentionality in relation to which it has meaning and function. Moreover, as Putnam informs us, "it is necessary to have standards of rational acceptability [coherence, consistency, and so on] in order to have a world [or a text] at all."[31] Otherwise, we would not know whether any detail was right, fitting, or appropriate (indeed, any detail would be as appropriate as any other). It is relative to the standards of the practice that the details are fitting, and whether they fit or not is an objective matter and not a matter of opinion.

Judged by the standards of euphony, the word "coccyx" is unpleasant (a bad sound, if you will), but within a certain sentence it may be absolutely perfect for the intended sense. Similarly, "I'll lug the guts into the other room" may be truly noisome from the point of view of sound values or of moral sensitivity, but within a particular context it is perfectly right as an indication of character. Comparably, a bad action may serve a plot well, and the unwholesomeness (by some standard) of many actions may be absolutely right and good for the work as a whole. The basic point of both critics and philosophers in the pluralist-pragmatic tradition is that there are no facts apart from values, and no (internal) goods apart from practices. But where there are values (acceptability standards) and practices, goodness and rightness are as objectively real as the facts themselves.

Finally, on this point, because we have a working understanding of what the details are right relative to, we are in a position to judge whether some detail, good and right as it is, is less fully or richly right than some other detail would be. In short, we are sometimes able to imagine how the overarching rationality could be more fully, powerfully, happily realized. Of course, whether we find any given category scheme or system of intentionality valuable will depend, as Catherine Elgin observes, on the value we place on "the truths it [manages] to state, the methods it permits [us] to employ, the projects it furthers, and the values it promotes."[32] In sum, the philosophical literature gives emphatic and detailed expression to the view of the Chicago critics that values in art works have reference to and are contingent upon form or system of intentionality, a view nowhere exhibited more forcibly than in Olson's "On Value Judgments in the Arts."

In presenting a brief overview of the intellectual bases of "Chicago criticism," with the end of demonstrating its enduring usefulness and its abiding philosophic rigor and timeliness, I have perhaps inadvertently contributed to the misrepresentation and oversimplification of the views of its advocates. This would be regrettable, though, to a large extent, unavoidable, for the fact is that those views can no more be adequately represented in short compass or by summary statement than the stateliness of a mansion can be represented by its unassembled bricks. I can only hope that this overview will instigate a renewal of interest in their arguments and, perhaps more important, in the views of art, language, and mind which they share with a goodly "field of folk" currently at work on the problems of meaning and understanding.[33]

# Chapter 7
# Genre: A Matter of Form,
# a Form of Matter

This chapter is designed to fill out some of the suggestive remarks on genre presented in Chapter 1 and to serve as a prolegomenon to a theory of genres. As such it is concerned both with principles of generic differentiation and, most immediately, with certain common assumptions underlying casual and loose ways of talking about genres. As a means of getting rather directly to fundamental issues, I have chosen to focus on a few general remarks relating to genre in a book of popular criticism, Paul Fussell's *Samuel Johnson and the Life of Writing*.[1] Fussell's remarks, though published aeons ago by the shelf-life standards of criticism today (when it seems that white bread lasts longer than the latest critical or theoretical fashion), are significant because they clearly exhibit widely held assumptions, at least among those who can borrow any time from gender, culture, and ideology studies to think about genre at all, and because they provide convenient access to matters especially relevant to the definition of genre and the identification of generic features of literary texts.

The following is divided into three sections. In the first, I deal with the notion that the recognition of a piece of writing as literature depends on a prior understanding of specific genre conventions, that subsumption by class is a prior condition of literary identification. The main object is to show that although nothing in particular can be understood without general concepts, the concepts upon which the assignment of literary status depends are not necessarily or regularly generic. The second section discusses broad problems involved in efforts to differentiate literary from non-literary composition. The final section concentrates on the necessary subordination of "genre" requirements to the peculiar formal ends of unique artistic particulars and on the nature of the various form-matter relationships necessarily implicated in any whole work. In the second and third sections, the aim is to demonstrate that the intrinsic form, or the system of rationality, of particular works does not and cannot derive from the requirements of genre or from any cultural, ideological, or historical constraints in any direct way, even though those requirements or, say, cultural constraints are necessary *material* limitations on the formal achievement of particular works. Taken together, the three sections seek to show that recognition of the literary status of a specific work does not depend on a prior understanding of the genre to which it belongs; rather, recognition of genre is contingent upon a prior understanding of the *sui generis* nature of individual works.

## Genre Conventions and Literary Identification

The primary assumption with which I am concerned in this section is stated pithily early in Fussell's study:

> The theory of literature I am relying on . . . is simple, empirical, and quite unoriginal. It derives largely from three well-known places: Harry Levin's essay of 1946, "Literature as an Institution"; Northrop Frye's speculations, in *Anatomy of Criticism*, about the autotelic world of literary forms; and E. H. Gombrich's demonstration, in *Art and Illusion*, of the indispensability of a "coded" or pre-structured or systematized medium if artistic communication is to take place at all. What I assume is that we recognize a piece of writing as literature only through our prior acceptance of the convention that its genre is literary: otherwise we do not notice it, or we do not notice it artistically.[2]

There is, I submit, nothing axiomatic about the assumption from which this reasoning begins. It is perhaps true that some readers have recognized and that some continue to recognize "a piece of writing as literature only through [a] prior acceptance of the convention that its genre is literary," but a moment's reflection on the diversity of past and present critical practice convinces us that recognition is not now and has not been in the past necessarily contingent upon such an acceptance. A comprehensive examination of the various ways critics have differentiated literature from "non-literary" pieces of writing is well beyond the scope of this chapter, but a few words on general tendencies might be useful.

Once we assume that literature can be differentiated from other forms of verbal communication,[3] we can proceed to make our actual discriminations by appealing to one or more of many possible differentia. Thus, if I assume that all writing is preeminently a sign of mental powers or activity and further that the production of literature, as distinct from that of other forms of verbal communication, requires in the writer either special faculties or general faculties in a special degree, then I may determine the literary or non-literary status of any piece of writing, whatever its kind, by noting whether or not the faculties in the requisite kind or degree are manifestly present (or, as is more often the case, by so reading the material as to disclose in it the distinctions on which my critical ingenuity has fastened). If, on the other hand, I derive my primary distinctions not from a consideration of the writer (or of the writing as a sign of the writer), but from a consideration of reader response, then I may recognize a piece of writing, whatever its kind, as literature whenever a work elicits the preferred response to it. Here recognition is the ineluctable consequence of my prior acceptance of the convention that a response distinct in nature or degree is peculiarly appropriate to literature, to which I could attach the distinguishing title, "literary response."

Again, literature may be identified by the special *means* it employs, recognition proceeding on the assumption that literature has a special *language*, relies on special resources of language, or uses language in special ways to convey meanings not possible to "non-literary" discourse (as the old "New Critics" and not a few others do). Similarly, we may conceive of literature as having a special *subject matter* and, thus, provide another basis for its recognition. This list of the ways we may go about the business of discriminating literature from other forms of discourse could be greatly extended, but the essential point is that recognition is a function of our basic differentia; we recognize as literature what our differentia compel us to recognize as literature, and as our differentia change, so also do our powers of recognition. Literature, like reference, has no essence; its identity, like that of all things else, follows the lines of our interests. Since the means of recognition are various, the objects identified by the various means are similarly various. In order to know the objects of recognition, we must first discover the intellectual bases of differentiation, since literature or, say, *Hamlet* (as a *kind*, that is) is not independent of our a priori determinations. We make *Hamlet* a kind of thing, though we do not, of course, make *Hamlet* (as an intentional system of rationality and justification), despite what some recent theoreticians who give preeminence to the creative powers of readers have boldly affirmed.

The more one thinks about the assumption, the more perplexing it becomes. Not only do many critics and theorists today treat as literature writings that belong to no recognizable or traditional literary class (writings, in fact, that many have recognized for various reasons as belonging to such particular branches of inquiry as history, philosophy, religion, science, and so forth), but they also betray no signs of having been induced to treat—and, hence, to recognize—these writings as literature as a result of having first found the means by which to subsume such works, at least temporarily, under legitimate literary genres.

On quite different grounds from those mentioned above, many critics would be unwilling to allow the assumption, because we can discover in literature no single attribute or set of attributes that distinguishes it from non-literary discourse. Under this banner march most postmodernist critics, for example, who discuss literature, not as a special category, but in terms of the qualities or values it shares with any other cultural product as a consequence of its dependence on one or another of the common causes of all discursive practices—language, history, politics, ideology, gender, psyche, or whatever. Of any attribute volunteered as distinctive of literature, we find either that it inheres in all word-based works (or in many that no one had ever recognized as literature), or that it inheres in too few, thus excluding from "literature" many works that not only post-structuralists but also the generality of readers, in different periods, had accepted as literature.

Moreover, even those modern critics who have done most to refine our notions of literary genres—the Chicago pluralists—would not be inclined to concur with the assumption that recognition as literature is contingent upon genre identification. Indeed, since theirs is essentially an *ex post facto* criticism, they would unequivocally reject, on principle, any critical position that attempted to fix (or assumed the fixation of) the forms that writings must assume to be considered as literature and all notions that implied that a piece of writing could be recognized as literature only through our prior perception of it as an example of an *existing* literary genre. On precisely this matter, R. S. Crane has written:

> It will be sufficient for all our purposes if we begin, simply, by taking as "poems" or "works of literary art" all those kinds of productions which have been commonly called such at different times, but without any supposition that, because these have the same name, they are all "poems" or "works of literary art" in the same fundamental structural sense. . . . And for such [diverse productions as *The Divine Comedy, The Faerie Queene, King Lear, Othello,* and so on*] we shall need to assume, in addition, only one common characteristic: that they are all works which, in one degree or another, justify critical consideration primarily for their own sake, as artistic structures, rather than merely for the sake of the knowledge or wisdom they express or the practical utility we may derive from them, though either or both of these other values may be importantly involved in any particular case. . . . [The task of criticism is to make] formal sense out of any poetic work before us on the assumption that it may in fact be a work for whose peculiar principles of structure there are nowhere any usable parallels either in literary theory or in our experience of other works.[4]

Formal literary structures may be types, but it is clear, to Crane at least, that some types may be known by only one example (once the work is created, other works, of course, may be constructed on the same formal principles). Further, it is clear that "typing" is not immediately prerequisite to recognition as literature, since, as Crane repeatedly affirms,[5] we have not begun to define (and, hence, to understand and recognize) the forms of a substantial number of pieces of writing that we have consented to treat as literature.

And if we bring to an end the enumeration of theoretical objections to the primary assumption and test it against common experience uninformed by precept, we still find skepticism refusing to submit to credulity. In practice, the way we go about recognizing a piece of writing as literature is actually both simpler and more complex than is generally assumed. For the most part, we treat as literature what we are asked or what, for one reason or another, we are inclined to treat as literature. There is, in short, no form of writing which in at least one of its incarnations cannot be discussed and recognized as literature, industry or ingenuity being as perverse as the understanding is tolerant and as the class "literature" is hospitable to divergent formulations.

As soon as anyone decides to discuss a selected piece of writing (for example, an editorial in a daily newspaper, a book of the Bible, a specific State Department paper, a particular sermon, a diary entry) in "literary" terms, according to "literary" criteria, as embodying particular "literary" devices, on its "literary" merits, or as operating under the governance of any terms, categories, or priorities that have been associated with the analysis or description of literature, we are willing, if only tentatively and temporarily, to recognize the legitimacy of calling that work, in response to the critic's specified conditions, literature, even though we may happen to disagree with her distinctions, analysis, or description, and we do this without once forgetting that the work under discussion is yet a sermon or an editorial, and without confounding the *Iliad* with a State Department paper. We may treat a sermon or a group of sermons as literature without believing for a moment that sermons necessarily constitute a literary genre. Indeed, if genre is defined principally in terms of principles of reasoning or of justification conditions, as I shall briefly argue later, then, since sermons are variously structured on various topics for the sake of various purposes, one would expect sermons to belong to several genres.

A student blissfully ignorant of any concept of genre may nevertheless be willing to recognize that *Beowulf* is literature. More generally, a person may glide through life accepting the literary status of works that he could not classify by genre, even upon being informed that unremitting and everlasting torment was the price of ignorance. We need not restrict our appeal to the novice or the "genre challenged," however. Even the dedicated literary critic or scholar may devote a lifetime to the study, contemplation, and discussion of a particular literary work (Dryden's *Absolom and Achitophel*, say) without ever determining to his own satisfaction to which genre it properly belongs.[6]

The fact is that "literature" is not a determinate class, delimiting in any meaningful way the forms of writing that may or may not be included within its legitimate jurisdiction. In acceding to any critic's request to consider a piece of writing as literature, we consent, in general, only to attend to a special way of construing a work for the purpose of disclosing in it what are taken to be devices, powers, attributes, or effects of literature. If we do not concur with the operative assumptions or conclusions or grant that attributes differentiating literature from other kinds of writing have been isolated, we still stand ready to acknowledge that some particular sermon, say, may be considered as literature. And it is because "literature" is not a fixed category of writing with a determinate set of universal attributes that we can be so tolerant.

Our reasons for accepting a piece of writing as literature are as manifold and diverse as are the terms, categories, doctrines, and principles that we employ in our discussions of literature. Like water, literature is largely known through the intellectual operations that we happen to apply to it. Water, construed in one way, is a medium for swimming, whereas under the construction sponsored by threatening flames, water is understood to be a fire extinguisher, even though a quite different construction of water has informed us that it is compounded of one element that sustains fire and another that is flammable).[7] Of course, in the first two instances I consider "water" as an artifactual kind—a substance variously defined by us in terms of use, in terms of its manifold functions—and, in the third instance, as a natural kind, with a determinate physical constitution. Literature is like "artifactual water" in not having a fixed essence, but each literary work, like each use of water, does have meaningful content relative to the functioning of its elements within some system of intentionality or rationality. In other words, particular works are like particular uses of water, functional constructs of justified constituents. Literature, then, is a protean entity that alters as it alteration finds in the observer (that is, in the interests and categories of the observer). Nevertheless, even if we do not approach texts with a limiting and, hence, restrictive conception of what differentiates literature from other forms of verbal discourse, we can still consent to recognize any piece of writing as literature, at least provisionally, if only because we can think of no compelling reason not to think so, if only because it is included in a "literature" course, if only because we sacrifice no intellectual principles, abrogate no argumentative prerogatives, invalidate no fundamental beliefs in allowing the designation.

The preceding discussion provokes, of course, many questions it refrains from answering. But for all its shortcomings, it does at least cast doubt on the adequacy of the notion that we recognize a piece of writing as literature *only* through our prior acceptance of the convention that its genre is literary.

## Literature and Non-Literature

In developing his position, Fussell observes that

An act of what observers will consent to consider literature can take place only when an individual talent engages and, as it were, fills in the shape of a preexisting form that a particular audience is willing to regard as belonging to the world of literature.[8]

For our present purposes, these remarks require attention because the whole issue of genre identification is implicated in them.

Now, since no particular audience will consent to consider every piece of writing as literature (this was true until quite recently at least), we must, to cover the ground, make explicit the corollary that is not articulated here: "An act of what observers will consent to consider 'non-literature' (or, say, philosophy, history, and so on) can take place only when an individual talent engages and, as it were, fills in the shape of a preexisting form that a particular audience is willing to regard as belonging to the world of 'non-literature' (or philosophy, history, and so on)."[9] Combined, these statements define the battleground or playground on which the warfare or sport of writing takes place. Unfortunately, by prior definition, the encounter between talent and tradition culminates in a predictable result. If talent does not yield to tradition (that is, preexisting form), we are placed in the awkward position of being witnesses to the thing which is not; the field must always be a playground, never a battleground where the outcome is uncertain. Yet, the definitions oblige us to conceive of the possibility of a battleground and of the forces of talent carrying the day.

The basic problem can perhaps be clarified by considering the subservience of talent to form. When individual talent encounters tradition, it must find the means to confine its rambunctious impetuosity within the limits prescribed by preexisting forms. If talent adjusts its activity to preexisting form—consents, that is, to play the "game" by the rules—then we can agree to call the result either literature or non-literature. The real source of difficulty here, as elsewhere, is the amorphous category "literature." Of course, there is no possibility of a meaningful use of *language* outside some rules, since a purely private language—one without proper and improper, permissible and impermissible moves—as Wittgenstein famously showed, is simply not possible or intelligible, even to its progenitor. Without allowability and disallowability rules any sequence of words is as permissible as any other sequence, and, hence, no sequence is better or more appropriate than any other. What has our concern here is the emergence of new rules and, consequently, new forms, not the dependence of meaning and reference on rules, on some system of rationality or intentionality. In our present scheme, if talent steadfastly refuses to submit to the demands of any preexisting form and decides rather to make, say, two or more preexisting forms bow before its strength, then, by definition, the audience must frankly admit the existence of a logical impossibility, admit that it has met a piece of writing that is neither literature nor non-literature: a piece of writing that is not a piece of writing.

This paradox is not insoluble, of course, but the first step toward solution involves, at the very least, a modification of what constitutes literature or, more sensibly still, an abandonment of the effort to determine the constituent nature of literature altogether, which should follow from our recognition that, as Thomas Nagel puts it, "the capacity to imagine new forms of hidden order, and [on the other side] to understand new conceptions created by others, [is] innate," a ground-floor feature of our evolutionary endowment.[10]

Oddly enough, support for the definition is found by our critic even in facts that would seem to invalidate it. For instance, in an effort to confirm his position, Fussell appeals to Stuart Gilbert's discussion of the reception in England of the "Sirens" episode of Joyce's *Ulysses*: "When it was sent by the author from Switzerland to England during the First World War, the Censor held it up, suspecting that it was written in some secret code. Two English writers (it is said) examined the work and came to the conclusion that it was not 'code' but literature of some eccentric kind."[11] As soon as we ask how they came to their conclusion, we immediately recognize that it could not have been achieved by relying on our critic's explanation of what constitutes literature. Their decision was reached before they had access to the whole work and presumably before they knew that the episode was indeed an episode—in advance, that is, of sufficient "genre" clues. Moreover, Gilbert's description tells us that the two writers did not think that Joyce had filled in the shape of a preexisting form (the work was deemed "eccentric," a member of no recognizable form) that they were willing to regard as belonging to the world of literature. On the contrary, they were willing for one reason or another to regard as belonging to the world of literature a piece of writing that they could not identify by genre. Decision preceded rather than followed genre identification.

A little later, we are informed that "It takes a mature and experienced sensibility . . . to do what Norman Mailer has done, to appropriate a genre not considered literary—the news story, the 'report,' the eyewitness account—and make it serve literary purposes."[12] But, in calling, say, *Armies of the Night* literature, we must apparently subordinate our notions of genre to what, for lack of other terms, we are willing to call, vaguely, "literary purposes." Recognition is based not on identification of literary genre, but on detection of "literary purpose." Mailer has not filled in the shape of a preexisting form that we are willing to regard as belonging to the world of literature. On the contrary, we are willing to regard as literature, on the basis of its "purpose," a piece of writing that belongs to a "genre" which, by prior consent, we do not recognize as literary. Moreover, it is clear that Mailer's success does not oblige us to add the "report," the news story to the list of literary genres.

In fact, of course, rather than filling in the shape of a preexisting form (literary or otherwise), Mailer has found the means to transcend or transgress the formal limitations (whatever they are exactly) of the news story, creating in the process a piece of literature that we are content for the time being to call, with Mailer's prompting, "novel-history, history-novel," a "new" genre. Mailer has written a news report with a difference, a difference depending upon and exemplifying the processes of imagination. A new type—even perhaps a unique type—has emerged from the dynamic coadunation of preexisting types, in much the same way that *highway* and *man* achieve something other than highway-ness and man-ness in *highwayman*. We have exhibited here what Alvin Goldman calls one of the pervasive aspects of human cognition, imagination, by which he means the "mental construction of new patterns, combinations, sequences, structures, and so on, out of old elements or parts."[13] In the end, we have not this form plus that form, but a dynamic whole demanding recognition in its own terms and governed by imperatives tending toward a peculiar formal completion. In sum, we understand that *Armies of the Night* is both like and unlike a news story and that Mailer has done more than appropriate a preexisting, non-literary genre in order to make it serve literary purposes.

Shortly before the commentary on Mailer, we are notified that, "like other sorts of public notices, what literature is at any moment depends wholly on conventions which appear and depart, wax and wane, fructify or deaden."[14] This seems sensible enough, but, operating from our working definition of literature, we are at a loss as to how to accommodate these fluctuations. How, indeed, can they take place? The definition of literature does not allow for waxing and waning. Indeed, one wonders how any piece of writing ever came initially to be identified as literature, if a particular audience can consent to recognize that and only that piece of writing as literature which takes a form previously acknowledged to be literary. We cannot logically agree both with this statement about fluctuation and with the prior definition, since the definition contains no implicit means by which to account for the comings and goings of recognizable forms of literature. The basic point here seems to be only that some forms are popular in one age, some in another.

To this innocuous truth we must add the qualification that the preferences of writers in these matters determine in no necessary way or absolute sense what we are willing, at any historical moment, to call literature. For example, the fact that no one today may choose to write heroic dramas or pastoral elegies does not prevent me from recognizing the literary status of works written in the past in those forms. Similarly, if someone today should choose to write a pastoral elegy, I would immediately recognize its "form," even though no one else today was writing in that form. The only thing I cannot do, of course, is recognize the literary status of an unformed form (existence precedes recognition), though I certainly know that new literary forms may in the time to come emerge.

Underlying the whole argument is the assumption of generic stability, for without any stable grounds of "genre" differentiation there can clearly be no sharp separation of talent from preexisting form, of what is inside from what is outside the writer. We are thus brought to the identification of "coded medium" with literary genre:

> The idea of the "coded medium" is a modern way of conceiving of a relatively fixed literary genre. *This coded medium comes inevitably from outside the writer:* otherwise it fails to transmit signals recognizable to the observer. Which is another way of saying what Northrop Frye has said: "The *forms* of literature can no more exist outside literature than the forms of sonata and fugue and rondo can exist outside music." The medium is a public property which is not inside the writer.[15]

Our assent to these remarks would be less than hesitant if they did not betray a loose way of talking about "medium" and "genre." In a sense, there is no startlingly new information offered here; part of the drift seems to be that a writer fashions material *already at hand* into a shape that the material, left to its own devices, would not naturally assume.

Of course, we always work from what is available (what else could we work from?), and what is true of the writer is likewise true of the architect, cabinet-maker, composer, potter, painter, and seamstress. But—leaving aside the problem of what any particular audience may or may not be willing to call the thing fashioned into a shape—I am reluctant to grant much of what goes beyond the obvious in these remarks. Why should we equate "coded medium" with relatively fixed literary genre and talk about a *form* of writing (a genre) as though it were a *medium* of writing? (What media are necessary to the realization of the form-medium?) Why should we interpret genre as the primary (only) medium with which an author (individual talent) engages? Why wouldn't it make more sense to talk about language as *the* (or *a*) medium used in the fashioning of a form of literature, a genre? Why should we stress the vulnerability of the writer and the rigid toughness of the genre? Could we not just as easily stress the strength of authorial will and the vulnerability of genre, since genre is finally subservient to the particular aims, purposes, and governing conceptions of the writer? How do we go about determining the extent to which artistic purpose yielded to a particular writer's *conception* of genre requirements (and it is essential to remember that with various writers we are dealing with varying conceptions of genre), or the extent to which *understood* genre requirements yielded to artistic purpose? How, in short, do we go about the job of adjusting vulnerabilities?

Can we not more safely say, in fact, that whenever a writer discovers that specific genre requirements inhibit rather than promote expression, whenever a writer finds that aspects of the specific genre in which she has *chosen* to write no longer serve as fundamental conditions of artistic freedom, enabling her to embody powerfully, vividly, and precisely her conception, she chooses rather to violate the rules or to disregard the generic imperatives than to revise her composition or to disrupt the ongoing integrity of her work? Even so timid and rule-conscious a man as Joseph Addison, who was willing to change much that his friends took exception to in *Cato*, chose rather to defend a violation of poetic justice than to conclude his play with the success of Cato. Rules guide practice only as long as they free expression and serve artistic purpose.

Moreover, is it not the case that knowledge of the genre[16] in which a writer is working is frequently the least useful information we can have about a particular work? Such knowledge, vague and various as it usually is, is less useful, for example, than knowlege about whether the work is "serious" or "comic," whether certain remarks are to be taken "literally" or "figuratively," and whether a given character is speaking ironically or straightforwardly. Is it not also true that in *choosing* to write in a particular genre, as he or she understands its nature and requirements, a writer frequently solves very few practical problems of composition?

To understand Dryden's *Astraea Redux*, for example, we must know a good deal more than that it belongs to the *genre* "occasional poetry" (assuming for the moment that this term identifies a genre, which, of course, it doesn't, since many *kinds* of poems on many different subjects and productive of many different effects can be occasional). We must know, in addition, more than what particular event occasioned the poem. To know that it was designed to celebrate the return of Charles II to England is to know very little about the poem, about how the poem is obliged to work; very few real problems were solved by Dryden in choosing to write on the return of Charles. The expression of Dryden's individual talent was restricted less by the occasion itself than by how he construed the problems involved in dealing with the return of Charles. His problems were immediate and practical: how to represent the exile as fortunate for Charles and for the people of England, without offending Charles and disturbing the people; how to make Charles acceptable to the people and the people acceptable to Charles, without creating fictions in which nobody could believe; how to suggest the way Charles should behave upon his return, without appearing to be impertinent or more astute than Charles himself, and so on. To understand *Astraea Redux* is to experience the resolution of problems such as these in the workingness of the justified parts in the interest of the poem.

It is worth noting here, I think, that occasional poetry is really not the exceptional, but the paradigmatic case. Every poem, however denominated, is, for the reader, like a new game, the rules for which he cannot presume to know prior to reading but must discover and learn by playing, that is, reading.[17] We must learn a new practice with the reading of each new work, depending as we go on our prior familiarity with a rich stock of mastered practices and on our imaginative capacity for improvising and understanding new possibilities. Our success in imagining and understanding new structures, new systems of justification and satisfaction, is impressive and may be owing to the fact, as Goldman suggests, that "the general lines of construction [are perhaps] species-specific. This would account for the commonality of the concepts we generate, the predicates we project, the possibilities we envisage."[18]

Every particular work is a "unique" product owing its peculiar coherence and integrity to the writer's playing out of those local options that are consonant with the functioning of the work as a whole, that are serviceable to that overall conception or aim, in relation to which the choice has meaning and function. To play the writer's game, to learn the writer's practice, we must construct what for lack of a better phrase I can only call a working "theory of meaning" or principle of form, intuiting as we proceed—on the basis of our experience competence and our familiarity with other literary texts and a host of other discourses—meaning conditions more comprehensive than the as yet disclosed information fully warrants, and altering our working theory or hypothesis in response to the demands of new information. Briefly, reading forces us to formulate and revise hypotheses, which are tentative, heuristic intuitions of systems of intentionality in advance of full evidence, as we encounter the work in its linear unfolding; for in the absence of such a theory of justified relations there is no meaningful content to the work at all.

Our confidence in the explanatory power of a particular theory or hypothesis increases as we get closer to the end of the work, because fewer choices (fewer possibilities and more necessities) are available to the writer at the end than at the beginning, and because our latest hypothesis is accountable to more material than the earliest. The latest, of course, may not be adequate to the richness and complexity of the work examined, but something that I am willing to call a theory of meaning or hypothesis is necessarily involved in the understanding or experiencing of any extended piece of writing, since without it the reader would be flooded with an incredible assortment of discrete units lacking relation, emphasis, or force. Without any theory, the reader is simply confused, overwhelmed, assaulted by data with uncertain boundaries that cannot be assimilated or rendered meaningful. The conception of understanding offered here is, of course, not that endorsed by or functional in most poststructuralist accounts (which are ultimately based on the Saussurean model of difference), but that informing the recent work of, among others, Donald Davidson and Michael Dummett. In Dummett's analysis, our understanding of language is determined by our theory of meaning, "for it is this that confers on [the writer's expressions] the senses that they bear." [19]

If reading is tainted by interpretation from the beginning and hypotheses, as prophecies, tend to be self-fulfilling, what prevents reading from being an exercise in self-imposition, a game in which each player takes out of the magic circle exactly what has been diligently put into it? Frequently, of course, nothing checks the steady progress of a self-initiated, self-sustaining, and self-justifying game. But, in general, readers are quick to modify their working theories or hypotheses as they confront new details, because they run crashing into recalcitrant material, because most early hypotheses are tentative, open to falsification as well as confirmation, because of a felt tension between the new details and the means of accounting for them, because, finally, of a failure of "fittingness." Throughout, we recognize that our task is to learn the rules that somebody else has devised for a game that we cannot be sure we know; the writer, in a manner of speaking, is our adversary, one whose choices may subvert the ongoing integrity of *our* controlling intuition.

When those choices cannot be accommodated to our "theory of meaning," we have at least the following three options available to us: we can attempt (1) to demonstrate that the new details are insignificant, unimportant, adventitious, in short, not theory-threatening; (2) to prove that they are "bad" choices, artistic flaws, mistakes, signs of carelessness, textual corruption, compositorial ineptness, in short, harmful to the text's best interests; or (3) to construct a new theory, in which such details function as necessary, contributing parts of an entirely different set of justification conditions, of a new theory, the sufficiency of our conception of which may again be tested (invalidated or confirmed) by subsequent disclosures. In the course of reading we perhaps rarely contemplate our "theoretical" intuitions in any self-conscious, deliberate way; our theory is a form of implicit knowledge, susceptible to revision. But, as stated above, if our experience with a work involves something more than an extended series of discrete, disjunct impressions, without history, future, or meaningful relation, then the ground of significant response is necessarily some more or less coherent cognition, for without "structure" or "pattern" there is neither thought nor meaning.

If we happen to be interested in the practice of interpretation, in explaining our understanding, we have an obligation to reason back from our specific, achieved hypothesis or theory to the details of the text. We must attempt to show that only this conception of justification conditions can adequately account for the text in all its particularity or, perhaps more exactly, attempt to show that by the standards of achievement to which we almost involuntarily resort as experienced readers—standards such as coherence, interest, beauty, moral significance, and so on—this conception of fittingness relations is more satisfying and less strained than other conceptions. This is perhaps the best we can do in the line of explanation, but in most cases this is more than good enough. As in all areas of explanation, there is no question here of achieving some "absolutely" right or correct interpretation. In themselves, the details of the text are not accidental or essential elements (indeed, they aren't even particular details apart from some reference scheme). And, as W. V. Quine and Joseph Ullian have noted, no matter how many details we have, even with the whole text before us, "there will still be many mutually incompatible hypotheses each of which implies those [details]. What confirms one hypothesis will confirm many, [since] the data are good for a whole sheaf of hypotheses and not just one." [20]

It is this situation that makes it necessary to establish such justification criteria as coherence, consistency, interest, moral significance, and so on. The parts, while prior to the whole which collectively they achieve, are seen and discussed as necessities following from the overall conception which generates their sequential unfolding; the informing conception here stands in relation to the details of the text as the meaning of a sentence stands in relation to the individual words of the sentence. (We know a meaning because of the words—the material cause—but the meaning is the cause—final cause—of the words being said, having a certain reference, value, and emphasis.) Having satisfied the demands of interpretation, we then may go on to note class correspondences obtaining between this work and several other works to which a "genre" name has been assigned. But "genre" distinctions (and here I use the term "genre" loosely, as we all generally do) control the artist's selection and the audience's responses only in a minimal sense, whereas the peculiar, constitutive principles of form control the meaningful relations of elements in a particular work, classifiable by genre, in a maximal sense. As one critic has said:

Sonnet form, for instance, is a perfectly comprehensible class term, but it implies very little for the form of any sonnet. It designates formal components which are largely fixated and do not interact. . . . While a critic recognizes a sonnet by virtue of features which sonnets possess in common [fourteen lines, discernible stanza divisions or patterns of imagery, etc.], he is usually not concerned to show that these features . . . are significant of anything in relation to the whole.[21]

The history of literature indicates that genre is more open than closed, is flexible rather than rigid. Are Jane Austen and James Joyce engaging with the same "coded medium," that is, the novel? As soon as we start designating the attributes of a genre, we find that we have inadvertently excluded works, which, in spite of our categorical specifications, seem to belong to the genre, or that we have allowed room for works which we would not want to enroll in the genre.

Underlying the position I have been dealing with is the false assumption that in any given period there is substantial agreement about what characteristics constitute the several distinct genres. A perfunctory examination of critical practice suggests that nothing could be further from the truth. Just as critics distinguish literary from non-literary discourse in various ways, so they differentiate among genres in various ways. Some critics define genre in terms of some more or less specific *quality* thought to be inherent in all works of the type: tragic quality, comic quality, satiric quality, ironic quality, and so on. Thus, narrative poems, long lyrics, novels, dramatic works and so forth may all be classified, say, as tragedies. Others fix upon subject matter as the discriminating sign of genre, so that we have, for example, domestic tragedy, bourgeois tragedy, social tragedy, and so on exemplified in dramatic works and extended prose and verse narratives. Still others define according to kinds of probability: fantastic, realistic, naturalistic, surrealistic, and so forth. And others differentiate on the basis of the kinds of techniques and conventions employed, for example, conventions of narration (omniscient author, first-person narration, stream of consciousness).

As Catherine Elgin has observed: "We [can] classify [works] by *subject*, as crucifixion pictures or medical bulletins; by *style* as impressionist paintings or symbolist poems. And we [can] classify them by *medium*, as watercolors or news reports; by *author*, as Monets or Flauberts; by *historical or cultural milieu*, as Renaissance or Victorian works." [22] The grounds of differentiation are many and various. And if critics discriminate among genres in many ways, writers also conceive of generic limitations in many radically disparate ways. In the absence of any consensus concerning the specific nature of genre limits or powers, there can be no general agreement about the ways in which talent adjusts to preexisting form.

## Genre Requirements and Principles of Form

I should now like to look briefly at the equation of coded medium with genre and to amplify earlier remarks. It seems to me that only confusion is served by talking about a "kind," a "form" as though it were a "medium," a "material" to be shaped, especially when genre is elsewhere described as the shape which the writer fills in. Now, the world of writing, not to mention the worlds of painting, music, sculpture, and so forth, is full of coded media, and considerable loss of precision results when we reduce media to medium. In fact, any distinguishable set of linguistic or conceptual units can be called a coded medium, a material, that is, which achieves specific expressive or representational meaning relative to pressures and controls exerted upon it, not pressures and controls intrinsic to or emanating from within the set.

This is simply another way of saying that lower-level elements cannot determine their own boundary conditions. Words, for example, cannot serve as the principle of their own arrangement, emphasis, and value. Or, nothing internal to signs—marks on a page or impact waves in the air—can determine reference. Words owe their significance to something outside themselves, and this something, to alter Wittgenstein slightly, concerns their function within the structure of meaning of which they are a part.[23] For example, in a rough and ready way of talking, we can say that phonemes are brought under the control of words (phonemes are formed into shapes—words—which they would not assume if left to amuse themselves); words are controlled by grammar and syntax; grammar and syntax by sentences; sentences by the comprehensive justification conditions (and these conditions are informative all the way down). This sequence does not exhaust the possibilities of matter-form relationships, of course, since between sentences and whole compositions a variety of conventions, including what we loosely call genre conventions, are brought under the governance of the overall shaping principle, which determines the expressive and representative relations of all the parts and the functional relevance and importance of them. Nevertheless, the sequence does indicate how form at one level of organization may become matter at a higher level.

From a whole composition, we can derive knowledge, albeit limited, of sentences, from sentences a knowledge of syntax, from syntax a knowledge of words, from words a knowledge of phonology. But we cannot infer a vocabulary from a knowledge of phonemes, a grammar from a familiarity with vocabulary. A grammar may limit the kinds of things that may be said, but it cannot predict or by itself generate meaningful sentences. And a whole composition, comprised of many sentences and ordered to a distinct end, cannot be derived from a knowledge of the individual sentences making up the whole. As John Searle has iteratively insisted, "semantics is not intrinsic to syntax,"[24] and Michael Dummett regularly reminds us that "the fundamental fact . . . is that our understanding of language is the grasp of a system or structure" of meaning, of justification conditions.[25] (Put all the sentences of, say, *Hamlet* in a box and then ask any student to return at the end of the term with a great play in hand. The play just ain't in the words—or in the terms and categories of the culture, for that matter.)

For our purposes, let us assume that the basic medium with which a writer deals is a particular language, with its lexicon and rules governing the values and the organizational possibilities of words. This language is not of his own devising and, hence, may be understood as belonging to his "speech community." Language is the primary "coded medium." At this point, we may invoke the aid of Fussell and Frye, applying what they say of genre to language: "*This coded medium comes inevitably from outside the writer*: otherwise it fails to transmit signals recognizable to the observer. . . . The medium is a public property which is not inside the writer."[26] What a person actually says or writes, however, does not exist outside the intentionality of the speaker or writer (a language community cannot speak or write). A statement is fashioned out of the materials of a particular language at a particular time and in a particular culture, though the language, historical period, and culture allow an indefinite number of statements and cannot prohibit the expression of contradictory or conflicting statements. We immediately recognize the statement as possible to the language (and culture). From the outset we know whether or not the writer is using a language that we understand.

On the other hand, we do not always know either immediately or ultimately what genre a writer is engaging with, and, furthermore, no realized work identifiable by genre, however defined, no result achieved by the specific choices of a writer, can be said to be outside the writer if we conceive of genre not as a material (a medium), but as a synthesis of material achieved by means of some shaping intentionality or principle of construction. By definition, a form—a structure or pattern—is the result of forces exerted upon materials that would not by themselves assume a distinctive shape.[27] But this statement needs to be refined, for even when the end peculiar to a particular genre can be clearly stated— a certain kind of tragedy is designed to effect the catharsis of pity and fear, for example—it is clear that every production not a mere copy of something already existing embodies artistic choices that culminate in a unique realization of the ends specified for the genre, in much the same way that every new declaratory sentence is a unique realization of the ends peculiar to that type of sentence.

In a radical sense, it is impossible for a writer to fill in the shape of a "preexisting form." Form is the result of specific acts of selection and arrangement, governed by locally operative intentionality constraints. The characteristics of a genre, however designated, are so many general conditions to be met or so many general limitations on the vagaries of imagination. But a unique synthesis of material, classifiable perhaps by genre, can only emerge as a result of a *writer's* taking advantage of those opportunities for choice in a genre (or a culture) which are consonant with and instrumentally useful to a specific artistic purpose. Otherwise, we would have statements of conditions and limitations, but no actual writings. If the conditions are met, we may be willing to recognize the work as an example of a certain genre, but the conditions cannot generate any specific form classifiable by genre any more than the conditions of possibility of an interrogatory sentence can generate a meaningful question in a specific context. For example, we can say that any sculptor working in clay and interested in representing a human being is severely limited, first, by the "material" in which the work is to be produced, and second, by the "form" that is to be represented (the "form" of a person is not the "form" of a toadstool). But no sculptor can represent the form of a person without at the same time forming a person.

The range of possible forms that the "form" of a person may assume is virtually infinite, just as the range of possible forms that, say, a novel may assume is virtually infinite. In relation to clay, "person" is a formal restraint; in relation to "person," a particular representation is a formal restraint. By way of refinement, we can narrow with increasing precision the type to which the formed person belongs. Thus, from person we can move to thin person, to thin person wearing a saffron robe, to thin person wearing a saffron robe, sitting, and knitting a sweater, to the same person qualified by signs of age, emotion, and so on, thus arriving at a type that includes one member. But whatever the final product, the formed person will be a unique synthesis of material conditions.

We can discuss genre requirements as coded media, but it is important to keep in mind that "genre" is not a primary coded medium, in the sense that a language is a primary coded medium, since (if for no other reasons) there is no consensus concerning genre requirements and since no genre requirements can be specified—for writing—that cannot be realized in language. In short, the material foundation of all genre requirements is language. Moreover, "genre," as we generally understand the term, is not a form, not a set of justification conditions to which all the discriminable parts are answerable and from which they derive their specific meaning and force (if such parts are justified, then they have definite content, for that is what justification entails). Rather, genre is a set of material conditions which, though they must be met, can be met in various ways in various works.

In a manner of speaking, we can say that when a writer *chooses* to write in one genre rather than another, he subordinates the various possibilities for formal development intrinsic to language to the control of genre requirements. The rules that apply to language achieve functional value relative to the rules specified for the genre, in just the way that the rules of language achieve functional value relative to the demands of kinds of sentences—assertoric, interrogatory, imperative. The rules of genre, however defined, are in turn *material* limitations on the formal potentialities of specific works, but the principle of form of any particular work does not derive from the rules of genre. Rather, the rules become functional in relation to *restraints imposed upon them by a local principle of form*. And what is true of "genre" limitations is likewise true of any "social," "historical," "cultural," "ideological" constraints as well. Such constraints can be met in indefinitely many ways, and, thus, they cannot determine the "specific content" of any writing whatsoever.

At this point, it may be noted that the conception of justification conditions determined by a system of intentionality on which this chapter depends derives its power and intelligibility from a philosophy of language and mind not widely known or understood in literary studies, one which requires, among other things, the recognition that meaning depends on use, and use on intentionality. Since there is no use apart from intentionality, this whole discussion of comprehensive justification conditions presupposes a rational agent involved in conscious, deliberative, voluntary activity. In short, it presupposes that writing is a kind of activity, a form of behavior; that behavior is explained by reference to the mental states (for example, belief and desire), propositional attitudes, or thoughts that are the cause of it; and that those mental states supply the representational or contentful context or "matter" of the activity or behavior. Too often today, it seems, critics and theorists devote time, energy, and ingenuity to ferreting out the latent, unintended functions of literary and all other artifacts, to giving agency, or something like agency, to such nonagentive abstractions as history, ideology, language, and so on. Speaking of correlative matters, John Searle, using italics to make his silent commentary, notes that if, for example, "you *think* that the *unintended latent* function of money is to maintain a system of oppression, then you will *claim* to have discovered a nonagentive function among the agentive status functions of money."[28]

To return to the topic at hand, in relation to the overall form of a work everything is material, including genre requirements and much that is not normally comprehended (or, because of our loose way of talking about such matters, may not be comprehended) under our conception of genre. In "realistic" works, for example, a writer's current, locally functional, working conception of the nature of external reality limits what can be said or done in a work and what sorts of probabilities can be actively contemplated. "Reality," as conceived, is then a "coded medium." With regard to "thought," limits are provided by the problems, ideas, and topics entertained, specifically by the particular manner of construing those problems, ideas, and topics.[29] Hence, the *thought* in the work, as limited in its aspects and subservient to artistic purpose, can be considered in terms of a coded medium. If a writer happens to rely regularly on specific devices or techniques not demanded or required by the genre (as defined), then we can examine those techniques and devices as coded media. They, too, are *means* to a determinate end. Similarly, imagery, symbolism, and so on may be considered as so many coded media subservient to the particular intentional interests of a particular work. In short, any distinguishable system of parts can be discussed as a medium.

What a definition of genre, no matter how detailed, cannot do, of course, is specify the nature, number, or value of all the various coded media with which a writer may actively engage in the production of a distinct piece of writing. Effective communication depends on the employment of coded media, but it is a mistake to assume that all the coded media used by a writer in making a particular work can be construed as so many aspects of a pervasive medium called "genre" or to imply that whatever is not comprehended under a particular conception of genre is an attribute of the writer's "individual uniqueness."[30] In every work tending toward completion, every choice made along the way limits the range of possible alternative choices that may be made subsequently (because, as Wittgenstein notes, "some developments would [be] absolutely wrong," given the way the work is unfolding). But few crucial choices— choices on which the peculiar artistic integrity of the work depends— are necessarily implicated in what we may abstractly identify as the attributes of a specific genre, even though it is also true that many particular choices are of a kind peculiar to the genre in which the writer happens to work.

In the end, what are assumed to be the fixed poles of the literary enterprise—talent and preexisting form—are no more than hypostatizations. Armed with these categories—or with categories derived from some prior analysis of history, culture, ideology, language, and so on— no critic could come to a detailed understanding of any particular work, if only because the critic could not reason from these ground terms to necessary literary particulars. The works, with their specific values, emphases, interests, and effects, cannot be deduced from or resolved into such broad "preconstructional categories" (to borrow once again one of R. S. Crane's happy phrases). The cognitive weakness of our critic's hypothesis is not on the side of *scope*, however, since every act of writing is comprehended under its polarities, but on the side of *precision*, since the necessary relations obtaining in any single piece of writing simply cannot be known by means of the preferred categories. Additionally, there is assumed in this view what even casual acquaintance with the history of literary criticism and practice would not seem to justify: that the persistence of names for types of writing (novel, lyric, tragedy, and so on) is a guarantee of the persistence of a commonly shared understanding of the meanings or significations of those names, and that this understanding provides a rational basis for discriminating between what in any piece of writing belongs to code and what derives from a writer's uniquely vulnerable self.

To know something about the power with which access to the "facts" of writing endows us, the reader should consider how skillfully and subtly I am managing in this sentence to exercise my individual talent—at this time in bourgeois culture when these rather than those power relations are in force—within the externally imposed limits of the coded medium in which I have elected to write, namely, the declarative English sentence. Now, from this sentence the reader may move to whole works and examine, say, *Tom Jones, Great Expectaions, Finnegans Wake*, and *Naked Lunch* (works that some audiences have been willing to regard, according to some criteria or other, as novels) as exemplifications of the felicitous conjunction of self and code. What we must inevitably recognize is that a distinction between self and code does not provide us with the first principles of either writing or reading. The terms of this distinction are not enabling terms, terms, that is, which enable us, without the specification of additional principles or categories, to reason to necessary conclusions about literary "facts."

The more general our sense of genre criteria, the more we necessarily attribute to individual talent. The more precise our generic criteria, the less we attribute to talent. In either case critical inquiry cannot go much beyond the naming of parts. More important, even if there were general agreement about the precise nature of the specific *forms* of writing which, in the absence of adequate definitions of literary forms, we tend to classify under such inclusive types as novel, lyric, tragedy, and so on, we would still have to deal with the fact that native force (or the uniquely vulnerable self) is not directly inferrable from the observable traits of the work itself. Many of those traits exhibit the effects of forces just as external to the writer as the "coded medium" is assumed to be. Some of those traits may be precisely what they are as a result of training, models, reading, social-political events, philosophical currents, and so forth. "Genre," however defined, is simply not the only element of writing with which an individual talent engages.

In its unimpeachable form the basic point (that to write anything a writer must employ coded media) is, for the writer or critic, without value or, at best, of nugatory significance, since the polarity or binary system on which it is based can achieve determinate meaning only when it is subordinated to a particular and coherent critical framework, incorporating primary assumptions about the nature of literary materials, forms, purposes, values, ends, and so on. Essentially, what is exhibited in the argument I have been examining is a particular version of what has virtually become the habitual mode of critical reasoning, the dialectical mode, based on an a priori conception of literature as discourse (or language) admitting of discussion in terms of content and form (or of the manifest and the latent, the literal and the figural, the overt and the covert, or the potent and the powerless). The "theory" underlying the discussion of literary writing is simply a cognitively inadequate tool of analysis.

In sum, it seems clear that an adequate understanding of genre can only proceed from an initial analysis of literary works in terms of local justification conditions.[31] Once a particular work has been constructed and then understood in light of the "theory of meaning" or system of intentionality that provides the conditions of possibility of its meaning, structure, and effect (once the work has been seen as the functional and consequential result of the writer's imposing some form upon some material in some fashion for some purpose), the work can then be discussed in relation to other works that are similarly formed out of similar materials in similar ways for similar purposes (with similarity being reflective, as always, of our ways of noting likeness). Works that we deem to be similar along all four of these lines of differentiation will be considered by us as representative of a distinguishable class of works. (Of course, we are free to establish categories along any lines of similarity that interest us, as long as we recognize that some categorizations are more rigorous, more satisfying, and, yes, better than others—not absolutely better, mind you, but better all the same, given our interests and capacities.) At any rate, analysis in terms of justification conditions precedes, because it is a basis for, generic classification. Finally, generic classification, of the rigorous kind hinted at here, involves the comparative analysis of works in terms of degrees of likeness/difference obtaining in the materials, manners, forms, and purposes of particular works, with priority being assigned to similarity in principles of construction or systems of justification. The rigorous work of genre identification has hardly begun, it seems, and the history of forms (genres) has yet to be written.

# Chapter 8
# Teaching Critical Principles in Introductory Literature Courses

It is a truth universally acknowledged that an instructor in possession of the first few days of a new term is often in want of material to fill that time when students are sizing up instructors, dropping and adding courses, buying books, and reading their first assignments. For my "Introduction to Fiction" courses I have developed a set of exercises to supply that want and to keep Cotton Mather from mounting the pulpit in my head and laying on about wasting time and doing the devil's work. These exercises enable me at once to address complex critical issues and to expose to daylight many of the unexamined assumptions that students bring to the reading of literary texts (e.g., any opinion, sincerely felt, is as good as any other opinion; there's no such thing as a correct interpretation of a literary work; there can be no argument about taste or response—the "this I like/that I don't," "loved her/hated him," "beauties/faults" approach to aesthetic evaluation).

The first exercise is presented as a typed version of handwritten notes that—so the fiction goes—I have found in a parking lot. The students are asked to construct or reconstruct the underlying human drama that informs these discrete particulars with specific point, emphasis, and value. In other words, they are asked to find or create a controlling, unifying conception that implies all the particular entries and is implied by them. They must try to accommodate all the entries to a central explanatory hypothesis, to justify the entries in terms of some intelligible narrative, to locate or make the conception for which these entries are the conditions of satisfaction. The entries or notations appear in the following not entirely random or arbitrary sequence, though no attention has been given to chronology—since once cannot know chronology in advance of a "theory of meaning" for the items:

Meet Jane at 9:00 P.M.
See lawyer on Tues.
Alice's plane leaves at 10:00 P.M. Thurs.; returns next Tues. at
    8:30 P.M.
Pick up tickets to concert Fri. morning
Susan sleeping at Paula's Fri. and Sat.
Mike's camping trip Fri., Sat., and Sun.
Send flowers with note to Jane on Fri.
Get key to cabin from Peter on Thurs.
Pick up chains from gas station
Pick up parcel from drugstore Fri. morning
Supper for Susan Sun. evening

After we explore a few of the manifold situational and relational possibilities (Is Jane the wife? Is Alice? Are Paula and Mike the children of
the notetaker? Is Peter a coworker? a real estate agent? and so on), someone, usually rather quickly, comes up with a tawdry, soap-operaish fiction
involving infidelity with Jane (the mistress) at a cabin in the mountains
while Alice (the wife) and Paula and Mike (the children) are away, a fiction that, once stated, achieves virtually unanimous acceptance as the
correct one or the most "fitting" or "satisfying" one. (Of course, there
are always a few holdouts, who remain partial, indeed, stubbornly loyal
to "organizing conceptions" that are usually stunningly different from
the "consensus" version, notable either for their convoluted perversity
or for their wholesome dullness.)

     There is, of course, no correct fiction underlying these diverse parti-
culars. Time, place, and kind of event are too uncertain; social relationships are hopelessly unsettled; things (chains, parcel, tickets, and so
forth) are too willing to participate in too many, indeed, innumerable
adventures, and so on. The data will support an indefinitely large number and assortment of human dramas. What the "consensus" fiction
does have, however, is explanatory power. It is not simply the case that
this hypothesis appeals to a cheap and tiresomely familiar scheme of
naughtiness (its acceptance is strongly, though not perhaps compell-
ingly, prompted by its cheapness), or that it is in any way "privileged."
Rather, it immediately satisfies the primary standards against which, intuitively and deliberately, all hypotheses are tested for their soundness,
that is, scope and precision. The fiction or hypothesis has sufficient
scope to account for the whole situation, and it has sufficient precision
to find a place for each particular. It implies all the data and is implied
by them. Moreover, the hypothesis, despite—perhaps because of—its
homely predictability, is inherently interesting. And it has economy.
Other explanations require either the generation of additional details

(that is, particulars not specified in the original notes) to account for the coherent organization of the "textual" givens or the postulation of a situation that is dull to the point of narcosis or narcolepsy.

Why bother to reconstruct a scene that contains intrinsically no latent drama at all? Rather than pestering anyone with these notes, it would be better simply to deposit the notes in the nearest trash can and to get dully on with one's own routine existence. Not many intelligences equipped by evolutionary endowment to fire more neurons per minute than a mollusk would be much gratified to learn, for example, that Jane is the note-taker's sister who is coming to town to have elective surgery—hence the parcel from the drugstore (a filled prescription) and the flowers—and that the lawyer's services are required because Alice and the notetaker are buying the cabin from Peter.

With or without the prompting of the instructor, the natural tendency of any mind confronted with these notes would be, I think, to impose upon them a pattern of significance. As beings, we are slanted in the direction of coherence; otherwise, we would die in a welter of particulars or randomness. If nature abhors a vacuum, mind or consciousness abhors sequentiality without consequentiality; mind is gestalt-prone. Indeed, as Mark Johnson has noted, "our most basic contact with rationality occurs in a culturally embedded process of story construction in response to standard sets of questions [for example, who, what, where, why, when questions] that can be answered by a limited range of sanctioned types of narrative."[1] John Searle makes a similar point when he notes that "Just as our particular experiences occur to us as aspectual, i.e., with aspectual shapes" (seeing, for example, is "seeing as"; we see something *as* a tree, *as* a fork, *as* a pop fly, and so forth), "so there is a narrative shape to sequences of experiences."[2] Rationality or structure would seem to be a basic feature of human thought, since it is only relative to some structure or system of rationality that items or objects have reference and meaning. Thus, we may properly speak of a rationality constraint on consciousness. To see something *as* something (and all seeing is seeing-as) is already to be implicated in a *system* of entailments, in which what we see belongs with or fits with some things and not other things.

Among other things, this little exercise gives students quick and easy access to the processes involved in hypothesis forming and testing: strong evidence must be adduced in support of any reading, and reading must be accountable to the particulars. Not so incidentally, it informs them that all reading involves the framing of hypotheses, that particulars cannot be understood at all except in reference to informing conceptions or justification conditions. Independently of Kant, they learn that there are no percepts without concepts. But the exercise also shows them that even to aspire to adequacy a reading (an interpretation, a sense of the whole) must imply and be implied by the specific details of the text. At the very least, I hope to make clear to students that reading literature is a rigorous undertaking and that our task is what Virginia Woolf said it was: to "free ourselves from the cramp and confinement of our own personalities" and to show that, for good and sufficient reasons, "our impressions hold good for others" as well.

What is learned quickly and somewhat surreptitiously or clandestinely by the students would undoubtedly take many days and weeks to unpack in a philosophically respectable way. At a minimum, however, I would note (in a more expansive manner than I have above) that there is no meaning in the disparate notes or in any other *list* of words, phrases, or sentences apart from some structure or pattern. To put the case more elaborately and formally, truth is prior to reference, inasmuch as the reference of terms, and hence their content, is determined by the conditions justifying their *use* on specific occasions. All words are like Wittgenstein's "rabbit-duck" figure in that they can be construed logically in many different ways. Indeed, as Crispin Wright observes, "it is no exaggeration to say that any piece of information may, in the context of an appropriate epistemic background, be relevant to any particular belief."[3] Elucidating a point made by Gottlob Frege and extended by Donald Davidson, Bjørn Ramberg observes that "Only in the context of a sentence does a word have meaning, . . . and only in the context of a language [a framework, a conceptual scheme, a "form of life"] does a sentence (and therefore a word) have meaning." Further, the "meanings of sentences and words are explained in terms of the role they play in the total structure."[4] To think about something in a particular way is to see it, as I noted earlier, as belonging or fitting with some other things and not a whole lot of other things, and what is most fitting is most satisfying, most satisfying at once to the things involved and to the agent (of making and interpretation).

The human story or drama adopted with alacrity by the students as the condition of possibility of the meaningful relation of the disparate items has no absolute status as the correct or right one. Still, it is certainly better, in the ways that we tend to determine "better," than all the proposed alternatives. It makes for the best system of intentionality—for the time being at least, until some better hypothesis is offered. And, unless there are compelling grounds for not doing so (and I can think of none), I see no reason why we would resist attributing the text's richest, most fitting, and, hence, "best" structure of virtuous (that is, "right"-tending) and satisfying entailments to the *author* of this exercise, no matter how tawdry and small a thing it finally is morally and artistically considered. Not so curiously or oddly, the fulsomely banal drama the class settled on was just the one from which *I* worked as I sought to supply apparently disparate items for this exercise.

The other two pieces of business in my opening routine involve a form of a game sometimes called "gossip." I select several students (usually five) from the class to participate in the retelling of two short narratives that I have written. Once we are in the hall, I read a narrative to the first student out of the hearing of the others; the narrative is then relayed to the other students seriatim; once the story has been passed on, the students return to the class, one by one, and relate what they have heard. (Read on, what you suppose will happen does not happen perhaps in precisely the way you suppose.) The two narratives are:

1. After listening to Johnny Sunshine and the Pipe Joint Company, three men, two wearing gray business suits and one wearing a saffron robe, walk to the corner of Lane and High, where they sit down and then proceed to chant and meditate. With eyes closed and voices droning, they appear to slip into a trance. Slowly, one of the men gets up and, after removing from his clothes a shiny metal object that he had concealed, goes directly into the small frame house behind him. Shortly thereafter, several screams are heard, and five minutes later, the man emerges from the house carrying a large black box and wearing a bright green hat.

2. After several months of marriage, a husband had come to suspect his wife's fidelity for a variety of reasons; particularly, he had noticed in recent weeks that, when greeting him at night in their two-bedroom, two-bath apartment, after he had spent a hard day working in the decentering room of the Derrida, de Man, and Hartman semiotic factory, his wife's ardor had diminished. He reluctantly entertained the idea that she had a paramour, plaguing his mind with lascivious visions.

Determined to ascertain the truth once and for all, he left the apartment one Tuesday morning, as usual, carrying, as usual, his Samsonite attaché case, and, after circling the block containing several modest, respectable, brownstone buildings very much like his own, he went immediately to Paul's Bar and Grill, which was situated directly opposite to his building. From the front booth he commanded an unobstructed view of the entrance to his building. Around eleven o'clock, he watched a young man, dressed in a manner totally out of keeping with the sartorial standards of the middle-class neighborhood, enter his building after looking furtively up and down the quiet street. When the young man had not left the building after fifteen minutes, the husband, consumed with rage, jealousy, and despair, rushed across the street, up the stairs, and into the apartment, all the time screaming his wife's name hysterically. Running into the large bedroom, he found his wife naked, but alone, in bed. Convinced that the young man had made a hasty retreat as he was dashing up the stairs, the husband proceeded to ferret him out. He ran from room to room opening and slamming doors and looking under furniture. In desperation, he ran back to the bedroom, looked under the bed, and checked the master bathroom. Finally, he opened the wardrobe closet. There, half-dressed, stood the young man, looking rather sheepish. Furiously, the husband screamed: "What the hell are you doing here?" With a puzzled and somewhat philosophical expression on his face, the young man replied: "Everybody's gotta be someplace."

Because I have tried these "stories" out on several classes and have witnessed many students of varying abilities and powers of retention do unto them remarkably similar things, I think I can safely say that the transformations the narratives undergo are attributable to, are caused by, the nature of the material and that no matter how often the experiment is repeated the same *kinds* of results will appear. Much of the first narrative, as might be expected, is lost, and what is lost in one telling is lost irretrievably. Invariably, each version becomes progressively shorter with each retelling until an easily transmittable brevity is achieved, and from first to last we are treated to a series of events lacking meaning, relation, or significance. (Interestingly, events may be lost, but they are never rearranged; there is a rudimentary chronological appropriateness to the details.) What I had hoped and originally assumed would happen—that the odd member of the group, the one wearing the saffron robe, would go into the house, that the shiny object would become a knife or gun, a weapon at any rate, or that among the events (the removal of the object from concealment, the entering of the house, the screaming, the emergence from the building, and the carrying out of a large black box) some connections would be established—never happens. If the first teller has a weak short-term memory, the exercise could be terminated after the second telling, for by then the "story" has been reduced to so few details that it is in no danger of suffering further truncation. Fidelity to and preservation of the narrative depends entirely upon powers of concentration and recall. The tale is very short, but I have not yet met five students for whom it was too short.

Why the mind, that beast with a rage for order, does not create the dramatic connections it does not find can be explained, I think, by considering that the tale lacks not order, but richness and significance; it is empty, but not "incomplete." The narrative has sequentiality, and apparently it does not aspire to consequentiality. If these events were presented to us in this fashion by a friend, we would feel compelled to ask for more information, to ask such questions as, "Well, so what?" "What happened?" "Why did she scream?" and so forth. But unlike the disparate notes in the previous example, the events of this story do not seek more formal completion than they already have. What is lacking here is not so much a principle of form, a principle of integration but, rather, a sufficient stock of details begging to be teased into a meaningful and coherent relationship. Chronological sequence in and of itself isn't very interesting or much of a crowd pleaser, but it is sometimes justification enough to satisfy us. The mind in this case exerts all its energy in recollection. There may be a million stories in the big city, but some of them do not make a good tale; some are pointless, characterized more by mere succession than by suspense, surprise, or emotional interest. Curiously, I'm moderately interested in all the events of this story. Each is inherently interesting, at least in a small sense. Taken together, however, they don't seem to belong to a single system of concatenation or justification.

Surprisingly enough, the second narrative, that of the outraged husband, though it is more than three times the length of the first (about 350 words to 110), survives the five retellings more or less intact, at least in its essentials. When I first presented this tale, I had hoped that much of it would be preserved, but as I watched the eyes of the student to whom I read it glaze over and saw the panic within become increasingly visible with the recitation of each additional sentence, I found my confidence in the likelihood of preservation diminishing. As I went on interminably, I could almost hear the brain cells crying out for relief, and during some parts of the reading, the student seemed to be attending only to his anxiety and not at all to the narrative. But, artistic structure and sound principles be praised, this student and all his successors have managed, in spite of their initial stark terror, to keep this tale (this trite, this lame joke) coherent and complete in all retellings.

Even more surprising, to me at least, is the fact that an unusually large number of indifferent, irrelevant, or nonessential details (the Samsonite attaché case, the number of baths in the apartment, the brownstone building, and so on) are retained in the several rehearsals of the tale. Moreover, in the repetition of this narrative a detail once dropped is not necessarily lost forever, as was the case with the saffron-robe narrative. For example, if one student neglects to mention looking under the bed, a subsequent teller may "re-introduce" it. Of course, in this as in other "recovered" details, the students display not clairvoyance or other supernatural powers but a readiness and a capacity to provide particulars intrinsic or appropriate to the situation or type of narrative. They supply material satisfactions to the internal needs of the operative system of rationality; they give the text what it wants or what at least it can use. Much of my language disappears, of course, but nothing essential to the narrative falls out. Indeed, throughout the retellings, my language is often presented in paraphrase. Nevertheless, where my language exits, new language, analogous in meaning and value to mine, enters. In the process of retelling the tale, students find suitable, adequate, and appropriate substitutes for my specific terminology.

When we discuss the differences between these two narratives and try to account for the drastic abridgment of one narrative and the essential preservation of the other, we quickly come up with what I take to be strikingly intriguing and sound answers. I am regularly (almost always, in fact) struck by the subtlety of the students' explanations. They immediately hit upon the obvious reasons for the differences and then quickly go beyond them, coming up with sophisticated ideas which they all instantly grasp but for which they do not have a developed critical vocabulary. That vocabulary I attempt to provide, even as I also try to expand on what is implicated in their remarks, by displaying their brachiating thought in full ramification. (This, as the *Beowulf* poet might say in characteristic understatement, is no unpleasant business.)

From the jealous-husband narrative, we together discover much that is useful. The narrative is retained because it is a consecutive, consequential, and complete comic action, one that is governed by a distinct, identifiable end—the punch line—that is the subsumptive, controlling principle of the work as a whole, the conditioning possibility from which the details derive, and to which they owe their full intelligibility and their emotional salience (or comic propensity). The writer, as well as the teller or reteller, has the punch line for security; it is in relation to that that all the antecedent parts must be ordered. With only the last couple of lines to work from, we could create a reasonable facsimile of our actual narrative, one that had not only situational perplexities but also tonal and attitudinal qualities in common with the Ur-text. Reasoning backward from the punch line, we are able to determine (or recall) that such and such a dilemma involving such and such characters in such and such a situation is necessary.

To make the essential elements of the action necessary and probable, it is only required that we get a minimum of three players in the right places at the right times. The action contains very few *essential* details (my narrative is only a highly elaborated—and unnecessarily gorgeous— version of one of Myron Cohen's old jokes), and they are suspicion, search, and resolution. Moreover, the tale has few *factorial* details. I borrow this term from Elder Olson and mean by it those details that are necessary to get the husband out of the house and into a place where he can observe his building, to get the young man into the house, and to get the husband involved in a search of the apartment. These, along with the essential details, are always retained, because the completion and formal effectiveness of the work depend upon them and because the form demands them. Writer and teller are governed by formal imperatives or what we have earlier called rationality or justification constraints.

Beyond the factorial and the essential we have an enormous number of what we can call (again following Elder Olson) *ornamental* details,[5] though in this narrative the nonessential particulars (Samsonite attaché case, name of the factory, and so on) function less in the service of making the scene interesting, beautiful, or vivid than in the service of confusion and unnecessary complication. That so many of these details are retained in retelling testifies, if perhaps quietly, to the security that knowledge of the end or purpose provides; they insinuate their way into remembrance almost incidentally, in large part because one does not have to strain to hold onto the narrative line.

From these facts of the text we can move easily into a discussion of synonymity (that is, of how different words satisfy the same justification conditions) and what E. D. Hirsch calls "intrinsic genres" and others call "principles of form." For what allows the substitution of analogous terms is a working conception of the kind of discourse one is involved with, an inexplicit sense of the whole that guides writing and recollection. It is that something only in relation to which the words have meaning and function, call it whatever you will—a "practice," a "theory of meaning," an intrinsic genre, a set of justification conditions, a principle of form. It is that which makes every *different* telling of the story a telling of the *same* story. If we never recollect even relatively short passages word for word, we regularly find terms that fall within the range of toleration constituted by the conditions of possibility of our task or tale, constituted by the form of our meaning.

This constitutive conception is the intrinsic genre that becomes explicitly realized only when the work is completed, or retold. Furthermore, all along the line alternative words can replace those in my version so long as those words are of a type compatible with the originals and consonant with the form. Sometimes, of course, small changes in the words can make a big and crucial difference in the meaning. (When that is the case the form is right to enjoin its patrons, "please, no substitutions.") But in general small differences are rectified by the overall intentionality. They are subsumed by or made functional (that is, meaningful) relative to the system of rationality to which they are subordinated, just in the way a multiplicity of phonemic differences in different voices and dialects are rectified by our understanding of their contribution to the expression of the same word or the same meaning within a sentence. For example, you say "fawg," and I say "fahg," but we both refer to—and understand that we refer to—*fog.*

Mental kinds (beliefs, meanings, experiences, understandings, de sires, intentions, and so on) are, in general, like artifact kinds in that both kinds admit multiple realizations, since content is always relative to function and is not a matter of features with underlying real essences. Simply, just as what is in some very fundamental sense the "same" duck (Donald, say) can be realized in wood, paper, clay, and so forth, so the same meaning can be realized in different words. As Colin McGinn notes, "citing the content of a mental state [like citing the content of any artifact] is giving its function" within a system of relationships.[6] Words are valuable and apt relative to their functions, and function determines the appropriateness of words. Hence, to expand on previous points for a moment, it is clear that we have more dictional latitude with ornamental than with factorial and essential details, though even the latter allow for substitutions. Deviation from original phrasing is possible at every point, but only so long as the substitution does not violate the ongoing integrity of the form or genre or overall justification conditions.

In class, I usually move next to the problems we encounter when we try to demonstrate the value and appropriateness of any given interpretation, but for the purposes of this chapter, and in deference to the overworked patience of the reader, I shall conclude by reviewing the three examples and commenting briefly on how I use them later in the term. In the first example (the string of "facts"), we have an instance of a presumably consequential but nonconsecutive action; in the second (the "saffron robe" story), an example of a consecutive but inconsequential action; and in the third (the "jealous husband" tale), a consecutive and consequential action. When all three examples are examined in the space of a couple of days, the students begin to learn how to participate effectively in the creation and testing of critical hypotheses; in addition, they are exposed to a wide range of critical problems. Throughout the term, we deal mainly, of course, with consecutive and consequential works (the "jealous husband" joke is the only illustrative piece which, with the gracious allowance of the reader, can be considered as art), but we are repeatedly reminded—as we run bump into recalcitrant works that cannot be assimilated by our working assumptions about form—that literary works are organized in marvelously diverse ways.

In this course I usually teach *Rasselas* and *Pride and Prejudice*, and sometime during the discussion of Austen's work I ask the students to recall as much as they can of the second and third tales discussed at the beginning of the term. The second comes back haltingly in *disjecta membra*, but the third returns more or less complete and well accommodated. I then ask them to locate a scene in *Rasselas* (for example, When exactly does Rasselas meet the philosopher of nature?) and in *Pride and Prejudice* (for example, When does Wickham's "history" of Darcy appear?). The Austen episode is easily and quickly placed, whereas the one from *Rasselas* is not. We have encountered the grounds of these differences earlier. Although massively superior to the joke in quality and human significance, *Pride and Prejudice* is, like the joke, a consecutive and consequential action, dependent for its effectiveness upon the initiation, complication, and resolution of problems about which we are made to care because (at least in the novel) of the ethical quality of the agents and the seriousness of their involvement in the events.

*Rasselas*, on the other hand, is like our first example of random notes, in that by and large the order of most of the events is not crucial to the purpose of the work. It is like the saffron robe narrative in that the nature and placement of specific details are not readily recalled. Yet, in spite of these similarities, we also recognize that *Rasselas* is a complete and effective work of art. What we come to realize, of course, is that although *Rasselas* uses the devices of the novel, that is, the devices of consequential action (for example, characters, dialogue, a sequence of events, and so forth), it is unified by something other than action. It is unified by ideas, by problems relating to the kinds and degrees of happiness possible to human beings in this contingent and probationary state of life. What concerns us is not character and action, but thought. When we consider the work as an apologue, a work governed in all its particulars by a body of ideas pertaining to a specific area of human concern, and not as a novel of consequential action, we discover something worth knowing about the diversity of artistic forms and the imperatives that underlie their integrity.

Among other things, students are reminded that whatever else they may be, works of literature (works of art generally) are artifactual practices, structures of intentionality with recoverable senses, emphases, and values. At this time in critical history, when the study of literature tends to focus on anything but the work as a unique product of artistic choices—when the focus is on, for example, the preconstructional conditions of the work's possibility in language, history, ideology, gender, race, class, and so on—it is important to remind ourselves that, as Catherine Elgin insists, "we design category schemes [including works of art] with more or less specific purposes in mind and integrate into the scheme such values and priorities [such concepts and details] as we think will serve those purposes."[7] What at this level of instruction students most need to understand, it seems to me, is that our texts are first and foremost artistic practices requiring appropriate moves. To borrow from Crispin Wright, a practice can be characterized as "any form of intentional, purposeful activity" and a move as "any action performed within the practice for its characteristic purposes."[8] This notion of practice squares perfectly with a view articulated by Kenneth Burke many years ago, and still relevant to our classroom activities: "the poet makes a poem; and his ways of making the poem are *practices* which implicitly involve principles, or precepts" (or, as I have been inclined to say, justification conditons). "The critic, in matching the poetry with a poetics, seeks to make these implicit principles explicit."[9] What we strive to understand is the workingness of the details within a system of artistic interest.

Because we have many interests that the texts have not (or that the texts have on the sly or *unintentionally*), and because so much talk is in the air about "theory" (by which is meant something generally subversive of authors, texts, and determinate meaning within knowable structures of intentionality, something involving the social construction of texts and the radical instability of reference), it is often useful in the first few days of class to distinguish between internal and external goods and internal and external causes. The notions of internal and external goods I derive, in large measure, from the work of Alasdair MacIntyre, though in my classes I revise and extend them in ways that he would not necessarily endorse. Like the critics and philosophers cited immediately above, MacIntyre thinks of artistic activities as practices, and internal goods, in his view, are those choices that serve the interests of the practice. Basically, a practice is a "coherent and complex form of activity through which goods internal to that form of activity are realized in the course of trying to achieve those standards of excellence which are appropriate to, and partially definitive of, that form of activity."[10] The external goods that a practice might bring (wealth, fame, or power, for example) can be achieved by many means unrelated to the practice in question, whereas the internal goods can only be specified in terms of the practice or artifact. The internal goods are "virtues," to use MacIntyre's term, or features of the practice; they are features, powers, and values within the possibilities of the system of realized intentionality. Internal and external causes will become apparent in the process of discussing an example.

Let our example be a portrait, one of a particular individual and one designed to meet the ordinary, person-in-the-street test of verisimilitude or likeness. Since in this case the formal object of intentionality is a "traditional" portrait (of my uncle Elmer, say), all the internal goods would be features contributing to the likeness. At this level, the artist would be obliged to get the nose "right," have only one ear on each side of the face, make the chin like Elmer's chin, and so on. The *internal causes* of such internal goods are such material and efficient things as paints, brushstrokes, coloring, shading, and so on. On the side of *external goods*, on the other hand, we have, for example, the current and potential market value of the portrait, its ability to hold open a window (this is a possible good of the portrait, but not a good internal to the functioning of the portrait as a portrait of Elmer), the admiration it brings from the family and the general public, and so on.

When we reach the *external causes*, we arrive at the scene where most of the critical and theoretical activity goes on today. These are the preconditional or preconstructional causes that operate in the background of the production of anything whatsoever, at any particular time or in any particular life. In short, here we are concerned with the historical, social, ideological, cultural, psychological, racial, gender determinants of production, which are responsible for all production but which can produce nothing in particular. Though necessary to and inevitably entangled with all making and producing, these are not causes into which particular practices can be resolved or from which particular products can be deduced, though because they are variously represented and implicated in particular works they can become independent sources of interest and can both inform and be modified by specific works.

Indeed, by close scrutiny of their variously exemplified features in particular productions, we can come to learn something interesting and valuable about mind, language, history, culture, ideology, and so forth. The "jealous husband" story, for instance, wears many of its class and gender biases on its sleeve, and a careful reader could clearly tease larger social implications out of its "middle-class" furnishings and surroundings and out of its not very deeply concealed ideological assumptions. In our early discussions of our exempla, in fact, we consider a few of the extra-intentional aspects of the three tales, but we regularly return to the main business of elucidating the internal conditions of our shared understandings of our texts. Our main business is not, alas, the main business of many literature classrooms today, but in a real sense it is, or seems to me to be, absolutely prerequisite to any other serious critical business. And there is in this business a collection of problems and difficulties equal to the most subtle and sophisticated understanding.

Each of us manages to get through the first days of every new term by one means or another, and what I have offered above are merely a few devices that work for me in my efforts to get students to think about artistic practices and their entailments, to integrate important critical principles into introductory literature courses (the devices will work for upper-divison courses as well, I think), and to establish a "level of discourse" for the rest of the term. The theoretical commitments that more than peep out at the reader of this essay are perhaps not for everyone, but I suspect that my examples, properly adapted, would be useful to instructors of many critical persuasions. What I do know with certainty is that, however sophisticated or clumsy my devices may be, they do accomplish one good thing: they get students into the habit of talking, of participating in class, and once that habit is established, it tends to extend itself, sometimes to the very end of the term.

# Notes

## Introduction. Language in Use, or the Semantics of Presence

1. The first quotation is from Michael Dummett, *The Seas of Language* (Oxford: Clarendon Press, 1993), 104; and the second from *Origins of Analytic Philosophy* (Cambridge, Mass.: Harvard University Press, 1994), 158.

2. My comments here roughly paraphrase Susan Hurley's definition of "pragmatic inconsistency"; see her "Martha Nussbaum: Non-Relative Virtues: An Aristotelian Approach," in *The Quality of Life*, ed. Martha C. Nussbaum and Amartya Sen (Oxford: Clarendon Press, 1993), 273.

3. Nagel's remark is taken from *The View from Nowhere* (Oxford: Oxford University Press, 1986), 84.

4. Michael Dummett, *Origins of Analytic Philosophy*, 187–88. In this passage, Dummett's focus is on Chomsky and on attempts to reduce meanings and mental states to brain states, not, as mine is, on attempts to reduce meaning and content to relational or differential states.

5. For one such discussion, in connection with the Chinese-room thought experiment, see John Searle, *Minds, Brains, and Science* (Cambridge, Mass.: Harvard University Press, 1984), 31–33.

6. David Papineau, *Reality and Representation* (Oxford: Blackwell, 1987), 47.

7. Papineau, *Reality*, 47.

8. Alvin I. Goldman, *Epistemology and Cognition* (Cambridge, Mass.: Harvard University Press, 1986), 162.

9. For these remarks, and others relevant to this discussion, see Donald Davidson, "A Coherence Theory of Truth and Knowledge," reprinted in *Truth and Interpretation: Perspectives on the Philosophy of Donald Davidson*, ed. Ernest Lepore (Oxford: Blackwell, 1986), 307–19. In his efforts to show a constraint on belief from experience (arguing that experience is conceptual as well as sensory), John McDowell qualifies Davidson by averring that "nothing can count as a reason for holding a belief except something else that is also in the space of concepts" (including "experiences" and "appearings"). See McDowell's *Mind and World* (Cambridge, Mass.: Harvard University Press, 1994), 143.

10. Hilary Putnam, *Renewing Philosophy* (Cambridge, Mass.: Harvard University Press, 1992), 123.

11. John Pollock, *Knowledge and Justification* (Princeton, N. J.: Princeton University Press, 1974), 12.

12. Donald Davidson, "Locating Literary Language," in *Literary Theory After*

*Davidson*, ed. Reed Way Dasenbrock (University Park: Pennsylvania State University Press, 1993), 298.

13. Donald Davidson, "Rational Animals," *Dialecta* 36 (1982): 317–27. The passage is quoted here from John Heil, *The Nature of True Minds* (Cambridge: Cambridge University Press, 1992), 194.

14. James F. Harris, *Against Relativism: A Philosophical Defense of Method* (La Salle, Ill.: Open Court, 1992), 149.

15. Hilary Putnam, *Realism with a Human Face*, ed. James Conant (Cambridge, Mass.: Harvard University Press, 1990), 139.

16. Michael Luntley, *Language, Logic, and Experience* (La Salle, Ill.: Open Court, 1988), 168.

17. Dummett, *Origins*, 188, 7.

18. Mark Johnson, *The Body in the Mind: The Bodily Basis of Meaning, Imagination, and Reason* (Chicago: University of Chicago Press, 1987), 75.

19. John Searle, *The Rediscovery of the Mind* (Cambridge, Mass.: MIT Press, 1992), 177.

20. Putnam, *Human Face*, 115.

21. John Heil, *The Nature of True Minds* (Cambridge: Cambridge University Press, 1992), 212.

22. Dummett, *Seas of Language*, 104.

**Chapter 1. Authors and Books: The Return of the Dead from the Graveyard of Theory**

1. Jonathan Culler, *On Deconstruction: Theory and Criticism after Structuralism* (Ithaca, N.Y.: Cornell University Press, 1982), 7.

2. J. Hillis Miller, *Topographies* (Stanford, Calif.: Stanford University Press, 1995), 292.

3. Julia Kristeva, *Desire in Language: A Semiotic Approach to Literature and Art*, ed. Leon S. Roudiez, trans. Thomas Gora, Alice Jardine, and Leon S. Roudiez (New York: Columbia University Press, 1980), 66.

4. Vincent B. Leitch, *Deconstructive Criticism: An Advanced Introduction* (New York: Columbia University Press, 1983), 3.

5. Jacques Derrida, *Of Grammatology*, trans. Gayatri Chakravorty Spivak (Baltimore, Md.: Johns Hopkins University Press, 1976), 18.

6. Hilary Putnam, *Renewing Philosophy* (Cambridge, Mass.: Harvard University Press, 1992), 124.

7. Hilary Putnam, *The Many Faces of Realism* (La Salle, Ill.: Open Court, 1987), 36.

8. John Searle, *The Construction of Social Reality* (New York: The Free Press, 1995), 159. "Reality," then, is a condition of the possibility of representation, of reference and meaning, not itself an existent object or collection of objects in space and time (as Searle explains at length; see, for example, pp. 183, 186, 187).

9. Donald Davidson, "The Myth of the Subjective," in *Relativisim: Interpretation and Confrontation*, ed. Michael Krausz (Notre Dame, Ind.: University of Notre Dame Press, 1989), 160.

10. Hilary Putnam, *Realism with a Human Face*, ed. James Conant (Cambridge, Mass.: Harvard University Press, 1990), 139.

11. James F. Harris, *Against Relativism: A Philosophical Defense of Method* (La Salle, Ill.: Open Court, 1992), 84–85.

12. Putnam, *Human Face*, 125.
13. Mark Sacks, *The World We Found: The Limits of Ontological Talk* (London: Duckworth, 1989), 81.
14. Michael Devitt, *Realism and Truth*, 2nd ed. (Oxford: Blackwell, 1991), 244. My emphasis.
15. Searle, *Social Reality*, 166.
16. W. V. Quine, *Ontological Relativity and Other Essays* (New York: Columbia University Press, 1969), 50.
17. Mark Johnson, *The Body in the Mind: The Bodily Basis of Meaning, Imagination, and Reason* (Chicago: University of Chicago Press, 1987), 75.
18. Ernest Lepore and Barry Loewer, "A Putnam's Progress," in *Realism and Antirealism*, ed. Peter A. French, Theodore E. Uehling, Jr., and Howard K. Wettstein, *Midwest Studies in Philosophy*, 12 (Minneapolis: University of Minnesota Press, 1988), 468.
19. Eddy M. Zemach, "On Meaning and Reality," in *Relativism: Interpretation and Confrontation*, ed. Michael Krausz (Notre Dame, Ind.: University of Notre Dame Press, 1989), 69.
20. John Searle, *The Rediscovery of the Mind* (Cambridge, Mass.: MIT Press, 1992), 155.
21. Simon Blackburn, "Losing Your Mind: Physics, Identity, and Folk Burglar Protection," in *The Future of Folk Psychology*, ed. John D. Greenwood (Cambridge: Cambridge University Press, 1991), 201.
22. Elder Olson, "The Dialectical Foundations of Critical Pluralism," *Texas Quarterly* 9 (1966): 207.
23. I borrow the "exciting sheep" example from Michael Devitt and Kim Sterelny, *Language and Reality: An Introduction to the Philosophy of Language* (Cambridge, Mass.: MIT Press, 1987). For their discussion of the weaknesses of the incommensurability thesis, see pp. 180–83.
24. Michael Polanyi, *The Tacit Dimension* (Garden City, N.Y.: Doubleday, 1967), 34.
25. Ralph Rader, "The Concept of Genre in Eighteenth-Century Studies," in *New Approaches to Eighteenth-Century Literature*, ed. Philip Harth (New York: Columbia University Press, 1974), 86.
26. Putnam, *Human Face*, 116.
27. Martha C. Nussbaum, *Love's Knowledge: Essays on Philosophy and Literature* (Oxford: Oxford University Press, 1990), 8, 9.
28. Michael Dummett, *The Seas of Language* (Oxford: Clarendon Press, 1993), 104–5.
29. W. V. Quine and J. S. Ullian, *The Web of Belief* (New York: Random House, 1970), 135.
30. R. S. Crane, "Critical and Historical Principles of Literary History," in *The Idea of the Humanities and Other Essays Critical and Historical*, 2 vols. (Chicago: University of Chicago Press, 1967), 2:105.
31. Catherine Z. Elgin and Nelson Goodman, *Reconceptions in Philosophy and Other Arts and Sciences* (Indianapolis: Hackett, 1988), 118–19. My emphasis.

### Chapter 2. The Inevitability of Professing Literature

1. Catherine Gallagher, "Re-Covering the Social in Recent Literary Theory," *Diacritics* 12 (1982): 40–48.

2. Jonathan Culler, *On Deconstruction: Theory and Criticism after Structuralism* (Ithaca, N.Y.: Cornell University Press, 1982); see especially the "Preface," pp. 7–13.

3. Richard Rorty, *Consequences of Pragmatism* (Minneapolis: University of Minnesota Press, 1982). See especially chapter 6, "Philosophy as a Kind of Writing: An Essay on Derrida."

4. Hayden White, *Metahistory: The Historical Imagination in Nineteenth-Century Europe* (Baltimore, Md.: Johns Hopkins University Press, 1973).

5. Alexander Pope, *An Essay on Man*, in *The Poems of Alexander Pope*, Twickenham Edition, vol. 3, pt. 1, ed. Maynard Mack (London: Methuen, 1950), 7. The relevant passage of "The Design" reads as follows in the original: "The disputes . . . have less sharpened the *wits* than the *hearts* of men against each other, and have diminished the practice, more than advanced the theory, of Morality."

6. In addition to Jonathan Culler's work (see note 2), the reader should note the following books, a mere sampling of output: Christopher Norris, *Deconstruction: Theory and Practice* (London and New York: Methuen, 1982); Vincent B. Leitch, *Deconstructive Criticism: An Advanced Introduction* (New York: Columbia University Press, 1983); Terry Eagleton, *Literary Theory: An Introduction* (Minneapolis: University of Minnesota Press, 1983); William Ray, *Literary Meaning: From Phenomenology to Deconstruction* (Oxford: Blackwell, 1984); William E. Cain, *The Crisis in Criticism: Theory, Literature, and Reform in English Studies* (Baltimore, Md.: Johns Hopkins University Press, 1984); Christopher Butler, *Interpretation, Deconstruction, and Ideology: An Introduction to Some Current Issues in Literary Theory* (Oxford: Clarendon Press, 1984); Raman Selden, *A Reader's Guide to Contemporary Literary Theory* (Brighton: The Harvester Press, 1985); Vincent B. Leitch, *American Literary Criticism from the Thirties to the Eighties* (New York: Columbia University Press, 1988); Roger Webster, *Studying Literary Theory: An Introduction* (New York: Arnold, 1989); Peter Collier and Helga Geyer-Ryan, eds., *Literary Theory Today* (Ithaca, N.Y.: Cornell University Press, 1990); and Richard Freadman and Seumas Miller, *Re-thinking Theory: A Critique of Contemporary Literary Theory and an Alternative Account* (Cambridge: Cambridge University Press, 1992).

7. Susan Hurley, "Martha Nussbaum: Non-Relative Virtues: An Aristotelian Approach," in *The Quality of Life*, ed. Martha C. Nussbaum and Amartya Sen (Oxford: Clarendon Press, 1993), 271.

8. I here paraphrase Michael Dummett; see his *Origins of Analytic Philosophy* (Cambridge, Mass.: Harvard University Press, 1993), 158. For the quotation from Colin McGinn, see his *Problems in Philosophy: The Limits of Inquiry* (Oxford: Blackwell, 1993), 65.

9. See, for example, J. Hillis Miller, "The Critic as Host," *Critical Inquiry* 3 (1974): 439–47.

10. See, for example, Paul de Man, *Allegories of Reading: Figural Language in Rousseau, Nietzsche, Rilke, and Proust* (New Haven, Conn.: Yale University Press, 1979).

11. Rorty, *Pragmatism*, 105.

12. Giovanna Borradori, *The American Philosopher* (Chicago: University of Chicago Press, 1994), 60.

13. Alasdair MacIntyre, *After Virtue: A Study in Moral Theory* (Notre Dame, Ind.: University of Notre Dame Press, 1981), 268–69.

14. John D. Greenwood, "Reasons to Believe," in *The Future of Folk Psychology: Intentionality and Cognitive Science*, ed. John D. Greenwood (Cambridge: Cambridge University Press, 1991), 72.

15. These standards achieve their fullest articulation in chapter 5 (pp. 197–232) of Wayne C. Booth's *Critical Understanding: The Powers and Limits of Pluralism* (Chicago: University of Chicago Press, 1979).

16. Alvin I. Goldman, *Epistemology and Cognition* (Cambridge, Mass.: Harvard University Press, 1986), 141.

17. The reader who wishes to know what can be said in defense of these propositions should consult Elder Olson, "*Hamlet* and the Hermeneutics of Drama," *Modern Philology* 56 (1964): 225–37.

18. Nelson Goodman, *Fact, Fiction, and Forecast* (Cambridge, Mass.: Harvard University Press, 1955), 67.

19. Putnam, *Renewing*, 122.

20. For one such approach to cure, see E. D. Hirsch, "Cultural Literacy," *American Scholar* 52 (1983): 159–69; for another, see M. H. Abrams, "What Is a Humanistic Criticism?," in *The Emperor Redressed: Critiquing Critical Theory*, ed. Dwight Eddins (Tuscaloosa: University of Alabama Press, 1995), 13–44.

## Chapter 3. Professionalism, Relativism, and Rationality

1. For a discussion of the autocrat/allocrat distinction, see E. D. Hirsch, Jr., "The Politics of Theories of Interpretation," *Critical Inquiry* 9 (1982): 240. Richard Rorty describes the hermeneuticist/epistemologist distinction in *Philosophy and the Mirror of Nature* (Princeton, N.J.: Princeton University Press, 1979), 315–56, and the kinds of Kantians in *Consequences of Pragmatism* (Minneapolis: University of Minnesota Press, 1982), 90–109. Extended commentary on the differences between traditionalists and their presumably more theoretically sophisticated colleagues can be found in Paul de Man, "The Return to Philology," *Times Literary Supplement* (10 December 1982): 1355–56. The realist/deconstructionist and the structuralist/poststructuralist dichotomies are virtually ubiquitous in recent criticism and hence figure in many books and essays. See, for example, Betty Jean Craige, *Literary Relativity: An Essay on Twentieth-Century Narrative* (Lewisburg, Pa: Bucknell University Press, 1982), especially chapter 1, "The Relativist Paradigm." Of course, Stanley Fish, whose relativism is a major focus of this essay, regularly distinguishes his position from that of the essentialists or "right-wing intellectuals." For responses to Fish that are particularly valuable for their analytic acuity, see, among others, Ralph W. Rader, "Fact, Theory, and Literary Explanation," *Critical Inquiry* 1 (1974): 245–72; Walter A. Davis, "The Fisher King: *Wille zur Macht* in Baltimore," *Critical Inquiry* 10 (1984): 668–94; and James Phelan, "Data, Danda, and Disagreement," *Diacritics* 13 (1983): 39–50; and Annette Barnes, *On Interpretation: A Critical Analysis* (Oxford: Blackwell, 1988).

2. Stanley Fish, "Anti-Professionalism," *New Literary History* 17 (1985): 106. This essay has been reprinted in *Doing What Comes Naturally: Change, Rhetoric, and the Practice of Theory in Literary and Legal Studies* (Durham, N.C.: Duke University Press, 1989), 215–46.

3. Fish, "Anti-Professionalism," 104.

4. Ibid., 94, 101.

5. Ibid., 93.

6. Ibid., 106.

7. Ibid., 104.

8. Ibid., 107.

9. This passage (and the preceding summary of "transperspectivity") is taken

from Mark Johnson, *Moral Imagination: Implications of Cognitive Science for Ethics* (Chicago: University of Chicago Press, 1993), 241. For Winter's full discussion, see his "*Bull Durham* and the Uses of Theory," *Stanford Law Review* 42 (1990): 639–93. I have elsewhere (in the Introduction) had occasion to quote Thomas Nagel's similar point: "the capacity to imagine new forms of hidden order, and to understand new conceptions created by others seems to be innate"; see his *The View from Nowhere* (Oxford: Oxford University Press, 1986), 84.

10. George Lakoff, *Women, Fire, and Dangerous Things: What Categories Reveal About the Mind* (Chicago: University of Chicago Press, 1987), 317.

11. For a fuller discussion of the defeasibility standard as it relates to interpretive communities, see Annette Barnes, *On Interpretation: A Critical Analysis* (Oxford: Blackwell, 1988).

12. W. V. Quine, *Theories and Things* (Cambridge, Mass.: Harvard University Press, 1981), 38.

13. Donald Davidson, "On the Very Idea of a Conceptual Scheme," *Proceedings and Addresses of the American Philosophical Association* 47 (1974): 16.

14. Donald Davidson, *Inquiries into Truth and Interpretation* (Oxford: Clarendon Press, 1984), 137.

15. Hilary Putnam, *Representation and Reality* (Cambridge, Mass.: MIT Press, 1988), 118.

16. Some critics—Barbara Herrnstein Smith, for example—try to "finesse" this argument out of respectability and authority, to usher it rudely out of court by insisting that its power or legitimacy, such as it is, depends upon a value (self-refutation) belonging to foundationalism or essentialism, to the universalist perspective that is being rejected or supplanted; thus, foundationalism applies its alien standard to matters outside its jurisdiction. See Barbara Herrnstein Smith, *Contingencies of Value: Alternative Perspectives for Critical Theory* (Cambridge, Mass.: Harvard University Press, 1988), 150–84. My answer, of course, is that "self-refutation" owes no special allegiance to foundationalism or essentialism. As a standard, it serves many causes on many fronts. It belongs to the class of transparadigmatic criteria discussed earlier; it is—like logic and rationality—a flexible, serviceable standard. The "self-refutation" argument may be easy to formulate, but it has our interest because it is a strong standard, capable of leading to a deep objection. Moreover, self-refutation, like rationality, is an operation of logic, and logic has no metaphysical allegiances but is, instead, a condition of the possibility of action or meaningful expression. As Hilary Putnam has observed, "Logic is a doctrine of the form of coherent thought. . . . [It] has no metaphyscial presuppositions at all. For to say that thought, in the normative sense of *judgment which is capable of truth* [a semantic, not a metaphysical matter], necessarily conforms to logic is *not* to say anything which a metaphysician has to explain." Putnam goes on to remark that "to explain anything presupposes logic. . . . [The laws of logic] are the formal presuppositions of thought" (Putnam, *Words and Life*, ed. James Conant [Cambridge, Mass.: Harvard University Press, 1994], 247). Akeel Bilgrami makes a similar point when he observes that "The norms of logic form an a priori constraint on the very possibility of interpretation" and that "Logical norms are highly context-free" (*Belief and Meaning* [Oxford: Blackwell, 1992], 101, 104).

17. One is reminded here of the positivist—at least we have analogous formations—whose tests for meaningfulness excluded from the category of the meaningful the very formulation by which the tests were expressed; the formulation was not itself "testable," for example.

18. Michael Polanyi uses the example of chess in several works; see, for example, his *The Tacit Dimension* (Garden City, N.Y.: Doubleday, 1967), 29–30, 34.

19. I have discussed above the *incomprehensibility* of the "incommensurability thesis" in connection with Davidson's analysis of radical interpretation. Here I stress that the understanding and comparison of theories depend on the sharing of referents across theories. To make the point, I draw once again on the pun or ambiguous sentence, on the yeomanly loyal "Alphonse likes exciting sheep" example. Understanding the ambiguity of this sentence requires us to see the same referents serving different meanings. In understanding such sentences, we daily perform with relative ease feats that the relativists (and incommensurabilists) have determined to be impossible.

20. Nelson Goodman, "Notes on a Well-Made World," *Partisan Review* 51 (1984): 279.

21. Ruth Anna Putnam, "Poets, Scientists, and Critics," *New Literary History* 17 (1985): 20.

22. For a similar discussion of methodological solipsism, as applied to Richard Rorty, see Hilary Putnam, *Realism and Reason* (Cambridge: Cambridge University Press, 1983), 234–40.

23. Stanley Fish, "Resistance and Independence: A Reply to Gerald Graff," *New Literary History* 17 (1985): 125.

24. In his response to Fish's essay, Gerald Graff makes a similar point, stating that he would "distinguish between critical standards which are 'institutional,' as all standards are by definition, and critical standards which are institutionally specific, as all are not." See Graff, "Interpretation on Tlön: A Response to Stanley Fish," *New Literary History* 17 (1985): 116.

25. Fish, "Resistance," 119.

26. Putnam, *Representation and Reality*, 104.

27. Davidson, "Very Idea," 7–14.

28. Davidson's view is here given as it is reported by Hilary Putnam in "The Craving for Objectivity," *New Literary History* 15 (1984): 233. See also Davidson, "Very Idea," 5–20.

29. Fish, "Resistance," 123.

30. Ibid., 122.

31. Ibid., 119.

32. Ibid., 120.

33. Ibid., 126.

34. Ibid.

35. In passing, we would note that this case has not been argued (it is merely asserted, repeatedly), and it seems to be one that gains in credibility and utility in proportion to its success in trivializing politics and ideology.

## Chapter 4. Ideology, Textual Practice, and Bakhtin

1. Louis Montrose, "The Elizabethan Subject and the Spenserian Text," in *Literary Theory/Renaissance Texts*, ed. Patricia Parker and David Quint (Baltimore, Md.: Johns Hopkins University Press, 1986), 305.

2. Simon Evnine offers us convenient access to Donald Davidson's complex and variously articulated conception of "charity" in interpretation, when he writes: "The Principle of Charity . . . is not a single principle which governs interpretation, namely, interpret so that the objects of interpretation are

generally true believers, but rather a collection of all those principles which together regulate the ways in which beliefs, desires, and actions rationally connect with each other." Evnine goes on to note that " 'belief,' 'desire,' 'action,' and 'linguistic meaning' are all, according to [the philosopher David] Lewis, theoretical terms, and the theory of which they are a part is the everyday theory of folk psychology. This theory is itself made up of a whole host of platitudes which are nothing other than the applications of the directives of the Principle of Charity. Indeed, the Principle of Charity could be taken as the skeleton of the theory of folk psychology. In relation to intentional concepts—e.g., belief, desire, and so on—the Principle of Charity is true by definition, or analytic. As David Lewis puts it, a person 'might have no beliefs, desires, or meaning at all, but it is analytic that if he does have them then they more or less conform to the constraining principles by which the concepts of belief, desire, and meaning are defined.' " See Evnine, *Donald Davidson* (Stanford, Calif.: Stanford University Press, 1991), 110, 112.

When I talk about psychological explanations, I talk about explanations in the sense meant by Davidson (and others). Put most basically, any explanation of any kind of intentional, purposeful action depends on the resources of folk psychology, and there are no contents of any kind (for us) in the absence of intentionality. In all, then, *charity* is a general term designed to comprehend all those platitudes on which we rely when we interpret action or meaning, or which govern the ways belief, desires, and actions rationally interact with each other. Charity is the name we give to all those rough and ready rules and assumptions we employ everyday whenever we assume that we are dealing not with mere movements or motions, but with actions and events which are by definition necessarily dependent on reasons (e.g., beliefs and desires) that are also the causes of the behavior.

3. M. M. Bakhtin, *The Dialogic Imagination: Four Essays*, trans. Caryl Emerson and Michael Holquist, ed. Michael Holquist (Austin: University of Texas Press, 1981), 333. All the quoted material can be found on page 333.

4. Bakhtin, *Dialogic Imagination*, 333–34. The quoted material is taken from these pages, with emphasis added to "discourse" here (and elsewhere in this discussion). It is important to note that in Bakhtinian—as in New Critical, deconstructive, and most forms of historicist—analysis, literature is treated "rhetorically"—that is, as a kind of "discourse." As discourse, it is concerned inevitably and chiefly with *meanings* or themes, theses, ideas, and, typically, with all these in binary or oppositional relations. Also, Bakhtin, like so many modern critics, writes in a style that is dense, dark, and obscure, one that does not easily give up its sense. He, like so many others riding the circumlocomotive of current theory, is caught up in what J. L. Austin somewhere calls the "ivresse des grands profondeurs."

5. Bakhtin, *Dialogic Imagination*, 361.

6. Ibid., 366.

7. One is not required to be a very astute reader to recognize here, albeit outfitted in different terminological dress, the logical distinctions and argumentative maneuvers that characterize not only the old New Criticism but also the newer "new criticism"—deconstruction and New Historicism. The method of reasoning is the "abstract" or "dialectical" method, in the exercise of which "occult entities" clash by night (in the fog); it deals, as Hume would say, in "matters of relation," in the logical and dialectical relations of terms, separated from contact with any referential entities or "facts." It is criticism at the formal, syntactic

level, not at the semantic, pragmatic level. Mystical agents and agencies operate heavy machinery (that is, abstractions) in a galaxy far away.

8. Bakhtin, *Dialogic Imagination*, 365. None dare call this passage translucent, yet apparently there are some for whom the passage is immediately intelligible.

9. Bakhtin, *Dialogic Imagination*, 349.

10. Hilary Putnam, *Realism with a Human Face*, ed. James Conant (Cambridge, Mass.: Harvard University Press, 1990), 115.

11. Donald Davidson, "Locating Literary Language," in *Literary Theory after Davidson*, ed. Reed Way Dasenbrock (University Park: Pennsylvania State University Press, 1993), 298. Davidson gives elaborated expression to the view that Quine puts more pithily when he, on various occasions, notes that there are no facts about reference beyond those established by use. In transporting "ideologemic" value from one context to another, Bakhtin and other historicists are engaged in a form of illegal traffic. It is difficult to see how the enterprise can be sustained in the absence of the (unwarranted and unwarrantable) belief in the inherent or instrinsic meaningfulness of linguistic units, which would commit these critics, it seems, to a "soft essentialism," a "culture-given essentialism."

12. Michael Dummett, *The Logical Basis of Metaphysics* (Cambridge, Mass.: Harvard University Press, 1991), 123.

13. See Akeel Bilgrami, *Belief and Meaning* (Oxford: Blackwell, 1992), 33.

14. Ibid., 142–43, 147.

15. Speaking of correlative matters, John Searle notes that "Just as one can 'impose' agentive functions on natural phenomena such as sunsets"—or, say, rivers, attributing to them a desire to reach the sea, for instance—"so one can 'discover' nonagentive functions among artifacts. If, for example, you accept the distinction between latent and manifest functions, and you believe that latent functions are unintended, then the discovery of latent functions of institutions is the discovery of a nonagentive function of an artifact. Thus, for example, if you think that the unintended latent function of money is to maintain a system of oppression, then you will *claim to have discovered* a nonagentive function among the agentive status functions of money." For this passage, see *The Construction of Social Reality* (New York: The Free Press, 1995), 121. Of course, in my conception of meaning and content, genuine functions depend upon the *intentional* states of agents.

16. Paraphrasing what Hilary Putnam says in a context of formal semantics, I would say that no matter what operational and theoretical constraints our culture may impose on our use of language, there are always infinitely many different reference and meaning relations that satisfy all of the constraints. In his own context, Putnam observes that "no matter what operational and theoretical constraints our practice may impose on our use of a language, there are always *infinitely many different reference relations* (different 'satisfaction relations,' . . .) which satisfy all the constraints." See Putnam, *Realism and Reason* (Cambridge: Cambridge University Press, 1983), ix.

17. Michael Devitt and Kim Sterelny, in differentiating syntax from semantics—the study of formal relations among linguistic units from the study of language use in meaningful contexts—note that language, though analyzable in formal, syntactical terms, differs from self-contained formal systems "in having representational powers; it represents situations in the world. It is because it does this that it has its central place in our lives." See *Language and Reality: An Introduction to the Philosophy of Language* (Cambridge, Mass.: MIT Press, 1987), 102.

### Chapter 5. Criticism: The More It Changes, the More It Is the Same Thing

1. My quotations of Levinson's remarks are taken from Morris Dickstein's "Damaged Literacy: The Decay of Reading," *Profession 93* (Modern Language Association, 1993): 38. For Levinson's remarks in context, see her *Wordsworth's Great Period Poems* (Cambridge: Cambridge University Press, 1986), 37, 45.

2. The terms "constative" and "performative" are appropriated from John Austin's speech-act theory, of course; de Man's use of them makes no contribution to and is not a gesture within the spirit of speech-act theory. For de Man, what a text says is undermined, subverted, or canceled by what a text performs. Or, perhaps more exactly, the text, as de Man affirms, both "asserts and denies the authority of its own rhetorical mode"; see his *Allegories of Reading: Figural Language in Rousseau, Nietzsche, Rilke, and Proust* (New Haven, Conn.: Yale University Press, 1979), 17.

3. "Review of a Free Inquiry into the Nature and Origin of Evil," in *Johnson: Prose and Poetry*, ed. Mona Wilson (Cambridge, Mass.: Harvard University Press, 1967), 355. The "system" to which Johnson refers is the "Great Chain of Being."

4. Jacques Derrida, *Positions* (Chicago: University of Chicago Press, 1981), 26.

5. For examples of this point, see Nelson Goodman, "Just the Facts, Ma'am," in *Relativism: Interpretation and Confrontation*, ed. Michael Krausz (Notre Dame, Ind.: University of Notre Dame Press, 1989), 80–85. Putnam's remark appears in his *Reason, Truth, and History* (Cambridge: Cambridge University Press, 1981), 65.

6. The "Sam–Boston Strangler" example I have borrowed from Mark Greenberg, "What Connects Thought and Action?" *Times Literary Supplement* (23 June 1995): 8.

7. For Goodman's discussion of this and related issues relating to the shifting relations of facts and conventions, see his "Just the Facts, Ma'am," 80–85.

8. Though often repeated in one or another variation, the person credited with originating the chiastic truism is Louis Montrose; see his "The Elizabethan Subject and the Spenserian Text," in *Literary Theory/Renaissance Texts*, ed. Patricia Parker and David Quint (Baltimore, Md.: Johns Hopkins University Press, 1986), 305.

9. See "Translator's Preface," in Jacques Derrida, *Of Grammatology*, trans. Gayatri Chakravorty Spivak (Baltimore, Md.: Johns Hopkins University Press, 1976), lxxv. For similar remarks, see pages lvii-lxii, lxxii-lxxviii.

10. Derrida, *Of Grammatology*, 158.

11. "Translator's Preface," *Of Grammatology*, xlix.

12. See G. Douglas Atkins, *Reading Deconstruction/Deconstructive Reading* (Lexington: University Press of Kentucky, 1983), 25. Despite this effort to distinguish deconstruction from New Criticism, it is clear, I think, that in terms of mode of argumentation and mechanism of inference building the bonds of kinship between the two are so close that they would not in most states be able to enter into the blissful state of holy wedlock.

13. The first quotation is taken from James F. Harris, *Against Relativism: A Philosophical Defense of Method* (La Salle, Ill.: Open Court, 1992), 149; the second quotation is from William P. Alston, *The Reliability of Sense Perception* (Ithaca, N.Y.: Cornell University Press, 1993), 53. Both writers, of course, are giving condensed expression to views expressed in Wittgenstein's *Philosophical Investigations*, trans. G. E. M. Anscombe (Oxford: Blackwell, 1953); see #258–70.

14. J. Hillis Miller, for example, has attempted to make a case for the political

proclivities of deconstruction; he does so, for instance, in "But Are Things the Way We Think They Are," *Times Literary Supplement* (17–23 June 1988): 676, 685. For another and quite differently slanted discussion of the political implications of deconstruction, see Peter Shaw, "The Politics of Deconstruction," *The War Against the Intellect: Episodes in the Decline of Discourse* (Iowa City: University of Iowa Press, 1989), 56–66.

15. I use the term "syntax" here metaphorically, of course, but I am thinking of syntax as that branch of semiotics which focuses on the relations of signs to one another, as distinct from semantics and pragmatics, which focus respectively on the referentiality (and, hence, intentionality) of signs and on the meanings of signs in contexts of use and interpretation.

16. An alternative conception of language is outlined in the introduction, in Chapters 1 and 2, and, very briefly, in the concluding section of this essay.

## Chapter 6. Philosophical Pluralism, Elder Olson, and Postanalytic Philosophy

1. Olson's agent-based views will become apparent shortly. Similar views are found in much of the current philosophical literature. For example, Michael Dummett observes that "Any adequate philosophical account of language must describe it as a rational activity on the part of creatures to whom can be ascribed intention and purpose." And on the dependence of thought (and, hence, specific content) on language, Dummett says that the "only effective means of studying thought is by the study of language." See Dummett, *The Seas of Language* (Oxford: Clarendon Press, 1993), 104, 99. A similar view is expressed by Donald Davidson in "Locating Literary Language": "Sentences express something only as *used* on particular occasions, and what they express depends, among other things [for example, context], on the intentions of the speaker or writer." Davidson's essay is in *Literary Theory after Davidson*, ed. Reed Way Dasenbrock (University Park: Pennsylvania State University Press, 1993), 295–308. Views such as these contrast sharply, of course, with those of, say, Barthes, Foucault, and most poststructuralists, who endorse "thinking without a subject" and are interested in language as a system of sign relations in which human agency and intentionality are minimized or eliminated or who view language as the medium in which power relations get expressed.

2. Davidson, "Locating," 298.

3. Elder Olson, *On Value Judgments in the Arts and Other Essays* (Chicago: University of Chicago Press, 1976), 3. All quotations from Olson will be taken from this text and will hereafter be cited by page number in the body of my essay. While enjoying virtually no credibility or influence within literary studies today (which are dominated by and large by a theory of language that ultimately derives from Saussure), Olson's view here is something of a commonplace in philosophical discussions of language and meaning. Michael Dummett, for example, variously and frequently affirms that the justification conditions of a sentence are its meaning: they are what determines specific content. For one such expression, see *The Seas of Language*, 94–116. And, of course, for Wittgenstein, the meaning of a concept is determined by its justification conditions; since words—or collections of words—do not possess meaning or reference intrinsically—they owe their significance to something outside themselves, namely, to their role in one or another particular practice or "form of life."

4. W. V. Quine and Joseph Ullian, *The Web of Belief* (New York: Random House, 1970), 122.

5. R. S. Crane, *The Languages of Criticism and the Structure of Poetry* (Toronto: University of Toronto Press, 1953), 31.

6. Stephen Stich, *The Fragmentation of Reason: Preface to a Pragmatic Theory of Cognitive Evaluation* (Cambridge, Mass.: MIT Press, 1990), 131. Stich goes on to note that "the consequences that may be considered in deciding whether to adopt a given [practice] are as rich and varied as the things that people find intrinsically valuable."

7. For a useful discussion of the views of Carnap and Quine on the acceptability and utility of frameworks, see James F. Harris, *Against Relativism: A Philosophical Defense of Method* (La Salle, Ill.: Open Court, 1992), 42–50. Interestingly, the "Chicago critics" also follow Carnap in distinguishing between "internal questions" (that is, questions internal to particular frameworks, questions answerable from within the assumptions of the operative framework) and "external questions" (that is, questions about the appropriateness of the framework itself, which are necessarily "external," because, as Putnam and others have argued, no theory can be *discussed* from within the theory). For an example of Crane's reliance on Carnap's distinction between kinds of questions, see *The Languages of Criticism and the Structure of Poetry*, 26.

8. Catherine Z. Elgin, "The Relativity of Fact and the Objectivity of Value," in *Relativism: Interpretation and Confrontation*, ed. Michael Krausz (Notre Dame, Ind.: University of Notre Dame Press, 1989), 88.

9. Nelson Goodman's illustration of this point concerns the guard who upon being instructed to shoot all the prisoners who move immediately shoots all of them, because each was moving around the earth's axis and orbiting the sun; see *Ways of Worldmaking* (Indianapolis: Hackett, 1978), 120–21. The guard is working within a fully justified category system; regrettably, for the prisoners, he is working in an *inappropriate* system.

10. Crane, *Languages of Criticism*, 28.

11. Dummett, *Seas of Language*, 452.

12. Hilary Putnam, *Realism with a Human Face*, ed. James Conant (Cambridge, Mass.: Harvard University Press, 1990), 211. See also my discussion of relativism in Chapter 2, "Professionalism, Relativism, and Rationality."

13. Susan Hurley, "Martha Nussbaum: Non-Relative Virutes: An Aristotelian Approach," in *The Quality of Life*, ed. Martha C. Nussbaum and Amartya Sen (Oxford: Clarendon Press, 1993), 271.

14. For one such discussion of the dependence of reference on use, and of the notion that reference is nonsense except relative to a conceptual framework (though within such a framework, reference is determinate), see W. V. Quine, *Ontological Relativity and Other Essays* (New York: Columbia University Press, 1969), 48–68.

15. As Dummett has observed; see *Seas of Language*, 155.

16. Akeel Bilgrami, *Belief and Meaning* (Oxford: Blackwell, 1992), 184.

17. This view of "aboutness," "the central concept of intentionality," is explored more fully in chapter 3, "A Theory of Reference," of Hilary Putnam's *Renewing Philosophy* (Cambridge, Mass.: Harvard University Press, 1992), 35–59.

18. John Searle, *The Rediscovery of the Mind* (Cambridge, Mass.: MIT Press, 1992), 155.

19. Catherine Elgin, "The Relativity of Fact and the Objectivity of Value," in

*Relativism: Interpretation and Confrontation,* ed. Michael Krausz (Notre Dame, Ind.: University of Notre Dame Press, 1989), 89.

20. I have not been able to locate this remark, though I know it to be Putnam's. It is consanguineous with Crane's observation (which I also cannot place) that "the number of relationships in which one thing can stand to another is virtually infinite." While I'm at this business of undocumentable recall, I should add to the previous two remarks one by Nelson Goodman—"regularities are where you find them, and you can find them anywhere"—and the other by C. S. Peirce— "any two things resemble one another just as strongly as any two others, if recondite resemblances are admitted." To me, these remarks make a happy foursome, especially since they belong to larger contexts that have deep affinities.

21. Martha C. Nussbaum, *Love's Knowledge: Essays on Philosophy and Literature* (New York: Oxford University Press, 1990), 96. Of course, Nussbaum, as she acknowledges, is playing a variation on Aristotle's observation that "there are many ways of missing the target . . . and only one way of hitting it."

22. Alvin I. Goldman, *Epistemology and Cognition* (Cambridge, Mass.: Harvard University Press, 1986), 128.

23. For this remark and also one of Burke's most incisive discussions of "poetics," see his essay "Poetics in Particular, Language in General," in *Language as Symbolic Action: Essays on Life, Literature, and Method* (Berkeley: University of California Press, 1966), 25–43.

24. I here give abbreviated expression to Davidson's complex view, as presented in Simon Evnine's useful summary in *Donald Davidson* (Stanford, Calif.: Stanford University Press, 1991), 41. For Davidson's more elaborated exposition of the rationality of action, including speech and writing, see his "Actions, Reasons, and Causes," reprinted in Donald Davidson, *Essays on Actions and Events* (Oxford: Clarendon Press, 1980), 3–19.

25. Frederick F. Schmitt, *Truth: A Primer* (Boulder, Colo.: Westview Press, 1995), 178.

26. John Heil, *The Nature of True Minds* (Cambridge: Cambridge University Press, 1992), 212.

27. Goldman, *Epistemology,* 141.

28. Colin McGinn, *Mental Content* (Oxford: Blackwell, 1989), 50–51.

29. For a fuller discussion formal differentiation and genre distinctions, see the next chapter, on genre.

30. Nelson Goodman, *Ways of Worldmaking* (Indianapolis, Ind.: Hackett, 1978), 35.

31. Hilary Putnam, *Reason, Truth, and History* (Cambridge: Cambridge University Press, 1981), 134. For a fuller discussion of the fact-value distinction, the reader should consult the entire chapter from which this quotation is taken, chapter 6, "Fact and Value."

32. Elgin, "The Relativity of Fact," 88.

33. In the review essay on which this chapter is partly based, I spend a considerable amount of time on how the essays in Olson's collection are not only in agreement but also in dialogue with one another, one piece at once echoing and expanding upon or sharpening points made in an earlier piece, or one piece anticipating the arguments of a later piece, on the stylistic felicities of various pieces, and on the argumentative concinnity of them all. All this, and more, I have omitted, in deference to the reader's sorely tested patience and severely imposed upon good will and in an effort to respond appropriately to the de-

mands of the chapter's new justification conditions, to satisfy the conditions of this chapter's intentionality.

### Chapter 7. Genre: A Matter of Form, a Form of Matter

1. Paul Fussell, *Samuel Johnson and the Life of Writing* (New York: Harcourt, Brace, Jovanovich, 1971). The reader should understand that I am using Fussell simply as a means to an independent discussion of large issues relating to genre definition and identification. This essay only attempts to establish a basis for a full-scale study of genres. Since my emphasis is on large, general assumptions, I have deliberately avoided any review or examination of particular conceptions of genre, such as those offered by, for example, Stanley Fish, Tzvetan Todorov, Wolfgang Iser, David Lodge, Alastair Fowler, or Adena Rosmarin. The reader will note, however, that I regularly proceed from principles and assumptions that run counter to those informing the works of most of these writers (as well as those informing most "postmodern" studies of the poststructuralist and historicist variety). In a subsequent work I hope to confront directly the theoretical shortcomings of alternative approaches to genre.

2. Fussell, *Life of Writing*, 63.

3. As Fussell does, at least implicitly, and as do many modern critics, including, for example, Todorov. The most recent tendency, of course, is to collapse all distinctions of kinds into one category, enlisting all kinds under the subsumptive heading of writing or literature. Philosophy, history, psychology, sociology, and so on, through all the erstwhile divisions of interest and inquiry, are engaged, so the modern theorists inform us, in the common enterprise of writing or literature, of creative writing and reading under the supervision of socially constructed categories or the imperatives of language-governed necessities.

4. R. S. Crane, *The Languages of Criticism and the Structure of Poetry* (Toronto: University of Toronto Press, 1953), 165–68. Of course, with his talk about works justifying consideration primarily for their own sakes, Crane articulates a view of concrete artistic achievements that is antithetical to virtually all postmodern positions, which tend to see all cultural products as curiously diverse manifestations of the same underlying social, political, or linguistic dynamic, the same colonialism, capitalism, or self-immolating system of inscription.

5. As he does, for example, in the chapter of *The Languages of Criticism* from which the above remarks were taken, "Toward a More Adequate Criticism of Poetic Structure."

6. If only because he, along with so many others, has never been particularly interested in questions of genre or in genre identification.

7. Part of this illustration has been taken from Julian Marias's "Philosophic Truth and the Metaphoric System," in *Interpretation: The Poetry of Meaning*, ed. Stanley Romaine Hopper and David L. Miller (New York: Harcourt, Brace, and World, 1967), 40–53.

8. Fussell, *Life of Writing*, 35.

9. Of course, to be truly faithful to the position, we would have to supply the corollaries for writings belonging to all the areas of non-literature, but in deference to Occam, we shall resist the temptation to multiply propositions.

10. Thomas Nagel, *The View from Nowhere* (Oxford: Oxford University Press, 1986), 84.

11. The quotation from Gilbert is taken from Fussell, *Life of Writing*, 36.

12. Ibid., 37.

13. Alvin I. Goldman, *Epistemology and Cognition* (Cambridge, Mass.: Harvard University Press, 1986), 139.

14. Fussell, *Life of Writing*, 37.

15. Ibid. In substituting "medium" for Frye's "form," Fussell is perhaps not confirming Frye's point. Here, as elsewhere, the reader should bear in mind that I am less concerned with specific aspects of Fussell's case than with assumptions variously and persistently embedded in general critical discussions of *form* and *genre*.

16. In general, "knowledge of genre" involves little more than the association of some few "material" aspects of works with various class names. When we think of *novel*, for example, we generally have very few differentiating characteristics in mind.

17. No poem, of course, plays by completely unique rules (we could not participate in or understand a game played by such rules), but by "rules" which we have the capacity to understand, by virtue of our linguistic skills and cognitive, primarily imaginative, abilities. Moreover, our cognitive and linguistic powers and limitations are also those of the writer. The range of meanings which the writer can express are limited, ultimately, by precisely the same conditions that control our understanding and, proximately, by the "satisfaction conditions" that are established by the work's system of intentionality. For both writer and reader alike early decisions, governed by some overall purpose or some particular end in view, impose severe restrictions on the subsequent development (or, in the case of the reader, understanding) of the work. If, as Gottlob Frege argued, a word has meaning and reference only relative to a sentence, and a sentence has meaning and reference only relative to a framework, scheme, language, or system of justification, then, once the literary work, say, gets underway and begins functioning for us, within a set of justification constraints, the work tends to prescribe its subsequent fittingness conditions and relations. Eddy Zemach, elucidating one of the later Wittgenstein's central ideas, puts the case this way: textual meaning is like a musical phrase, in that although we can do anything with the phrase (considered in isolation), "given the way we see it, having heard the work up to this point, [we recognize that] some developments would look absolutely wrong to us. The phrase in that work has a meaning: it 'asks' to be dealt with in a certain way and not others." See Zemach, "On Meaning and Reality," in *Relativism: Interpretation and Confrontation*, ed. Michael Krausz (Notre Dame, Ind.: University of Notre Dame Press, 1989), 69.

18. Goldman, *Epistemology*, 140.

19. Michael Dummett, *The Seas of Language* (Oxford: Clarendon Press, 1993), 100. For Davidson, interpretation involves bringing a "theory of truth" to the reading of texts; it supplies a means of linking sentences produced to sentences understood. One of the fullest accounts of the processes of interpretation as Davidson understands them can be found in "Radical Interpretation," reprinted in his *Inquiries into Truth and Interpretation* (Oxford: Clarendon Press, 1984), 125–39.

20. W. V. Quine and J. S. Ullian, *The Web of Belief* (New York: Random House, 1970), 97.

21. Arthur K. Moore, "Formalist Criticism and Literary Form," *Journal of Aesthetics and Art Criticism* 19 (1970): 23.

22. Nelson Goodman and Catherine Z. Elgin, *Reconceptions in Philosophy and Other Arts and Sciences* (Indianapolis, Ind.: Hackett, 1988), 118–19.

23. For one discussion of these matters, see Ludwig Wittgenstein, *The Blue and Brown Books* (Oxford: Blackwell, 1958), especially pp. 3–12. Of course, I substitute "structure of meaning" for his "form of life."

24. For one expression of this principle, see John Searle, *Minds, Brains, and Science* (Cambridge, Mass.: Harvard University Press, 1984), especially pp. 31–33.

25. For one expression of this view, see Michael Dummett, *Origins of Analytical Philosophy* (Cambridge, Mass.: Harvard University Press, 1993), 191.

26. Fussell, *Life of Writing*, 37.

27. I refer here to "artificial," functional forms designed by humans to meet certain ends or purposes (plays, lyric poems, sonatas, paintings, and so on), not to "natural" forms (trees, shrubs, horses, gladiolas, and so on). With Elder Olson, I would distinguish between the two kinds as follows: natural kinds have certain characteristics because they belong to a class (a class defined, as Hilary Putnam might say, by experts and in terms of their constituent parts), whereas artificial kinds belong to a class because they have certain functional characterisics. The preceding is indeed a paraphrase of Olson's comments in "On Value Judgments in the Arts," *Critical Inquiry* 1 (1974): 76.

28. John Searle, *The Construction of Social Reality* (New York: The Free Press, 1995), 121. The agentive function of money, for example, is simply *our counting* or *treating* pieces of paper or metal *as* money, our collective agreement that X (pieces of paper) counts as Y (money) in C (certain contexts or circumstances), the formula "X counts as Y in C" serving in Searle's judgment as the basic, constitutive structure of all institutional or social reality.

29. For example, no character discusses jealousy as such, but only so much of the topic as is dictated by his or her particular dilemma or his or her particular way of construing the topic and its implications.

30. If a writer happens to accept as valid or appropriate certain conventions sponsored, say, by particular notions of propriety or decorum—that in a tragedy, for example, a king should speak in a "high" style and exhibit no habits of thought or behavior which general opinion associates, again as a result of particular notions of propriety or decorum, with "low" characters—he is still faced with the practical problem of making a specific character functional in his play and necessary to its sequence of events. That is, the conventions define a more or less specific boundary of permissibility, beyond which is the area of the artistic "thou shalt not," but they do not determine how the area of legitimacy is to be filled in. A critic, if she happens to be interested in such matters, may recover the reasoning governing the way the writer actually filled in that area, but she cannot arrive at any very useful grounds of necessity in the actual details by reasoning from what is stated or implied in the conventions. In other words, knowledge of these "genre" requirements—and I consent to call them such because they have been treated as such by some writers and critics—may tell you why a king did *not* do something other than what he did (why Caesar was not a drunk), but not why he behaved as he did. To understand his behavior we would have to consider the contents of the mental states (his beliefs and desires, say) that were the *reasons* for that behavior. We would have to consider the intentional states that could most reasonably account for that behavior, however strange, unacceptable, or irrational it might seem to us in our personal and private capacities. Nothing in the "rules" or "requirements" can determine specific action, thought, or speech.

31. For a useful and rigorous discussion of a related matter, that is, how meanings and explanations are always local (governed by immediate local conditions

of intentionality and action), see Akeel Bilgrami, *Belief and Meaning* (Oxford: Blackwell, 1992), 143–47.

### Chapter 8. Teaching Critical Principles in Introductory Literature Courses

1. Mark Johnson, *Moral Imagination: Implications of Cognitive Science for Ethics* (Chicago: University of Chicago Press, 1993), 179.

2. John Searle, *The Construction of Social Reality* (New York: The Free Press, 1995), 134.

3. Crispin Wright, *Truth and Objectivity* (Cambridge, Mass.: Harvard University Press, 1992), 45.

4. Bjørn Ramberg, *Donald Davidson's Philosophy of Language: An Introduction* (Oxford: Blackwell, 1989), 35.

5. For Olson's discussion of "factorial," "essential," and "ornamental" details, see his "A Letter on Teaching Drama," *Chicago Review* 11 (1957): 80–91.

6. Colin McGinn, *The Problem of Consciousness* (Oxford: Blackwell, 1991), 131.

7. Catherine Z. Elgin, "The Relativity of Fact and the Objectivity of Value," in *Relativism: Interpretation and Confrontation*, ed. Michael Krausz (Notre Dame, Ind.: University of Notre Dame Press, 1989), 88.

8. Wright, *Truth and Objectivity*, 15.

9. Kenneth Burke, "Poetics in Particular, Language in General," in his *Language as Symbolic Action: Essays on Life, Literature, and Method* (Berkeley: University of California Press, 1966), 33.

10. Alasdair MacIntyre, *After Virtue: A Study in Moral Theory* (Notre Dame, Ind.: University of Notre Dame Press, 1981), 188.

# Bibliography

Abrams, M. H. *Doing Things with Texts: Essays in Criticism and Critical Theory.* New York: Norton, 1989.

———. "What Is a Humanistic Criticism?" In *The Emperor Redressed: Critiquing Critical Theory,* ed. Dwight Eddins, 13–44. Tuscaloosa: University of Alabama Press, 1995.

Alston, William P. *The Reliability of Sense Perception.* Ithaca, N.Y.: Cornell University Press, 1993.

Anscombe, G. E. M. *Intention.* Oxford: Blackwell, 1957.

Arvon, Henri. *Marxist Esthetics,* trans. Helen Lane, with an introduction by Fredric Jameson. Ithaca, N.Y.: Cornell University Press, 1973.

Atkins, G. Douglas. *Reading Deconstruction /Deconstructive Reading.* Lexington: University Press of Kentucky, 1983.

Audi, Robert. *Action, Intention, and Reason.* Ithaca, N.Y.: Cornell University Press, 1993.

Baker, G. P., and P. M. S. Hacker. *Wittgenstein: Rules, Grammar, and Necessity.* Oxford: Blackwell, 1985.

Bakhtin, M. M. *The Dialogic Imagination: Four Essays,* trans. Caryl Emerson and Michael Holquist, ed. Michael Holquist. Austin: University of Texas Press, 1981.

———. *Speech Genres and Other Late Essays,* trans. Vern W. McGee, ed. Caryl Emerson and Michael Holquist. Austin: University of Texas Press, 1986.

Barnes, Annette. *On Interpretation: A Critical Analysis.* Oxford: Blackwell, 1988.

Barrett, Robert, and Roger Gibson, eds. *Perspectives on Quine.* Oxford: Blackwell, 1990.

Battersby, James L. *Paradigms Regained: Pluralism and the Practice of Criticism.* Philadelphia: University of Pennsylvania Press, 1991.

Battersby, James L., and James Phelan. "Meaning as Concept and Extension: Some Problems." *Critical Inquiry* 12 (1986): 605–15.

Berger, Peter L., and Thomas Luckmann. *The Social Construction of Reality: A Treatise in the Sociology of Knowledge.* Garden City, N.Y.: Anchor-Doubleday, 1967.

Bernstein, Richard J. *Beyond Objectivism and Relativism: Science, Hermeneutics, and Praxis.* Philadelphia: University of Pennsylvania Press, 1983.

Bilgrami, Akeel. *Belief and Meaning.* Oxford: Blackwell, 1992.

Blackburn, Simon. *Spreading the Word: Groundings in the Philosophy of Language.* Oxford: Clarendon Press, 1984.

———. "Losing Your Mind: Physics, Identity, and Folk Burglar Protection." In

*The Future of Folk Psychology*, ed. John Greenwood, 196–225. Cambridge: Cambridge University Press, 1991.

———. *Essays in Quasi-Realism.* Oxford: Oxford University Press, 1993.

Boër, Steven E. "Substance and Kind: Reflections on the New Theory of Reference." *College of Humanities Inaugural Lectures*, 20–66. Columbus: Ohio State University, College of Humanities, 1984–85.

Boolos, George, ed. *Meaning and Method: Essays in Honour of Hilary Putnam.* Cambridge: Cambridge University Press, 1990.

Booth, Wayne C. *Critical Understanding: The Powers and Limits of Pluralism.* Chicago: University of Chicago Press, 1979.

Borradori, Giovanna. *The American Philosopher.* Chicago: University of Chicago Press, 1994.

Boruah, Bijoy H. *Fiction and Emotion.* Oxford: Clarendon, 1988.

Bourdieu, Pierre. *Outline of a Theory of Practice*, trans. Richard Nice. Cambridge: Cambridge University Press, 1977.

Bratman, Michael E. *Intention, Plans, and Practical Reason.* Cambridge, Mass.: Harvard University Press, 1987.

Bruner, Jerome S. *Actual Minds, Possible Worlds.* Cambridge, Mass.: Harvard University Press, 1986.

Burke, Kenneth. "Poetics in Particular, Language in General." In *Language as Symbolic Action: Essays on Life, Literature, and Method*, 25–43. Berkeley: University of California Press, 1966.

Butler, Christopher. *Interpretation, Deconstruction, and Ideology: An Introduction to Some Current Issues in Literary Theory.* Oxford: Clarendon Press, 1984.

Cain, William E. *The Crisis in Criticism: Theory, Literature, and Reform in English Studies.* Baltimore, Md.: Johns Hopkins University Press, 1984.

Carruthers, Peter. *Introducing Persons: Theories and Arguments in the Philosophy of Mind.* London: Croom Helm, 1986.

Cherniak, Christopher. *Minimal Rationality.* Cambridge, Mass.: MIT Press, 1986.

Churchland, Patricia Smith. *Neurophilosophy: Toward a Unified Science of the Mind/Brain.* Cambridge, Mass.: MIT Press, 1986.

Churchland, Paul M. *Matter and Consciousness*, rev. ed. Cambridge, Mass.: MIT Press, 1988.

Clark, Peter, and Bob Hale, eds. *Reading Putnam.* Oxford: Blackwell, 1994.

Collier, Peter, and Helga Geyer-Ryan, eds. *Literary Theory Today.* Ithaca, N.Y.: Cornell University Press, 1990.

Craige, Betty Jean. *Literary Relativity: An Essay on Twentieth- Century Narrative.* Lewisburg, Pa.: Bucknell University Press, 1982.

Crane, R. S. *Critics and Criticism: Ancient and Modern.* Chicago: University of Chicago Press, 1952.

———. *The Languages of Criticism and the Structure of Poetry.* Toronto: University of Toronto Press, 1953.

———. "Critical and Historical Principles of Literary History." In *The Idea of the Humanities and Other Essays Critical and Historical.* 2 vols., II: 45–156. Chicago: University of Chicago Press, 1967.

———. *Critical and Historical Principles of Literary History.* Chicago: University of Chicago Press, 1971.

Cresswell, M. J. "The World Is Everything That Is the Case." *Australasian Journal of Philosophy* 50 (1972): 1–13.

Crews, Frederick. *The Critics Bear It Away: American Fiction and the Academy.* New York: Random House, 1992.

Culler, Jonathan. *Structuralist Poetics: Structuralism, Linguistics, and the Study of Literature.* Ithaca, N.Y.: Cornell University Press, 1975.

———. *On Deconstruction: Theory and Criticism after Structuralism.* Ithaca, N.Y.: Cornell University Press, 1982.

Cummins, Robert. *Meaning and Mental Representation.* Cambridge, Mass.: MIT Press, 1989.

Dasenbrock, Reed Way, ed. *Redrawing the Lines: Analytic Philosophy, Deconstruction, and Literary Theory.* Minneapolis: University of Minnesota Press, 1989.

———, ed. *Literary Theory after Davidson.* University Park, Pa.: Pennsylvania State University Press, 1993.

Davidson, Donald. "On the Very Idea of a Conceptual Scheme." *Proceedings and Addresses of the American Philosophical Association* 47 (1974): 5–20.

———. *Essays on Action and Events.* Oxford: Clarendon, 1980.

———. "Rational Animals." *Dialecta* 36 (1982): 317–27.

———. *Inquiries into Truth and Interpretation.* Oxford: Clarendon Press, 1984.

———. "Radical Interpretation." In *Inquiries into Truth and Interpretation,* 125–39. Oxford: Clarendon Press, 1984.

———. "Thought and Talk." In *Inquiries into Truth and Interpretation,* 155–70. Oxford: Clarendon Press, 1984. Originally in *Mind and Language,* ed. Samuel Guttenplan. Oxford: Oxford University Press, 1975.

———. "A Coherence Theory of Truth and Knowledge." Reprinted in *Truth and Interpretation: Perspectives on the Philosophy of Donald Davidson,* ed. Ernest Lepore, 307–19. Oxford: Blackwell, 1986.

———. "The Myth of the Subjective." In *Relativism: Interpretation and Confrontation,* ed. Michael Krausz, 159–72. Notre Dame, Ind.: University of Notre Dame Press, 1989.

———. "Locating Literary Language." In *Literary Theory after Davidson,* ed. Reed Way Dasenbrock, 295–308. University Park: Pennsylvania State University Press, 1993.

Davis, Steven, ed. *Pragmatics: A Reader.* Oxford: Oxford University Press, 1991.

Davis, Walter A. "The Fisher King: *Wille zur Macht* in Baltimore." *Critical Inquiry* 10 (1984): 668–94.

de Man, Paul. *Blindness and Insight: Essays in the Rhetoric of Contemporary Criticism.* New York: Oxford University Press, 1971.

———. *Allegories of Reading: Figural Language in Rousseau, Nietzsche, Rilke, and Proust.* New Haven, Conn.: Yale University Press, 1979.

———. "The Return to Philology." *Times Literary Supplement* (10 December 1982): 1355–56.

———. "Dialogue and Dialogism." *Poetics Today* 4 (1983): 99–107.

———. *The Resistance to Theory.* Manchester: Manchester University Press, 1986.

Dennett, Daniel C. *The Intentional Stance.* Cambridge, Mass.: MIT Press, 1987.

———. *Consciousness Explained.* Boston: Little, Brown, and Co., 1991.

Derrida, Jacques. *Of Grammatology,* trans. Gayatri Chakravorty Spivak. Baltimore, Md.: Johns Hopkins University Press, 1976.

———. *Writing and Difference,* trans. Alan Bass. Chicago: University of Chicago Press, 1978.

———. *Positions,* trans. Alan Bass. Chicago: University of Chicago Press, 1981.

de Sousa, Ronald. *The Rationality of Emotion.* Cambridge, Mass.: MIT Press, 1987.

Devitt, Michael. *Realism and Truth,* 2nd ed. Oxford: Blackwell, 1991.

Devitt, Michael, and Kim Sterelny. *Language and Reality: An Introduction to the Philosophy of Language.* Cambridge, Mass.: MIT Press, 1987.

Diamond, Cora, and Jenny Teichman, ed. *Intention and Intentionality: Essays in Honour of G. E. M. Anscombe.* Brighton: Harvester, 1979.

Dickstein, Morris. "Damaged Literacy: The Decay of Reading." *Profession 93*: 34–40. Modern Language Association, 1993.

Dretske, Fred. *Explaining Behavior: Reasons in a World of Causes.* Cambridge, Mass.: MIT Press, 1988.

Dummett, Michael. *Truth and Other Enigmas.* Cambridge, Mass.: Harvard University Press, 1978.

———. *The Logical Basis of Metaphysics.* Cambridge, Mass.: Harvard University Press, 1991.

———. *Origins of Analytic Philosophy.* Cambridge, Mass.: Harvard University Press, 1993.

———. *The Seas of Language.* Oxford: Clarendon Press, 1993.

Eagleton, Terry. *Literary Theory: An Introduction.* Minneapolis: University of Minnesota Press, 1983.

Eddins, Dwight, ed. *The Emperor reDressed: Critiquing Critical Theory.* Tuscaloosa: University of Alabama Press, 1995.

Elgin, Catherine Z. *With Reference to Reference.* Indianapolis: Hackett, 1983.

———. "The Relativity of Fact and the Objectivity of Value." In *Relativism: Interpretation and Confrontation,* ed. Michael Krausz, 86–98. Notre Dame, Ind.: University of Notre Dame Press, 1989.

Elgin, Catherine Z., and Nelson Goodman. *Reconceptions in Philosophy and Other Arts and Sciences.* Indianapolis: Hackett, 1988.

Ellis, John M. "What Does Deconstruction Contribute to a Theory of Criticism?" *New Literary History* 19 (1988): 259–79.

Elster, Jon. *Making Sense of Marx.* Cambridge: Cambridge University Press, 1985.

Evnine, Simon. *Donald Davidson.* Stanford, Calif.: Stanford University Press, 1991.

Fauconnier, Gilles. *Mental Spaces.* Cambridge, Mass.: MIT Press, 1985.

Fish, Stanley. "Normal Circumstances, Literal Language, Direct Speech Acts, the Ordinary, the Everyday, the Obvious, What Goes Without Saying, and Other Special Cases." *Critical Inquiry* 4 (1978): 625–44.

———. *Is There a Text in This Class? The Authority of Interpretive Communities.* Cambridge, Mass.: Harvard University Press, 1980.

———. "Anti-Professionalism." *New Literary History* 17 (1985): 89–108.

———. "Resistance and Independence: A Reply to Gerald Graff." *New Literary History* 17 (1985): 119–27.

———. *Doing What Comes Naturally: Change, Rhetoric, and the Practice of Theory in Literary and Legal Studies.* Durham, N.C.: Duke University Press, 1989.

Fodor, Jerry A. *Psychosemantics: The Problem of Meaning in the Philosophy of Mind.* Cambridge, Mass.: MIT Press, 1987.

Fodor, Jerry A., and Ernest Lepore. *Holism: A Shopper's Guide.* Oxford: Blackwell, 1992.

Foucault, Michel. *Madness and Civilization: A History of Insanity in the Age of Reason,* trans. Richard Howard. New York: Vintage, 1973.

———. *The Archaeology of Knowledge and the Discourse on Language,* trans. A. M. Sheridan Smith. New York: Harper, 1976.

Fowler, Alastair. *Kinds of Literature: An Introduction to the Theory of Genres and Modes.* Cambridge, Mass.: Harvard University Press, 1982.

Freadman, Richard, and Seumas Miller. *Re-thinking Theory: A Critique of Contemporary Literary Theory and an Alternative Account.* Cambridge: Cambridge University Press, 1992.

Fussell, Paul. *Samuel Johnson and the Life of Writing.* New York: Harcourt, Brace, Jovanovich, 1971.

Gadamer, Hans-Georg. *Philosophical Hermeneutics,* ed. and trans. David E. Linge. Berkeley: University of California Press, 1976.

Gallagher, Catherine. "Re-covering the Social in Recent Literary Theory." *Diacritics* 12 (1982): 40–48.

Gardner, Howard. *Art, Mind, and Brain: A Cognitive Approach to Creativity.* New York: Basic Books, 1982.

Garfinkel, Alan. *Forms of Explanation: Rethinking the Questions in Social Theory.* New Haven, Conn.: Yale University Press, 1981.

Geertz, Clifford. *The Interpretation of Cultures.* New York: Basic Books, 1973.

Goldman, Alvin I. *Epistemology and Cognition.* Cambridge, Mass.: Harvard University Press, 1986.

———. *Philosophical Applications of Cognitive Science.* Boulder, Colo.: Westview Press, 1993.

Gombrich, E. H., " 'They Were All Human Beings—So Much Is Plain': Reflections on Cultural Relativism in the Humanities." *Critical Inquiry* 13 (1987): 686–99.

Gombrich, E. H., Julian Hochberg, and Max Black. *Art, Perception, and Reality.* Baltimore, Md.: Johns Hopkins University Press, 1972.

Goodman, Nelson. *The Structure of Appearance.* Cambridge, Mass.: Harvard University Press, 1951.

———. *Fact, Fiction, and Forecast.* Cambridge, Mass.: Harvard University Press, 1955.

———. *Languages of Art: An Approach to a Theory of Symbols.* Indianapolis: Hackett, 1976.

———. *Ways of Worldmaking.* Indianapolis, Ind.: Hackett, 1978.

———. "Notes on a Well-made World." *Partisan Review* 51 (1984): 276–88.

———. *Of Mind and Other Matters.* Cambridge, Mass.: Harvard University Press, 1984.

———. "Just the Facts, Ma'am." In *Relativism: Interpretation and Confrontation,* ed. Michael Krausz, 80–85. Notre Dame, Ind.: University of Notre Dame Press, 1989.

Goodman, Nelson, and Catherine Z. Elgin. *Reconceptions in Philosophy and Other Arts and Sciences.* Indianapolis, Ind.: Hackett, 1988.

Gordon, Robert M. *The Structure of Emotions: Investigations in Cognitive Philosophy.* Cambridge: Cambridge University Press, 1987.

Graff, Gerald. "Interpretation on Tlön: A Response to Stanley Fish." *New Literary History* 17 (1985): 109–17.

Grandy, Richard. "Reference, Meaning, and Belief." *Journal of Philosophy* 70 (1973): 439–52.

Greenberg, Mark. "What Connects Thought and Action?" *Times Literary Supplement* (23 June 1995): 7–8.

Greenblatt, Stephen. *Renaissance Self-Fashioning.* Chicago: University of Chicago Press, 1980.

Greenwood, John D., ed. *The Future of Folk Psychology: Intentionality and Cognitive Science.* Cambridge: Cambridge University Press, 1991.

Gregory, Richard L., ed. *The Oxford Companion to the Mind.* Oxford: Oxford University Press, 1987.

Grice, Paul. *Studies in the Way of Words.* Cambridge, Mass.: Harvard University Press, 1989.

Grunbaum, Adolf, and Wesley C. Salmon, ed. *The Limitations of Deconstruction.* Berkeley: University of California Press, 1988.

Hacking, Ian. *Why Does Language Matter to Philosophy?* Cambridge: Cambridge University Press, 1975.

Hampden-Turner, Charles. *Maps of the Mind.* New York: Collier-Macmillan, 1982.

Harris, James F. *Against Relativism: A Philosophical Defense of Method.* La Salle, Ill.: Open Court, 1992.

Harris, Wendell V. *Interpretive Acts: In Search Of Meaning.* Oxford: Clarendon, 1988.

———. *Literary Meaning: Reclaiming the Study of Literature.* New York: New York University Press, 1996.

Harth, Philip, ed. *New Approaches to Eighteenth-Century Literature.* New York: Columbia University Press, 1974.

Hartman, Geoffrey H. *Saving the Text: Literature/Derrida/Philosophy.* Baltimore, Md.: Johns Hopkins University Press, 1981.

Harvey, Irene E. *Derrida and the Economy of Difference.* Bloomington: Indiana University Press, 1986.

Heil, John. *The Nature of True Minds.* Cambridge: Cambridge University Press, 1992.

Hesse, Mary. "Texts Without Types and Lumps Without Laws." *New Literary History* 17 (1985): 31–48.

Hintikka, Jaakko. *Knowledge and Belief.* Ithaca, N.Y.: Cornell University Press, 1962.

———. *The Intentions of Intentionality and Other New Models for Modalities.* Dordrecht: Reidel, 1975.

Hirsch, E. D., Jr. *Validity in Interpretation.* New Haven, Conn.: Yale University Press, 1967.

———. "The Politics of Theories of Interpretation." *Critical Inquiry* 9 (1982): 235–47.

———. "Past Intentions and Present Meanings." *Essays in Criticism* 33 (1983): 79–98.

———. "Cultural Literacy." *American Scholar* 52 (1983): 159–69.

———. "Meaning and Significance Reinterpreted." *Critical Inquiry* 11 (1984): 202–25.

———. "Transhistorical Intentions and the Persistence of Allegory." *New Literary History* 25 (1994): 549–67.

Hollis, Martin, and Steven Lukes, ed. *Rationality and Relativism.* Cambridge, Mass.: MIT Press, 1982.

Hopper, Stanley Romaine, and David L. Miller, ed. *Interpretation: The Poetry of Meaning.* New York: Harcourt, Brace, and World, 1967.

Howard, Jean E. "The New Historicism in Renaissance Studies." *English Literary Renaissance* 16 (1986): 13–43.

Hurley, S. L. *Natural Reasons: Personality and Polity.* Oxford: Oxford University Press, 1989.

———. "Martha Nussbaum: Non-Relative Virtues: An Aristotelian Approach." In *The Quality of Life,* ed. Martha C. Nussbaum and Amartya Sen, 270–76. Oxford: Clarendon Press, 1993.

Jackendoff, Ray. *Semantics and Cognition.* Cambridge, Mass.: MIT Press, 1983.

———. *Consciousness and the Computational Mind.* Cambridge, Mass.: MIT Press, 1987.

———. "Conceptual Semantics." In *Meaning and Mental Representation,* ed. Umberto Eco, Marco Santambrogio, and Patrizia Violi, 81–97. Bloomington: Indiana University Press, 1988.

————. *Patterns in the Mind: Language and Human Nature.* New York: Basic Books, 1994.

Jameson, Fredric. *The Political Unconscious: Narrative as a Socially Symbolic Act.* Ithaca, N.Y.: Cornell University Press, 1981.

Johnson, Mark. *The Body in the Mind: The Bodily Basis of Meaning, Imagination, and Reason.* Chicago: University of Chicago Press, 1987.

————. *Moral Imagination: Implications of Cognitive Science for Ethics.* Chicago: University of Chicago Press, 1993.

Johnson, Samuel. "Review of a Free Inquiry into the Nature and Origin of Evil." In *Johnson: Prose and Poetry*, ed. Mona Wilson. Cambridge, Mass.: Harvard University Press, 1967.

Johnson-Laird, Philip N. "How Is Meaning Mentally Represented?" In *Meaning and Mental Representation*, ed. Umberto Eco, Marco Santambrogio, and Patrizia Violi, 99–118. Bloomington: Indiana University Press, 1988.

Johnson-Laird, Philip N., and P. C. Wason, eds. *Mental Models: Towards a Cognitive Science of Language, Inference, and Consciousness.* Cambridge: Cambridge University Press, 1983.

Juhl, P. D. *Interpretation: An Essay in the Philosophy of Literary Criticism.* Princeton, N.J.: Princeton University Press, 1980.

Kiser, Lisa J. *Telling Classical Tales.* Ithaca, N.Y.: Cornell University Press, 1983.

Krausz, Michael, ed. *Relativism: Interpretation and Confrontation.* Notre Dame, Ind.: Indiana University Press, 1989.

Kripke, Saul A. *Naming and Necessity.* Cambridge, Mass.: Harvard University Press, 1972.

————. *Wittgenstein on Rules and Private Language.* Oxford: Blackwell, 1982.

Kristeva, Julia. *Desire in Language: A Semiotic Approach to Literature and Art*, ed. Leon S. Roudiez, trans. Thomas Gora, Alice Jardine, and Leon S. Roudiez. New York: Columbia University Press, 1980.

Kuhn, Thomas S. *The Structure of Scientific Revolutions.* Chicago: University of Chicago Press, 1962.

Lakoff, George. *Women, Fire, and Dangerous Things: What Categories Reveal About the Mind.* Chicago: University of Chicago Press, 1987.

————. "Cognitive Semantics." In *Meaning and Mental Representation*, ed. Umberto Eco, Marco Santambrogio, and Patrizia Violi, 199–54. Bloomington: Indiana University Press, 1988.

Lakoff, George, and Mark Johnson. *Metaphors We Live By.* Chicago: University of Chicago Press, 1980.

Leitch, Vincent B. *Deconstructive Criticism: An Advanced Introduction.* New York: Columbia University Press, 1983.

————. *American Literary Criticism from the Thirties to the Eighties.* New York: Columbia University Press, 1988.

Lepore, Ernest, ed. *Truth and Interpretation: Perspectives on the Philosophy of Donald Davidson.* Oxford: Blackwell, 1986.

Lepore, Ernest, and Barry Loewer, "A Putnam's Progress." In *Realism and Anti-realism*, ed. Peter A. French, Theodore E. Uehling, Jr., and Howard K. Wettstein, 459–73. *Midwest Studies in Philosophy*, 12. Minneapolis: University of Minnesota Press, 1988.

Levinson, Marjorie. *Wordsworth's Great Period Poems.* Cambridge: Cambridge University Press, 1986.

Lewis, David. *On the Plurality of Worlds.* Oxford: Blackwell, 1986.

————. "Putnam's Paradox." *Australasian Journal of Philosophy* 64 (1986): 221–36.

Lilla, Mark. "Philosophy: On Goodman, Putnam, and Rorty." *Partisan Review* 51 (1984): 220–35.

Lloyd, Dan. *Simple Minds.* Cambridge, Mass.: MIT Press, 1989.

Longuet-Higgins, Christopher H. *Mental Processes: Studies in Cognitive Science.* Cambridge, Mass.: MIT Press, 1987.

Lucas, John. "Absence into Presence: Changes in Literary Criticism." *Times Literary Supplement* (14 November 1986): 1280.

Luntley, Michael. *Language, Logic and Experience.* La Salle, Ill.: Open Court, 1988.

McCormick, Peter J. *Fictions, Philosophies, and the Problems of Poetics.* Ithaca, N.Y.: Cornell University Press, 1988.

McDowell, John. *Mind and World.* Cambridge, Mass.: Harvard University Press, 1994.

McGinn, Colin. *Mental Content.* Oxford: Blackwell, 1989.

———. *The Problem of Consciousness.* Oxford: Blackwell, 1991.

———. *Problems in Philosophy: The Limits of Inquiry.* Oxford: Blackwell, 1993.

MacIntyre, Alasdair. *After Virtue: A Study in Moral Theory.* Notre Dame, Ind.: University of Notre Dame Press, 1981.

Margolis, Joseph. *Pragmatism Without Foundations: Reconciling Realism and Relativism.* Oxford: Blackwell, 1986.

Marias, Julian. "Philosophic Truth and the Metaphoric System." In *Interpretation: The Poetry of Meaning*, ed. Stanley Romaine Hopper and David L. Miller, 40–53. New York: Harcourt, Brace, and World, 1967.

Marshall, John C. "Routes and Representations in the Processing of Written Language." In *Motor and Sensory Processes of Language.*, ed. Eric Keller and Myrna Gopnik, 237–56. Hillsdale, N.J.: Lawrence Erlbaum, 1987.

Merrill, G. H. "The Model-Theoretic Argument against Realism." *Philosophy of Science* 47 (1980): 69–81.

Miller, George, and Philip Johnson-Laird. *Language and Perception.* Cambridge, Mass.: Harvard University Press, 1976.

Miller, J. Hillis. "The Critic as Host." *Critical Inquiry* 3 (1974): 439–47.

———. "But Are Things the Way We Think They Are." *Times Literary Supplement* (17–23 June, 1988): 676, 685.

———. *Topographies.* Stanford, Calif.: Stanford University Press, 1995.

Millikan, Ruth Garrett. *Language, Thought, and Other Biological Categories: New Foundations for Realism.* Cambridge, Mass.: MIT Press, 1984.

Montefiore, Alan. "Philosophy, Literature and the Restatement of a Few Banalities." *The Monist* 69 (1986): 56–67.

Montrose, Louis. "The Elizabethan Subject and the Spenserian Text." In *Literary Theory/Renaissance Texts*, ed. Patricia Parker and David Quint, 303–40. Baltimore, Md.: Johns Hopkins University Press, 1986.

Moore, Arthur K. "Formalist Criticism and Literary Form." *Journal of Aesthetics and Art Criticism* 19 (1970): 21–32.

Nagel, Thomas. *The View from Nowhere.* Oxford: Oxford University Press, 1986.

Newton-de Molina, David, ed. *On Literary Intention.* Edinburgh: Edinburgh University Press, 1976.

Norris, Christopher. *Deconstruction: Theory and Practice.* London and New York: Methuen, 1982.

———. *Contest of Faculties: Philosophy and Theory after Deconstruction.* New York: Methuen, 1985.

Novitz, David. "The Rage for Deconstruction." *The Monist* 69 (1986): 39–55.

Nussbaum, Martha C. *Love's Knowledge: Essays on Philosophy and Literature.* Oxford: Oxford University Press, 1990.

Nussbaum, Martha C., and Amartya Sen, eds. *The Quality of Life.* Oxford: Clarendon Press, 1993.

Olson, Elder. "A Letter on Teaching Drama." *Chicago Review* 11 (1957): 80–91.

———. "*Hamlet* and the Hermeneutics of Drama." *Modern Philology* 56 (1964): 225–37.

———. "The Dialectical Foundations of Critical Pluralism." *Texas Quarterly* 9 (1966): 202–30.

———. "On Value Judgments in the Arts." *Critical Inquiry* 1 (1974): 71–90.

———. *On Value Judgments in the Arts and Other Essays.* Chicago: University of Chicago Press, 1976.

Palmer, F. R. *Semantics.* 2nd ed. Cambridge: Cambridge University Press, 1981.

Papineau, David. *Reality and Representation.* Oxford: Blackwell, 1987.

Pastan, Linda. "Marks." In *PM/AM: New and Selected Poems.* New York: Norton, 1982.

Phelan, James. "Data, Danda, and Disagreement." *Diacritics* 13 (1983): 39–50.

———. *Reading People, Reading Plots: Character, Progression, and the Interpretation of Narrative.* Chicago: University of Chicago Press, 1989.

Plantinga, Alvin. "Actualism and Possible Worlds." *Theoria* 42 (1976): 139–60.

Polanyi, Michael. *Personal Knowledge: Towards a Post-Critical Philosophy.* Chicago: University of Chicago Press, 1958.

———. *The Tacit Dimension.* Garden City, N.Y.: Doubleday, 1967.

———. *Knowing and Being.* Ed. Marjorie Grene. Chicago: University of Chicago Press, 1969.

Polanyi, Michael, and Harry Prosch. *Meaning.* Chicago: University of Chicago Press, 1975.

Pollock, John. *Knowledge and Justification.* Princeton, N.J.: Princeton University Press, 1974.

Pope, Alexander. *An Essay on Man. The Poems of Alexander Pope.* Twickenham Edition, vol. 3, ed. Maynard Mack. London: Methuen, 1950.

Popper, Karl R. *The Poverty of Historicism.* New York: Harper and Row, 1964.

———. *Objective Knowledge: An Evolutionary Approach.* Rev. ed. Oxford: Clarendon, 1979.

Prickett, Stephen. *Words and "The Word": Language, Poetics and Biblical Interpretation.* Cambridge: Cambridge University Press, 1986.

Putnam, Hilary. *Mind, Language and Reality.* Cambridge: Cambridge University Press, 1975.

———. *Meaning and the Moral Sciences.* London: Routledge and Kegan Paul, 1978.

———. *Reason, Truth, and History.* Cambridge: Cambridge University Press, 1981.

———. *Realism and Reason.* Cambridge: Cambridge University Press, 1983.

———. "The Craving for Objectivity." *New Literary History* 15 (1984): 229–39.

———. "A Comparison of Something with Something Else." *New Literary History* 17 (1985): 61–79.

———. *The Many Faces of Realism.* La Salle, Ill.: Open Court, 1987.

———. *Representation and Reality.* Cambridge, Mass.: MIT Press, 1988.

———. *Realism with a Human Face,* ed. James Conant. Cambridge, Mass.: Harvard University Press, 1990.

———. *Renewing Philosophy.* Cambridge, Mass.: Harvard University Press, 1992.

————. *Words and Life*, ed. James Conant. Cambridge, Mass.: Harvard University Press, 1994.

————. *Pragmatism: An Open Question*. Oxford: Blackwell, 1995.

Putnam, Ruth Anna. "Poets, Scientists, and Critics." *New Literary History* 17 (1985): 17–21.

Quine, Willard Van Orman. *Word and Object*. Cambridge, Mass.: MIT Press, 1960.

————. *Ontological Relativity and Other Essays*. New York: Columbia University Press, 1969.

————. "On the Reasons for Indeterminacy of Translation." *Journal of Philosophy* 67 (1970): 178–83.

————. "Worlds Away." *Journal of Philosophy* 73 (1976): 859–63.

————. *Theories and Things*. Cambridge, Mass.: Harvard University Press, 1981.

————. *Quiddities: An Intermittently Philosophical Dictionary*. Cambridge, Mass.: Harvard University Press, 1987.

————. *Pursuit of Truth*. Cambridge, Mass.: Harvard University Press, 1990.

Quine, Willard Van Orman, and Joseph S. Ullian. *The Web of Belief*. New York: Random House, 1970.

Rader, Ralph. "The Concept of Genre and Eighteenth-Century Studies." In *New Approaches to Eighteenth-Century Literature*, ed. Philip Harth, 79–115. New York: Columbia University Press, 1974.

————. "Fact, Theory, and Literary Explanation." *Critical Inquiry* 1 (1974): 245–72.

Ramberg, Bjørn. *Donald Davidson's Philosophy of Language: An Introduction*. Oxford: Blackwell, 1989.

Ray, William. *Literary Meaning: From Phenomenology to Deconstruction*. Oxford: Blackwell, 1984.

Rorty, Richard. *Philosophy and the Mirror of Nature*. Princeton, N.J.: Princeton University Press, 1979.

————. *Consequences of Pragmatism*. Minneapolis: University of Minnesota Press, 1982.

————. "Texts and Lumps." *New Literary History* 17 (1985): 1–16.

Rumelhart, David E., James L. McClelland, and the PDP Research Group. *Parallel Distributed Processing: Explorations in the Microstructure of Cognition*. Vol. 1, *Foundations*. Vol. 2, *Psychological and Biological Models*. Cambridge, Mass.: MIT Press, 1986.

Sacks, Mark. *The World We Found: The Limits of Ontological Talk*. London: Duckworth, 1989.

Salmon, Nathan. "How *Not* to Derive Essentialism from the Theory of Reference." *Journal of Philosophy* 76 (1979): 703–74.

Schaff, Adam. *Language and Cognition*, ed. Robert S. Cohen, with an introduction by Noam Chomsky. New York: McGraw-Hill, 1973.

Schauber, Ellen, and Ellen Spolsky. *The Bounds of Interpretation: Linguistic Theory and Literary Text*. Stanford, Calif.: Stanford University Press, 1986.

Scheffler, Israel. *Science and Subjectivity*. 2nd ed. Indianapolis: Hackett, 1982.

Schiffer, Stephen. *Remnants of Meaning*. Cambridge, Mass.: MIT Press, 1987.

Schmitt, Frederick F. *Truth: A Primer*. Boulder, Colo.: Westview Press, 1995.

Searle, John. *Expression and Meaning: Studies in the Theory of Speech Acts*. Cambridge: Cambridge University Press, 1979.

————. *Intentionality: An Essay in the Philosophy of Mind*. Cambridge: Cambridge University Press, 1983.

————. "The World Turned Upside Down." Review of *On Deconstruction: Theory and Criticism after Structuralism,* by Jonathan Culler, *New York Review of Books* (27 October 1983): 74–79.

———. *Minds, Brains, and Science.* Cambridge, Mass.: Harvard University Press, 1984.

———. *John Searle and His Critics,* ed. Ernest Lepore and Robert van Gulick. Oxford: Blackwell, 1991.

———. *The Rediscovery of the Mind.* Cambridge, Mass.: MIT Press, 1992.

———. *The Construction of Social Reality.* New York: The Free Press, 1995.

Selden, Raman. *A Reader's Guide to Contemporary Literary Theory.* Brighton: The Harvester Press, 1985.

Shaw, Peter. "The Politics of Deconstruction." In *The War Against the Intellect: Episodes in the Decline of Discourse,* 56–66. Iowa City: University of Iowa Press, 1989.

Shusterman, Richard. "Analytic Aesthetics, Literary Theory, and Deconstruction." *The Monist* 69 (1986): 22–38.

———. "Organic Unity: Analysis and Deconstruction." In *Redrawing the Lines: Analytic Philosophy, Deconstruction, and Literary Theory,* ed. Reed Way Dasenbrock, 93–115. Minneapolis: University of Minnesota Press, 1989.

Smith, Barbara Herrnstein. *Contingencies of Value: Alternative Perspectives for Critical Theory.* Cambridge, Mass.: Harvard University Press, 1988.

Spivak, Gayatri Chakravorty. "Translator's Preface." In *Of Grammatology,* by Jacques Derrida, trans. Gayatri Chakravorty Spivak. Baltimore, Md.: Johns Hopkins University Press, 1976.

Staten, Henry. "The Secret Name of Cats: Deconstruction, Intentional Meaning, and the New Theory of Reference." In *Redrawing the Lines: Analytic Philosophy, Deconstruction, and Literary Theory,* ed. Reed Way Dasenbrock, 27–48. Minneapolis: University of Minnesota Press, 1989.

Stich, Stephen. *The Fragmentation of Reason: Preface to a Pragmatic Theory of Cognitive Evaluation.* Cambridge, Mass.: MIT Press, 1990.

Stout, Jeffrey. "The Relativity of Interpretation." *The Monist* 69 (1986): 103–18.

Strawson, Galen. *Mental Reality.* Cambridge, Mass.: MIT Press, 1984.

Tallis, Raymond. *In Defense of Realism.* London: Arnold, 1988.

Todorov, Tzvetan. *The Fantastic: A Structural Approach in a Literary Genre.* Ithaca, N.Y.: Cornell University Press, 1975.

———. *Mikhail Bakhtin: The Dialogical Principle,* trans. Wlad Godzich. Minneapolis: University of Minnesota Press, 1984.

———. *Genres in Discourse,* trans. Catherine Porter. Cambridge: Cambridge University Press, 1990.

Watson, Walter. *The Architectonics of Meaning: Foundations of the New Pluralism.* Albany, N.Y.: SUNY Press, 1985.

Webster, Roger. *Studying Literary Theory: An Introduction.* New York: Arnold, 1989.

Weightman, John. "On Not Understanding Michel Foucault." *American Scholar* 58 (1989): 383–406.

Wheeler, Samuel C., III. "The Extension of Deconstruction." *The Monist* 69 (1986): 3–21.

———. "Wittgenstein as Conservative Deconstructor." *New Literary History* 19 (1988): 239–58.

———. "Metaphor According to Davidson and de Man." In *Redrawing the Lines: Analytic Philosophy, Deconstruction, and Literary Theory,* ed. Reed Way Dasenbrock, 116–39. Minneapolis: University of Minnesota Press, 1989.

White, Hayden. *Metahistory: The Historical Imagination in Nineteenth-Century Europe.* Baltimore, Md.: Johns Hopkins University Press, 1973.

Whiteside, Anna, and Michael Issacharoff, ed. *On Referring in Literature.* Bloomington: Indiana University Press, 1987.

Williams, Bernard. *Ethics and the Limits of Philosophy.* Cambridge, Mass.: Harvard
University Press, 1985.

Winter, Steven. "*Bull Durham* and the Uses of Theory." *Stanford Law Review* 42
(1990): 639–93.

Wittgenstein, Ludwig. *Philosophical Investigations,* trans. G. E. M. Anscombe. Oxford: Blackwell, 1953.

———. *The Blue and Brown Books.* Oxford: Blackwell, 1958.

———. *Remarks on Colour.* Berkeley: University of California Press, 1987.

Wright, Crispin. *Realism, Meaning, and Truth.* Oxford: Blackwell, 1987.

———. *Truth and Objectivity.* Cambridge, Mass.: Harvard University Press, 1992.

Zemach, Eddy M. "On Meaning and Reality." In *Relativism: Interpretation and Confrontation,* ed. Michael Krausz, 51–79. Notre Dame, Ind.: University of Notre
Dame Press, 1989.

# Index